PENGUIN BOOKS

A Social History of Canada

Born in Winnipeg, George Woodcock spent most of his first 37 years in England. After returning to Canada in 1949, he became widely known as a literary journalist and historian.

His first published book, a collection of poems called *The White Island*, appeared in 1940. His political writing, particularly *Anarchism* (1962), established him as Canada's pre-eminent social thinker. Works that combine history and travel include *Faces of India* (1964) and *South Sea Journey* (1976). His works of literary criticism include *Dawn and the Darkest Hour: A Study of Aldous Huxley* (1972); *The Crystal Spirit* (1966), a study of George Orwell; *Hugh MacLennan* (1969); *Mordecai Richler* (1970); and two books of literary essays: *Odysseus Ever Returning* (1970) and *The World of Canadian Writing* (1978). Woodcock has also published two volumes of autobiography: *Beyond the Blue Mountains* (1983) and *Letter to the Past* (1987). His most recent works are *Anarchism and Anarchists* (1992), and *The Monk and His Message* (1992), an attack on determinist theories of history. The founder of the quarterly journal *Canadian Literature*, George Woodcock lives in Vancouver, British Columbia.

A SOCIAL HISTORY OF CANADA

George Woodcock

Penguin Books

PENGUIN BOOKS
Published by the Penguin Group
Penguin Books Canada Ltd, 10 Alcorn Avenue, Toronto, Ontario,
Canada M4V 3B2
Penguin Books Ltd, 27 Wrights Lane, London W8 5TZ, England
Penguin Books USA Inc., 375 Hudson Street, New York,
New York 10014, U.S.A.
Penguin Books Australia Ltd, Ringwood, Victoria, Australia
Penguin Books (NZ) Ltd, 182-190 Wairau Road,
Auckland 10, New Zealand

Penguin Books Ltd, Registered Offices: Harmondsworth,
Middlesex, England

First published in Viking by Penguin Books Canada Limited,
1988

Published in Penguin Books, 1989
10 9 8 7 6 5 4 3 2

Copyright © George Woodcock, 1988
Illustrations copyright © René Demers, 1988
Illustrations © National Archives of Canada, National Map
Collection NAC-8517
All rights reserved

Manufactured in Canada

Canadian Cataloguing in Publication Data
Woodcock, George, 1912-
A social history of Canada

ISBN 0-14-010536-0

1. Canada — Social conditions.   I. Title.

HN103.W66 1989   971   C87-094918-7

To Barry and Dorothea Leach,
celebrating a long friendship.

CONTENTS

INTRODUCTION

This is a history of peoples rather than of politics, of the folk from many tribes and lands who over the millennia came to the vast land mass we call Canada and formed the nation of many languages, origins and ethnic strains we call the Canadians. It was a long process of breaking away and forming anew, for in human terms Canada has always been a land of immigrants, people who have detached themselves from old worlds to recombine in a new world. Even the oldest of our peoples, the ancestors of our Indian tribes, came to our country from the northernmost areas of Asia at a time that in geological terms is extremely recent: roughly twelve thousand years ago.

We have all started from some other place, and the break with the past elsewhere has never been complete. In their cultures Canadian peoples, even the most ancient of them, have retained something of their pre-Canadian past: an obstinate cluster of beliefs and techniques of ecstasy, like the shamanism our native peoples shared with the tribes of Siberia and Mongolia, or a language and a whole historic culture such as those the French, the English and later immigrant groups share with the people who have remained in their mother countries. These tenuous and various continuities have enriched our traditions, our cultures, our social lives. We have contributed our original differences as well as our acquired similarities to the nation we have become. And thus there is no such thing as a

1

homogeneous Canadian society, just as there is no such thing as a Canadian *tout simple*, without links — however unconsciously sustained — elsewhere.

Paradoxically, this often subliminal link between the distant past and an urgent present has in the long run been a unifying factor. For our pasts, after all, are mostly histories of escape; we share the experience of departure. Whether fleeing from famine or poverty, from persecution or merely from a sense of stagnation in a conservative society, generations of immigrant ancestors who came to Canada viewed the new land as more attractive than the land they were leaving, and in the long run, despite the well-known trials and tribulations of the pioneers, that new land gave a better and more spacious kind of life to those who worked to establish themselves.

But the past was never entirely lost. We carry our social and cultural heritages with us as we carry our genes. That is why the plurality we see in Canadian life — the differences of styles and aims and standards — and the ever-recurring cycles of dispute and reconciliation that punctuate our history have been determined by collective impulses and geography as well as by those of individuals in moments of decision in their lives. Goldwin Smith, the nineteenth-century historian and journalist who was himself a distinguished immigrant to Canada, likened Canada after Confederation to a bundle of "fishing-rods tied together by the ends," meaning that the combination was too flexible to be strong. But a study of our past might also suggest that the reason for Canada's durability, in spite of the successive crises that have threatened its unity, lies precisely in the flexibility of our society. Like a well-built structure in an earthquake zone, it absorbs the shocks by yielding to them in the right places.

IT IS NOT ONLY HISTORY THAT has contributed to Canada's pluralism as a nation and a society. Geography has

But societies are rarely identical with nations. Sometimes, when the nation is a small one, embracing a single geographical region with a unified ethnic stock, they do coincide; people in a small city of ancient Greece, in a remote island community like Tonga or in a tiny, self-contained community, like Liechtenstein in modern Europe, may share a single undifferentiated culture. In such cases the local society and the nation coincide with each other. But even in countries as small as Switzerland or Belgium, there may be several cultures differentiated by language and tradition, and the nation, though it seeks a *modus vivendi* between the societies that have united to create it, is never identical to any one of them, nor is it a collective projection of them, since it exists as a unity only to accommodate their diversity. The societies are realities, but the state is a political arrangement. In the same way, Canadian society, in all its historical and geographical diversity, is far from identical to the governmental structure that gives it a semblance of unity, though in the case of Canada, as in that of Switzerland, the double-level political structure suggests the diversity of societies that underlies and, in its own way, supports the unity of the nation.

THIS BOOK IS A SOCIAL HISTORY, not a political one. People form societies to satisfy collectively needs that they would not be able to satisfy individually. They develop languages and other systems of communication; they evolve shared beliefs; they contrive means of avoiding conflict and complementary patterns of mutual aid. But a social organization does not necessarily imply a political one or dictate its form. Some societies have had quite elaborate patterns of life maintenance and rich shared traditions but almost no political organization at all; Inuit society was like this. In other situations, where an alien political structure rests on an older social structure, the original society has often continued to exist, substantially disregarding the superimposed order, as traditional Hindu society did in India under both the Mogul Empire and the British Raj.

In modern democracies, of course, the link between the society and the political structure — the polis — is closer because the people have at least some intermittent say in the shaping of political events and decisions. And though this is a study of Canada as a society, in all the diversity that underlies its appearance of unity, it cannot entirely avoid the discussion of politics. A political event like the Conquest of 1760 or the Confederation of 1867 obviously has permanent and fundamental effects on the society and on the lives of its members. Nevertheless, even those events are different when we see them from below, as it were, rather than from above through the eyes of those who shape policies and who wield political power.

How various peoples have come together, how they have lived together, how as individuals and collectivities they have affected each other, so that various groups have struggled with, and sometimes replaced, others: these will be the beginnings of our inquiry. For, as Leo Tolstoy recognized long ago and showed in his great novel, *War and Peace*, it is in society that true history begins, and the great men, with their armies and their policies, are the products of society rather than its makers and shapers. And so our story begins, quite appropriately, with men who certainly developed societies, but almost certainly had no politics: the wandering hunters of the age when the vast glaciers began to melt and the land that is Canada began to emerge from under its mantle of ice, when the gigantic mammals of the Pleistocene era began to roam over the reborn terrain with humanity in pursuit.

PART
I

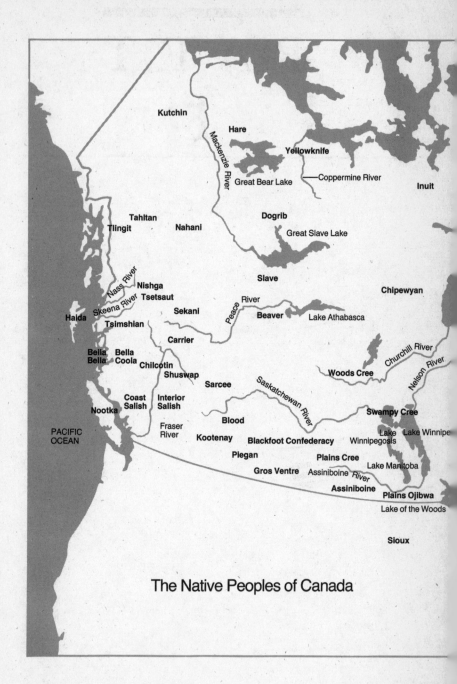

The Native Peoples of Canada

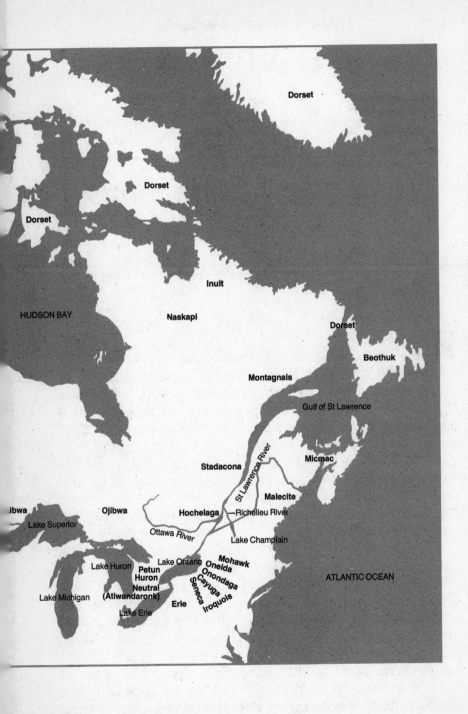

CHAPTER

1

The Earliest Immigrants

People who lived in ages or places where written records did not exist really entered history only at the point when they encountered other people who were able to make a record of experience in writing. For this reason our earliest approximately reliable knowledge of the native peoples of Canada begins at that point of fatal encounter when the first literate men met them and began to describe their ways of life. From that point onward these earliest inhabitants of the land start to live for us, as persons within a pattern of recorded events, within written history.

Of course, even written history never tells the whole story, for there are always gaps where facts fall out of memory or out of record. There are also psychological shifts from period to period, in the way people see themselves and their world, so that the greater the distance from which we observe a past era, the more difficult it becomes to put ourselves into the minds of the people who lived at that time. Still, we do have some specific knowledge of the individuals who appear in history, of their temperaments and sometimes even of their looks. We possess some of the words they spoke or wrote and know in some detail, because it has been described by contemporaries, the physical nature of the world they lived in. We often know a great deal about the events in which they took part. When we follow Alexander Mackenzie through the Rockies to the Pacific Ocean and he tells us what he wrote there in 1793 on a rock above salt water on a shore that is not yet even Canadian, we can form a fairly exact picture in our minds of what went on and we feel a personal rapport with this man who lived nearly two hundred years ago. We do so thanks to literacy, to the gift of the written word.

But with people who lived before literacy and therefore before written history, no such intimate rapport is possible. We have no knowledge of how they spoke or thought and very little idea of how they looked. We know only scattered facts about them, and these are the material facts conveyed by the few physical relics they left behind them — usually only the relics of imperishable materials. We have little access into their minds, even indirectly, and the broader picture of the past to which they belong has to be filled in with inspired conjecture.

Even the first literate Europeans to encounter the native peoples of Canada did not always keep records, and when they did so, the usefulness of their records was limited by the fact that their interests did not coincide with those of history scholars in later times. The earliest encounter between Canadian native peoples and Europeans actually took place in the early eleventh century A.D. when the Icelandic Norsemen, who had established their settlements in Greenland, came down to Vinland (which was later rediscovered and called Newfoundland) and established an ephemeral little settlement on the bay at L'Anse aux Meadows with a few houses and a blacksmith's forge to make rivets for their longships. There they became involved in hostile encounters with a mysterious people they called the Skraelings. The

Norsemen, who did not persist for more than two or three winters in their tiny settlement on Vinland, were themselves only a recently literate people, whose sagas — like the oral poems that had preceded them — were still concerned with heroic deeds rather than mundane descriptions. So the Skraelings appear as menacing but undifferentiated presences appearing on raids out of the dark hinterland, though we must assume they were ancestors of the Indian people found by the next wave of European visitors to this region centuries later. Archæological evidence actually suggests that the Norsemen did sustain a peaceful trading relationship with the Inuit of Greenland, Baffin Island and possibly even Labrador, but such trading activity entailed no heroic deeds and so finds no place in the sagas. We have to wait for the arrival of more sophisticated strangers before the native peoples of Canada really move into history.

From the late fifteenth century onward, English, French and Portuguese fishermen sailed year after year to the great cod-fishing banks off the shores of Newfoundland and Nova Scotia and even penetrated the Gulf of St Lawrence. But they were too narrowly concerned with their seasonal occupations to gather much knowledge of the lands whose beaches they visited or of the people who inhabited them. Other Europeans, however, had motives that made them pay closer attention to the indigenous inhabitants and establish lasting contact with them. They were traders who sought to win profits by exploiting the Indians as fur gatherers; priests who sought to win souls by converting them to Christianity; aristocrats and adventurers who wanted to acquire real estate and build up imperial prestige for their countries by occupying and annexing the lands to which the native peoples claimed no property rights. (Personal property was a concept unknown to them.) And when these Europeans came to Canada with the intent of taking up more or less permanent residence and began to assess their surroundings and the people already occupying the land, the native folk began to take on character and life as historical beings.

The French, who made their first appearance in the sixteenth century when Jacques Cartier entered the mouth of the St Lawrence in 1534, combined all three motives, and so it is to them that we owe our earliest real accounts of the native peoples of eastern Canada. The peoples of the interior of the continent, the northern woodlands and the great plains entered history in the seventeenth and eighteenth centuries, when the London-based Hudson's Bay Company and French explorers like La Vérendrye penetrated the great central expanse of the land where the brief, flamboyant history of fur trade took place. With the arrival of Captain Cook and the Spanish explorers by sea in the late eighteenth century, the richly ceremonial society of the Pacific coast tribes finally became a matter of record. As for the most northerly of the native peoples, the Inuit, they were encountered not only by the Norsemen, probably in the late eleventh century, but also by sixteenth-century English adventurers, such as Martin Frobisher, who in 1575 was shot in the buttock by an Inuit arrow on the bay that bears his name. However, detailed descriptions of their way of life did not begin to appear until the nineteenth century.

BUT THE STORY OF THE PEOPLES OF CANADA begins in prehistory, the long ages before men began to keep written records. To make history out of anything before that fateful moment of contact with literate people, we can rely on only two sources: the mythical stories about their own past, and the actual relics of past cultures that archæologists have discovered and assessed.

Myths, which precede literacy, also precede rational thinking based on empirical data. Primitive man sees not merely the physical, concrete world that his five senses offer to him. For him that world is permeated with spirit. Animals, trees and stones have their own spiritual nature, so that beyond the obvious and everyday physical world there lies a world of magical relations, access to which can give special powers to bring about good or evil. Visions and various forms of mystical experience provide links between these two worlds, and the lives of men are often seen as being determined by the intervention of spirit helpers or familiars from the other world, who often appear in animal form. All this means that the account of the past presented by myths will differ notably, because of its extensions into the supernatural, from the account an objective record-making historian might present.

This does not mean that myths are devoid of truth. That was proved dramatically when the great German amateur archæologist, Heinrich Schliemann, using the mythical *Iliad* as a kind of archæological guide, excavated the great mound of Hissarlik beside the Bosporus in 1871, and discovered that the Troy of the myth had likely existed and that the Trojan War had probably taken place on this spot.

But the Trojan War, likely fought in the twelfth century B.C., was still a comparatively recent event when its myth was incorporated into the oral epic of the *Iliad* during the eighth century and even when the epic was set down in writing in the sixth century B.C. As the past recedes, myths become less precise in their relation to it; Greek myths about the much earlier deeds of the hero Herakles, for example, contain much less historically authentic data than the stories of the Trojan War. Migration myths are particularly susceptible to the erosion of time. People like the Maori, whose Polynesian ancestors left Samoa for New Zealand in relatively recent times, still have their tales of exodus. But the Melanesians who live on other South Sea islands and whose ancestors must have arrived at a much earlier time, do not see themselves as migrants at all, but as the autochthonous inhabitants, descended from ancestors who somehow emerged from the land.

The same applies to native peoples in Canada. Some of them, who changed their habitat in fairly recent periods, have tales to tell of their ancestral wanderings. Others, who have been a long time in the same place, do not. Recently I talked to a federal government commissioner appointed to investigate the land claims of the Nishga Indians on the Nass River in British Columbia. Archæologists suggest that the Nishga culture may have started in this region five thousand years ago. Yet modern Nishga believe that their ancestors lived beside the Nass River and in the neighbouring mountains from time immemorial. When they talked to the commissioner they denied any suggestion that their remote forefathers could have come from Asia ten or twelve thousand years ago, as historians and archæologists generally accept. The white men were clearly wrong, they argued, for the Nishga traditions made no mention of any such movement of peoples.

There is, in fact, no mythical account of any great migration of the ancestors of all Indian and Inuit peoples from the neighbouring continent. The only non-material evidence of such a connection lies in the observation that the peoples on both sides of the northern Pacific share an ancient complex of spiritual and magical beliefs and ecstatic practices generally known as shamanism. Otherwise we have to rely on the archæological record to present its facts, which, scanty as they are, lead to the conclusion that beings of the species *Homo sapiens* first entered North America at its far northwestern extremity, using the land bridge where the Bering Strait now is, towards the end of the last great Ice Age, in about 10,000 to 9500 B.C.

THERE IS NO EVIDENCE THAT EARLIER human types like Peking man or Neanderthal man reached the American continent, nor are there any relics — either skeletal remains or tools — to suggest that men arrived earlier than about twelve millennia ago. This is late in the geological calendar and even in the calendar of *Homo sapiens* as a distinct species. But it was a time of dramatic changes on the earth's surface. Between 20,000 and 10,000 B.C. virtually the whole of Canada and part of the American Midwest had been submerged under gigantic glacial formations spanning the whole continent from the Pacific to the Atlantic. The Cordilleran Ice Sheet, as geologists call it, covered the Pacific coast and the western mountain ranges of what is now Canada, including the Rockies. The Laurentide Ice Sheet covered the rest of the country, including Newfoundland. They joined in present-day Alberta.

Because so much water was locked into the ice, the seas of that period were much lower than they are today. Areas that are now seabed, such as the Grand Banks of Newfoundland, were above the water then, and where the Bering Sea now flows a land bridge stretched from Siberia to the one part of northern North America not covered by ice: the greater part of Alaska and the Yukon basin. About 9500 B.C. the great ice sheets began to melt. A broad corridor opened down the eastern side of the Rockies, and great glacial lakes began to line the receding edge of the Laurentide Ice Sheet. The tundra moved southward down this corridor to meet the thin woodland moving upward from the central plains of the subcontinent, and into this space the massive mammals that had survived from the Pleistocene era wandered down from Alaska: the great hairy elephants, mammoths and mastodons; bison of a much larger breed than those known to history; wild horses and sloths; and some species still familiar to us, such as the caribou and the beaver.

With these animals the first hunters came from Siberia. They were wandering peoples who left little by which they could be remembered. They built no structures of stone — not even fish traps, bison pounds or cult circles. They had no pottery and they do not appear to have used any metal. What they did leave, in abundance, were the chipped stone heads of throwing spears that earned them the name "Fluted Point People" among archæologists; out of every spearhead a flute was chipped so that the haft could be fitted in and more securely bound, presumably with rawhide thongs.

The fluted points used by this ancient people have been found all down the corridor between the ice sheets, eastward through the southern prairies to the St Lawrence valley, and throughout the United States as far south as the Gulf of Mexico. There seems no doubt that in this initial migration, which perhaps continued in waves for several centuries while the land bridge still held, humankind spread throughout North America and the flow continued over the Isthmus of Panama into South America, where other derivative cultures developed.

The migrants were simple people, hunting and gathering wild products and clothing themselves in skins. They must have had some kind of communal organization, since they were able to kill the enormous mammoth and mastodon. This would have been impossible for single hunters equipped only with stone-pointed spears. In parts of eastern Canada large deposits of bones have been found, which suggests that they organized collective hunts of the caribou, perhaps driving them into enclosures made of intertwined branches. They may even have had rudimentary trading patterns linked with the quarries where they dug out and worked the stone suitable for their weapon heads. Often stone from a particular quarry has been found shaped into spearheads, in areas far from the quarry. These peoples seem to have developed ceremonial patterns of a kind, linked with a belief in life after death, since skeletons from this period have been found with red ochre — already a sacred substance — scattered around them and spearheads lying beside them.

But there are vast gaps in our knowledge of these first Canadians — even in our knowledge of their material lives. Did they use canoes or other watercraft, or did they rely on simple rafts as some modern primitive groups have done? Did they use hand sleighs for transport? How did they shelter themselves during their nomadic wanderings? What did they eat apart from the big game whose bones have survived? We know they had fire, since heat-cracked stones have been found at their living sites — but how did they cook their food? What were their languages, or did they arrive in North America speaking a single language that later gave rise to the historical Indian tongues? How were they organized socially? Merely in families like the wandering Inuit of historical times, or in rudimentary tribal structures like those of the Chippewa? What did they believe in apart from an afterlife and the rituals of primitive shamanism? To understand truly the outer and inner lives of a people, these questions need to be answered, but we have no answers to them, and so our earliest immigrants, the ancestors of our native peoples, remain shadowy figures, moving incessantly through the wilderness in their search for food.

Most archæologists now think that once they settled into different parts of what is now Canada the descendants of the Fluted Point People ceased to be mobile except in a few areas where seasonal movements linked to the migrations of game or fish took place. Increasingly specialized cultures began to develop in the separate regions, as the people adapted to changing climatic patterns and local food supplies. New and more specialized tools and techniques were developed. Many of the great beasts that man had accompanied into the Canadian land mass became extinct, probably before 8000 B.C., but people hunted or gathered whatever could be found, and by 7000 B.C. there were peoples on the plains who were already devoting themselves mainly to the bison hunt, others in the boreal forests who depended mainly on caribou, and fishermen on the Gulf of St Lawrence who hunted marine animals, seals and walruses, with harpoons. The heads of these weapons detached from the haft once they pierced the animal's hide, but they were attached to cords, so the animal could be played and drawn in.

As the millennia went on, Stone Age techniques became increasingly sophisticated. New tools appeared — axes and adzes, drills and burins, skin scrapers and pestles — and new weapons, including stone maces and bows and arrows. Stone was ground as well as chipped, and some groups of Indians learned to beat spearheads out of the natural copper found in their regions.

By about 8500 B.C. the waters from the melting ice sheets had raised sea levels appreciably, so that the Bering land bridge was submerged, and there is no evidence of any major migration from that time until about 3000 B.C., when the ancestors of the Inuit came over the Bering Strait either in umiaks (large skin boats), or over the winter ice; their culture was the precursor of the Dorset culture, which during the next millennium moved rapidly across the northern Arctic as far as Greenland.

In about 3000 B.C. more complex social patterns also began to develop. The peoples of the plains started to supplement the spearman's individual pursuit of the bison with the communal hunts that drove herds of bison into stone- or wood-walled pounds where they could be killed easily or over the cliffs that later became known as buffalo jumps. The fishermen of the Pacific coast began to organize themselves into villages consisting of various clan houses whose inhabitants moved collectively to summer sites for fishing and other food gathering, and back to winter sites for the season of leisure and ceremonial celebration.

SOME TIME AFTER THE END OF THE ICE AGE the Indian languages began to develop. They must have become

differentiated many centuries ago, as the tongues are
now mutually incomprehensible, and the Haida spoken
by the people of the Queen Charlotte Islands off the
west coast seems entirely unrelated to the Algonkian dialect spoken by the Micmac in Nova Scotia on the east
coast. Twelve language groups developed altogether, including the Inuktitut spoken by the Inuit of the North
and the Beothuk spoken by the native people of Newfoundland, who became extinct soon after their encounter with Europeans. Some languages were spoken over a
great area. Algonkian, for instance, was spoken
throughout a vast sweep of country stretching over
what is now southern Canada, from Labrador and the
Maritimes across the Shield and the prairies as far as the
foothills of the Rockies. Athapascan-speakers occupied a
large area of boreal woodland and tundra in northwestern Canada, including the present Yukon Territory and
much of the district of Keewatin, as well as northern
British Columbia, Alberta and Saskatchewan. But some
language groups occupied such small territories that in
British Columbia, in addition to the Athapascan-
speaking Dene tribes in the north, no less than six language groups existed, and five of these were on the
Pacific coast: Haida, Tsimshian, Tlingit, Wakashan and
Salish. Kootenay was spoken inland in the area which
now bears that name. Some of these languages were
spoken only by a few thousand people. The Siouan and
Iroquoian languages were spoken in small areas just
north of the central plains and the eastern woodlands of
the United States, respectively.

The extraordinary fact about these language areas is
that they did not coincide with cultural zones, which
tended to be environmentally determined. This phenomenon has never been explained satisfactorily by either
linguists or ethnologists. The Algonkian-speakers included not merely the Naskapi of Labrador, who had a
mixed fishing and hunting economy, but also the cari-
bou-hunting Ojibwa, the Woods and Swampy Cree, the

bison-hunting Plains Cree and the tribes of the Blackfoot Confederacy. At the same time the plains bison-hunting culture was shared by the Athapascan-speaking Sarcee and the Siouan-speaking Assiniboine, as well as the Kootenay, who had a language of their own. The remarkably homogeneous Pacific coast culture was also shared by many different language groups, who would have been unable to communicate without the trading *lingua franca*, known as Chinook, which was already flourishing when the Europeans arrived. A simplification of the language of a tribe living at the mouth of the Columbia River, Chinook was a kind of North American pidgin which whites themselves later used in dealing with the Indians who lived on the west coast.

It is hard even to guess how this situation originated, and the most one can offer as explanations are reasoned guesses. My guess is that the vast spread of the Algonkian language group over so many environmental and cultural zones suggests that the language was there before cultural differentiations took place in response to the environment. In other words, the root language of this group of Indians may have been an archaic, lost tongue close to the one the Fluted Point People brought with them from Asia about twelve thousand years before the first Europeans arrived. There is little doubt that Inuktitut has remained very close to its ancestral Asian language, since Inuit now living in Siberia speak a dialect of it. But the Indian language groups are now so unrelated that linguists have to work hard to discover even small points of similarity. Were the differing languages derived from the languages of smaller groups who already spoke distinct tongues when they came across the land bridge? Or was twelve thousand years time enough for these peoples to develop out of an ancestral Algonkian the radically different languages the first European explorers and traders found them speaking? Even the rashest of linguists has offered no convincing solution to this most challenging problem.

Differences of language do not seem to have prevented the native peoples of Canada from interacting on a number of levels — in commerce, diplomacy and war — and when the Europeans first arrived they found that many Indians spoke more tongues than their own. Multilingualism was particularly common on the prairies, and the linguistic ability of the nineteenth century Métis leader Gabriel Dumont, who spoke six Indian languages, was probably not unusual among members of the Indian tribes. Such linguistic exchanges must have been necessitated by the trading networks that were established soon after the first human beings arrived in the Americas.

The only trade routes of which we have certain knowledge are those along which visible and imperishable relics were left. From what we know of the commerce between Indian groups in historic times, however, there was probably considerable traffic in foodstuffs, skins and other perishables, as well. For example, we know of trade in oolachon oil from the Nishga of the Nass River to inland peoples, along routes known traditionally as "grease trails." They derived their name from the trade goods that travelled along them just as the main trade route of central Asia became known as the Silk Road. But all traces of ancient traffic in perishables have vanished; the evidence that survives is of mineral products and the seashells that became trade goods.

Certain kinds of stone, such as obsidian, prized for its sharp cutting edge, and siliceous flint, which flaked easily, were particularly valued and extensively traded from an early time. Not long after the arrival of human beings in the Americas, obsidian was being sent out from quarries in Alaska, in northern British Columbia, on the Chilcotin plateau and in inland Oregon, and by the seventh millennium B.C., as tools became more specialized, flints were finding their way across the continent from a few widely scattered quarries. It is also possible that native copper — copper in a pure state that did not need to be smelted — was being mined and exported from around the western end of Lake Superior as early as six thousand years ago. The deposits on the Coppermine River were already being worked at least three thousand years ago and the metal traded throughout the central Arctic and as far south as Hudson Bay.

Seashells show up later in the archæological calendar (perhaps because of their greater fragility), but their appearance about four thousand years ago is important. It represents the first known commerce in goods intended not merely for use but for personal ornamentation and prestige — the beginning of conspicuous consumption. By this time large groups of native people must have been living well enough from the land not only to have surpluses to purchase luxury goods but also the leisure to develop a lifestyle with its own social and ceremonial graces.

The white shells called wampum, which came from the eastern seaboard of what is now the United States, were exported northward from about 2000 B.C. into the eastern woodland areas of Canada and northwestward into the prairies. In historical times they were used as ornaments and as money, but more importantly as ceremonial gifts during the negotiation of treaties between Indian groups. It is likely that these uses had been current for many centuries before the white men arrived in North America to observe and record them. Dentalium shell and abalone shell served similar purposes on the Pacific coast. Harvested off Vancouver Island and off the shores of what are now the states of Washington and Oregon, they were being traded long before the Christian era began, not only northward, eventually as far as Alaska and the Aleutians, but also inland across the Rockies where they reached the Blackfoot in the prairies.

Some cultural innovations also moved out along the routes of trade and probably along the routes of warfare, but many innovations were no doubt exclusively local, with no influence from outside regions. For example, it is likely that the birchbark canoe and the sleigh, the snowshoe, and the wigwam were all developed in the areas to which they were so superbly adapted with no apparent outside influence.

CERTAIN ANCIENT CULTS — LIKE THE ONE associated with medicine wheels on the prairies — were so closely adapted to a local culture that they must have been of indigenous origin. Medicine wheels are round areas in which stones are arranged in radiating patterns. They were in fact large-scale magical symbols connected with practices intended to ensure the continued return of the bison. Some medicine wheels were started as early as 3000 B.C., and were constantly added to in historical times. Astronomers who have studied them have concluded that the wheels were linked with celestial phenomena, notably the summer solstice. This conclusion, along with some of the solar myths of the Haida and other Pacific coast Indians, suggests that the most advanced prehistoric native peoples of Canada may have had cosmological notions at least as developed as those of the builders of Stonehenge.

Elsewhere on the prairies there were other stone formations, laid out in serpentine forms. These are generally regarded as representing Mishikenahbik, the Algonkian snake manitou, or godly spirit, whose role was to sustain a link between the living and the dead. Serpent cults are almost universal among precivilized peoples: they occur in every age and in every land where a snake is to be encountered. They represent archetypal reactions whose origin probably lies less in any kind of cultural derivation or diffusion than in the collective unconscious of the species. This reaction may even extend to the whole natural order of primates to which man belongs, for monkeys react as passionately to snakes as humans do. Fear and reverence for the snake, the symbol of wisdom and healing as well as the conveyor of death, are emotions so bound up with human experience that we must assume the ancestors of the Indians had acquired them before they made their great journey from Asia into the Americas only to find that here, too, in other forms, the serpent lurked in the solitudes. Encountering snakes must have been a matter of recognition rather than discovery.

Other complexes of belief that were widely held among both Inuit and Indians in ancient Canada had arrived with the cultural baggage of the original immigrants. Indian beliefs were essentially Manichean, based on the conception of eternal conflict between dark powers and bright ones. The shaman exemplified this struggle. He could contact helpers from the spirit world who gave him supernatural powers, so that he could be the great healer and the voyager into the shadows in search of the lost souls of the sick. But he could also use his powers negatively and become a malign, destructive sorcerer. Another ancient cult, found in Neanderthal times before *Homo sapiens* embraced it, was sustained by tribes in Siberia, by the Ainu of Japan and by many groups of Indians in Canada. It was the cult of the bear. Many believed they had a special relationship with this animal and appeased the bear spirit with special rituals whenever they killed a member of the species.

In addition to beliefs like these that probably accompanied the native peoples from Asia, they developed religious practices for themselves in response to their needs as hunters and fishermen. (The Pacific peoples, for instance, had ceremonies to recall the salmon just as the prairie tribes had rituals to recall the bison.) Apart from these there were cults that came northward from what is now the United States, forming part of the pattern of cultural diffusion that profoundly changed certain aspects of the living patterns of the early Canadian peoples.

These were largely funerary cults, connected with the ceremonial burial of the dead. They were almost certainly linked to changing views of life after death and to the need for propitiation of the dead and were similar to ancestor worship among the Chinese. However, the earliest manifestations of this kind of cult actually occurred in an out-of-the-way part of the continent: the coast of Labrador and the north shore of the St Lawrence, where about seven thousand years ago bodies were buried in earth which was then covered by a high mound of stones almost twenty or thirty feet across. There is no sign that this practice was derived from any other culture. It may well have developed on the spot as an extension of a practice still widespread in the Arctic, where the ground is frozen most of the year, of covering a body, whether in or out of a coffin, with a pile of stones large and heavy enough to protect it from carnivores. Care for the body implies a continuing reverence for the dead, out of which an ancestral cult could easily have developed. Later death cults which spread northward out of the Ohio Valley in the first millennium B.C. involved not only burial mounds but also offerings of objects whose variety suggested a widespread trade in what were then considered valuables (including copper and seashells) in the area south of the Great Lakes.

EVEN IF THEY WERE UNCONNECTED, such cults show how strong a force diffusion was in prehistoric cultures. Except on a minor scale the peoples seem by this time to have ceased migrating and to have located themselves within their own hunting, fishing and food gathering areas. In a land where population put very little pressure on resources, actual invasion and annexation of the territory of other groups was unusual until after the white men came. By distributing firearms, they changed the balance of forces that was maintained naturally in prehistoric times. In fact, cultural invasions were more likely than military ones. This happened in the case of the Tahltan people of northern British Columbia, an inland Athapascan group that during the nineteenth century adopted the intricate system of inherited ranks and titles of the neighbouring Tlingit and the elaborate ceremonial patterns that went with it. Assimilation on a narrower scale took place between the Gitksan, an inland group of Tsimshian extraction who had taken their coastal culture far up the Skeena River, and the more primitive Carriers, who were their neighbours.

But such wholesale adoptions of the social patterns of other groups seem to have been rare and less important in their overall effect than a number of technological innovations that changed the old patterns of life. The most important of these were the introduction of the dog sleigh into the Arctic, the arrival of the horse on the prairies and the appearance of agriculture in the St Lawrence Basin. Of slightly less importance was the introduction of pottery-making techniques in eastern Canada.

Late in the first millennium B.C. an Inuit people who were part of what is called the Thule culture (Thule being the ancient Greek word for the most northerly part of the world) began to move eastward across the Arctic from Alaska. Their culture was distinct from the older Dorset culture, which was so named because it was first identified at Cape Dorset in 1925 by the archæologist and ethnologist Diamond Jenness. After a thousand years the Thule people reached Baffin Island and Greenland, about the same time as the Norsemen established their settlements or perhaps even a little later. They either killed off or assimilated the Dorset people, and their descendants became the Inuit of history. It was they who developed the complex techniques of survival in a land of extreme temperatures and unreliable stocks of wild food that we associate with the contemporary Inuit. They developed the kayak, that craft superbly adapted to hunting marine animals in Arctic waters, and its heavier counterpart, the skin-covered umiak, for transporting people and goods. They had acquired the bow and arrow, probably from the Siberians. They built houses of stone and whalebone, some of which have survived virtually intact in the special climatic conditions of the Arctic, forming the only existing examples of the kind of homes in which prehistoric Canadians lived. Later the Thule people devised the igloo.

But of all the Thule innovations, the dog-drawn sleigh was the most important because of the ease and speed with which it allowed hunting groups to range over areas where game might be thinly scattered. Despite the almost visceral hatred that existed between Inuit and Indian, the dog-drawn sleigh spread far south, to the Indian peoples of the wooded zone, and even after the white men arrived it was long the principal form of overland transport in the Canadian North.

It is not known whether the Inuit tamed and bred the sleigh dog or whether they acquired it from other peoples. The Indians of the plains, for instance, were probably using dogs for drawing travois — frames made of poles — even before the Inuit used them to draw sleighs. In any event dogs remained the only domestic animals living among the native peoples of Canada for almost the entire prehistoric era. The horse did not appear until that crucial period when the native peoples of Canada were stepping from prehistory into history.

Anthony Henday was the first European to encounter Indians who possessed horses and were expert in their use. He travelled to the west in 1754 in the company of a group of wandering Indians, sixty years after Henry Kelsey, who was likely the first white man to sight the prairies. The Blackfoot were using horses in the bison hunt, shooting the great beasts with bows and arrows from their steeds, and Henday mentioned meeting a group of Assiniboine who were using horses as pack animals "loaded with provisions." His evidence shows that at some time between 1690 and 1750 the Indians of the prairies acquired, by trading or raiding, the horses that more southerly tribes had originally obtained from the Spaniards in Mexico. By the end of the prehistoric era, the patterns of hunting and transport in the prairies were therefore undergoing radical changes as a result of the appearance of this animal. It combined usefulness and beauty and to own one meant prestige as well as convenience. Obtaining horses also provided an excuse for raids and intermittent warfare.

Nevertheless, the introduction of the horse did not radically change the life of the bison-hunting prairie peoples; they merely hunted more effectively on horseback than their ancestors had done on foot. The introduction of agriculture, on the other hand, had widespread effects on the lives of the Iroquoian peoples of the St Lawrence Basin and the Great Lakes — effects that are quite noticeable even in the archæological record.

Indian corn, or maize, had been cultivated by the Mayas of Central America as early as 3500 B.C. In Mexico the practice of growing corn, beans, squash and sunflowers together, thus providing a relatively balanced diet that was rich in carbohydrates, protein and vegetable fat, seems to have developed very early. It took four thousand years for the seeds of cultivated plants and the lore of growing them to move northward as far as the Iroquois of the Five Nations, in what is now New York state. From there knowledge of this form of agriculture spread to the related Huron tribes who lived between Lake Ontario and Lake Huron and to the other peoples of Iroquoian stock who lived on the lower St Lawrence River. It seems to have taken several more centuries for the other Central American food plants to find their way into this area, but it is likely that beans, squash and sunflower were all being grown by Iroquoian-speaking peoples on Canadian soil in about A.D. 1200 and that they quickly learned how to press oil from the sunflower seed. Extensive cultivation of tobacco also began during this period. By the time the Europeans arrived, one small Iroquois group, the Petun, were pursuing such an active trade in tobacco they had grown that they became known as the Tobacco Indians.

Tobacco and the pipes in which it was smoked quickly assumed a central role in Indian ceremonies and diplomacy.

Techniques of baking clay and making cooking vessels that could be placed on a fire probably reached eastern Canada in about the tenth century B.C. as part of the general northward drift of cultural innovations developed by the peoples of Mexico. (Interestingly, their ancestors had passed through Canada long before on their way to Central America.) Tobacco pipes, many of them ingeniously worked to mark their ceremonial function, were among the last developments in a craft that was never widely or consistently practised in Canada. Pottery never even reached the prairies or the Far West; the Pacific coast tribes, for all their artistic sophistication, cooked by dropping red-hot stones into cedarwood boxes filled with water. Some of the Canadian Indians who adopted pottery did not continue to use it. The Micmacs of Nova Scotia were pottery users for a time, if one can judge from their prehistoric relics, but they had reverted to cooking with hot stones in birchbark baskets by the time the white men came. Did this mean that they themselves had never actually made their pottery and that their source for some reason had dried up? Or had they been baking clay for themselves and come to the conclusion that it was not worth the effort? We can never know. We can only note how much less indispensable pottery was to most of the prehistoric Canadian Indians than it was to the settled civilizations of the world. Most of the Indian cultures in prehistoric Canada were nomadic, and so they would have been hostile to a ceramic tradition that relied on the sedentary complex of claypits and kilns.

Among the agrarian Iroquois, pottery was much more evident. This was because the cultivation of corn and other food plants entailed a settled village life. In fact, apart from providing a more varied and certain supply of food the most important effect of the introduc-

tion of agriculture was that it altered the nomadic hunting lifestyle. If the native peoples of Canada as a whole
can be regarded as our first immigrants, the Iroquois can
be regarded as our pioneer settlers.

Once settlement occurs, the archæological record becomes fuller, not only because of the accumulation of
waste of various kinds on continually used sites, but
also because when dwellings burnt down, which happened quite often, plant substances that would normally
decay were carbonized. They were therefore more likely
to survive for the archæologist to uncover. So, even before history, we know more about the eating habits of
the Iroquois than of the other groups, and we can guess
more about their social organization. Their villages were
built within defensive palisades, which suggests a condition of intermittent warfare. Each village consisted of a
number of longhouses with pole frameworks and covered with cedar, ash or elm bark. The dwellings were
collective, some of the larger ones having a floor area of
as much as two thousand feet and containing five
hearths in the middle, each shared by two families. So
each house might have contained as many as fifty inhabitants. The average longhouse would probably house
thirty people, doubtless united by some kind of clan
connection, so that living in one of them was probably
more like sharing space in a large joint family than mix-
ing with a crowd of strangers in a rooming house.

As successful farming provided larger supplies of
food, the population grew and the villages became
larger. Remains of ninth-century villages are likely to
show seven or eight relatively small longhouses, which
would have housed two or three hundred people. By
the fourteenth century some villages covered five acres,
and contained more and larger longhouses and perhaps
a thousand inhabitants. Often these villages had double
palisades. In one instance there was a small house between the two palisades at the entrance to the settlement, which might have been used to accommodate

visitors whom the tribe did not want to admit within
their defences. Later, villages became even larger, and
in one case archæologists have traced the expansion of a
Huron settlement built in the early sixteenth century
from a small original nucleus with about six hundred inhabitants to a community of thirty-eight longhouses,
whose expanded defences embraced more than ten acres
of land and gave home to two thousand people.

In prehistoric times the only other part of Canada
where a stable form of village life appeared was the
Pacific coast. The abundance of seafood there offered as
regular a source of food as the cornfields of the Iroquois
and their kin. Because Pacific salmon and other fish and
shellfish were food sources not introduced from outside,
the cultures associated with them were considerably
older than the agrarian culture of the Iroquois. Around
the harbour at Prince Rupert, the foundation outlines of
large rectangular buildings on sites five thousand years
old can still be traced. They were predecessors of the
well-carpentered dwellings built of split cedar planks in
which the Tsimshian Indians were still living when the
first Europeans — English and Spaniards — arrived at
the end of the eighteenth century. These were the winter houses of the tribes, to which they brought back the
stores of dried and smoked fish and fish oil and the
dried berries they had gathered in their summer camps.
Such villages, inhabited for millennia, are the oldest Canadian communities and older than most European
cities. Out of them emerged the great artistic traditions
of the Pacific coast culture.

Although they were considerably more advanced
than the campsites of nomads, the Iroquois villages
were never entirely permanent settlements. Both the
supplies of firewood available within a reasonable distance and the fertility of the unmanured land would diminish as the years went by, and in ten or fifteen years
the band would shift to another site where they would
burn off the forest cover to obtain land for cultivation. If

we can judge from accounts of these peoples in historic times, these villages were not occupied all the year round either. There were times when the people would leave their villages for months on end to trade or hunt or fish. In fact, having corn and beans, which were easily transportable and relatively imperishable, the Iroquois could make such expeditions with less risk of starvation. The availability of such foods made it possible to launch military expeditions that were more lengthy and more highly organized than the raids that were more typical of Indian warfare. As a result, the Iroquois generally had greater military success than other Indian peoples and were dreaded by the white men when they became their enemies.

But in the beginning the Iroquois were not enemies. They welcomed the new arrivals as friends. On his first voyage in 1534 Jacques Cartier encountered Iroquois who lived on the lower St Lawrence. He was almost certainly not the first European to deal with the Canadian native peoples; the Basque and Breton fishermen who penetrated the Gulf of St Lawrence early in the century had already begun trading with them for furs by the time Cartier arrived. But he was the first to write about them, and about the large village of Stadacona on the site of present-day Quebec. The next year he returned, and proceeded upriver to the palisaded Iroquois village of Hochelaga, which had about 1,500 inhabitants and covered a small fraction of the area of present-day Montreal. He and his men were the first Europeans the people of Hochelaga had ever seen, and the description of their welcome is a striking example of the goodwill that so often marked the first encounters between the aboriginal peoples and those visitors who rather oddly became known as the "founding peoples": the French and the British.

And on reaching Hochelaga, there came to meet us more than a thousand persons, both men, women

and children, who gave us as good a welcome as ever
father gave to his son, making great signs of joy; for
the men danced in one ring, the women in another,
and the children also apart by themselves. After this
they brought us quantities of fish, and of their bread
which is made of Indian corn, throwing so much of it
into our longboats that it seemed to rain bread. Seeing
this, the captain, accompanied by several of his men,
went on shore; and no sooner had he landed than
they all crowded about him and about the others, giving them a wonderful reception. And the women
brought their babies in arms to have the captain and
his companions touch them, while all held a merry
making which lasted more than half an hour. Seeing
their generosity and friendliness, the captain had the
women all sit down in a row and gave them some tin
beads and other trifles; and to some of them he gave
knives. Then he returned on board the longboats to
sup and pass the night, throughout which the Indians
remained on the banks of the river, as near the longboats as they could get, keeping many fires burning
all night and calling out every morning *aguyase*, which
is their term of salutation and joy.[1]

Such was the dawn of trust, which faded quickly. It
was also the portentous moment when the native peoples of Canada began to take on face and voice, to
emerge as recognizable human beings with their relationships and their societies. They stepped out of the
anonymous past in which they are represented only by
the ruins of their homes, the detritus of their rubbish
heaps and the conjectures of archæologists. The moment
that the native peoples encountered the literate Europeans was the moment they entered history. So the very
different societies and polities and ways of life of the
first Canadian peoples are now viewed largely through
the eyes of these strangers — through the curious eyes
of a people who would eventually displace them as the
lords of the Canadian lands.

CHAPTER

2

The Moment of History

In looking at the European version of Canadian history, it is easy to pass by two important facts about Canada's native peoples. The first is that these peoples represented and still represent many cultures, not just one. Although in the late twentieth century the native groups may seek to make common cause against the non-Indian majority, there never was a unified Indian nation. We call one group of the native peoples Indians because that was the name Columbus gave the natives of the Caribbean when he thought that he had reached the real Indies, the outlying islands of India. But in fact they were and are as various as the inhabitants of the true India, and any unity they have recently acquired has been achieved through the presence of a common enemy, the non-Indian majority. The original lack of connection between Indian societies was crucial to the Europeans' being able to establish ascendancy over them eventually. They were dealt with regionally, tribe by tribe, and in that way they succumbed to the domination of the materially more sophisticated and therefore more powerful intruders.

But they did not succumb immediately. In hindsight we can see the triumph of the Europeans as inevitable, but the European conquest did not always appear so sure. After the first moments of discovery and encounter, the native peoples were not only much more numerous than the new peoples in many areas of what is now Canada, but they also maintained virtual control over their lands. They continued to live their traditional lives while the aliens — the fur traders and others — sojourned on sufferance. During the earlier periods of their penetration into the land that became Canada, the Europeans in many areas were in fact no more than an intrusive minority in the heart of still-functioning native societies.

This last fact has been obscured by most political and social historians of Canada. They have treated Canadian history essentially as a history of the Europeans whose descendants eventually formed the vast majority of Canadians. They have seen that history primarily in terms of cod fishing and the fur trade, of settlement and urbanization, of modern transport and communication, of the development of Canadian political structures from European ones, and of anglophone and francophone literatures and artistic traditions.

But while such developments of course took place, the native peoples were never absorbed completely into the dominant European social patterns and yet they were never eliminated. In the period between Cartier's arrival in 1534 and the decline of the bison herds in the 1870s, Indian groups in large parts of Canada carried on their traditional lives almost without change. They even maintained their identities and the substance if not the details of their ways of life throughout the dismal decades between the 1870s and the 1940s when their aboriginal cultures were in decay and "the vanishing Indian" was a phrase on everyone's lips. They survived to increase in numbers once again and to play a notable role in the social and political life of late twentieth-century Canada.

Up to the end of the 1860s, the white population of Rupert's Land, which stretched from the western end of Lake Superior to the Rockies, was of meagre proportions. Apart from the inhabitants of the tiny settlement of Red River, about two thousand Hudson's Bay officers and employees plus a handful of missionaries were scattered among the tens of thousands of Indians and Métis who still led a hunter's life on the prairies. When British Columbia entered Confederation in 1871 about three-quarters of its population was made up of Indians, whose rich local culture was at the height of its productivity. It was not until the late 1880s that the whites became a majority in that province. In the great Canadian North, with the exception of the Yukon Territory, European whalers or explorers might have been found along the coastline, but the great mass of the Arctic territory did not see a European from one generation to the next until after World War I. The fur traders were latecomers there, and the ancient Inuit way of life continued almost unchanged in many areas until after World War II. Even in New France, where attempts were made to create a miniature late feudal European society with lords and peasants, priests and bishops and a viceregal court, the hold of the few thousand Frenchmen over the territory was precarious until late in the seventeenth century. It was perpetually threatened by the warriors of the Five Nations Confederacy. Only in Newfoundland, where the Beothuks were already a declining people, were the European intruders completely in charge from the beginning.

Ironically, the European records, which give the impression of early European dominance and usually fail to describe the diversity of the Indian and Inuit cultures, also provide the most detailed written accounts. Unless we ignore the written record altogether, we must to some extent view the first Canadian peoples through the eyes of the first Europeans. At the same time, however, we can redress the balance by looking at each group individually, as they were first encountered by the small groups of explorers, fishermen, traders and missionaries who spearheaded the thrust of European penetration.

IN THE GREAT OUTER ARC FROM THE Alaskan border across to Baffin Island and northern Labrador, the Inuit thinly populated the coastline and islands of the Arctic Ocean and much of the tundra of Keewatin to the west and Ungava to the east of Hudson Bay. The coastal Inuit depended on marine mammals and fish, and their inland relatives had developed a life based on the seasonal caribou hunt. By the sixteenth century they had long abandoned the villages of stone and whalebone built by the early Thule people and were living in skin tents in summer and snow houses or igloos in winter. But they continued to use dog sleighs, and these were adopted both by the Indians who lived in nearby regions and by the Europeans who came to live in the North.

The Inuit were among the most practical and versatile of the native peoples of Canada. They developed the skills to survive in a rigorous environment which was gripped by a continuing northern night for long periods of the year and was subject to dangerous changes of climate. They had learned to locate and hunt the wild animals that lived scattered over the land or even hidden beneath the ice. Their artifacts, like the kayaks and the harpoons with which they killed seals and even hunted small whales, were extremely well adapted to the purpose for which they were used. Before Europeans arrived many of the Inuit were making semicircular knives and other tools from the deposits of native copper found in the North.

Even the early Dorset people were skilful carvers, making images of birds and sea mammals from bone and walrus teeth. The Thule people and their descendants used the same materials and also discovered that

soft soapstone could be used to make the lamps that
kept their igloos warm and cooked their food. They also
carved figures from the stone, mainly of the animals
they hunted. The carvings were small enough to be held
in the hand and doubtless had a magical function. It
was an intimate and personal kind of art, unlike the
other notable tradition among the native peoples of
Canada, that of the Pacific Coast Indians, whose art was
public and declarative, designed to assert social status.

At the same time the Inuit were perhaps the least
politically organized of all Canadian peoples — so unorganized that they have sometimes been held up as an
example of natural communistic anarchism. They had no
tribal or band organization and wandered over the tundra or the ice in small groups, since food supplies were
relatively scanty. Sometimes a group would consist of
one family, sometimes two or three. There was no semblance of political authority. The father exercised a pa-
ternal primacy within his family, but there were no
chiefs, perhaps because there were no larger groups
over which they could wield authority. Whenever the
small groups assembled for seasonal activities, they mingled naturally and freely and seem to have found no
need to establish a structure of public order. Intermin-
gling of the groups was made easier by the fact that a
single language — Inuktitut — was spoken all the way
from Alaska to Greenland. Although there were variant
dialects, Inuit from different regions could usually
understand each other without great difficulty.

Gatherings might take place when the Arctic char
were running or when the caribou were migrating and
the hunters gathered at river crossings. Particularly in
the more populated eastern Arctic, groups also joined
together for festivals aimed at magically ensuring that
the creatures on which they depended for food would
not disappear. During the long winters, when hunting
was confined to the twilight hours in the middle of the
day, families living close together would visit each other

in the evening, often sitting long into the night, singing songs that described their experiences and adventures. The men sometimes danced with drums while the woman sang, frequently poetic ballads. There was no social ranking among the Inuit, and no real economic disparity, no gulf between rich and poor. Their homes were shelters whose temporary character was most dramatically exemplified in the igloo, the house of snow that melted as soon as the short Arctic spring began. Because of their largely nomadic existence they were prevented from accumulating large amounts of property. Sharing was essential in a life as precarious as theirs, and a hunter who had been fortunate would always divide up the animals he had killed and give parts to the other members of his group.

The one figure who wielded a kind of influence over the Inuit was the shaman, whose role and functions had developed in Siberia before either the Inuit or the Indians reached Canada. The shamans' authority was by no means political. They were magicians who learned their art from other shamans or from encounters with spirit helpers out on the lonely hunting grounds. In ecstatic states they would utter oracles, and it was their duty to placate the angry spirits when game was scarce, when bad weather prevented the hunters from going out, and when the people were threatened with starvation. But they probably owed most of their influence to the fact that the Inuit had no system of even primitive medicine. Although they knew how to deal with accidents and injuries and could treat a wound or splint a broken leg, they had no lore of herbs or other means of dealing with sickness, always ascribing illness to causes outside nature: an enemy had bewitched the sufferer, a spirit was angry with him for violating a taboo, or his soul had just gone wandering away from his body. With rituals of various kinds the shamans would deal with such situations, struggling in their ecstasies with the malevolent spirits, believing that they could draw from the patients' bodies foreign substances implanted by sorcerers or going on dream journeys in search of errant souls. The shamans seemed to protect the Inuit in a world which they saw as being inhabited by spiritual as well as physical dangers. In their concept of the world, there were few positively benevolent spirits beyond nature and many potentially harmful ones.

The perils of the two worlds in which they saw themselves living often seemed to be reflected in the ambivalence strangers observed in Inuit lives. Children were loved and treated with indulgence. Women, who were valued for their expert tailoring of the close-fitting garments needed to hunt in the Arctic cold, enjoyed more equality of status than women in most Indian groups. Marriages were easy and could be dissolved by either partner at will, though they usually endured once children had been born. Little store was set by chastity and jealousy was virtually unknown. Wives regularly slept with their husbands' friends and more than one European visitor staying in an igloo was surprised by the pressing attentions of the lady of the house.

Yet the very people who in such aspects of their lives seemed to live like the parents of mankind in Eden, also showed a darker side. Accustomed to the sharp edge of need, to times when the available food supply could feed no surplus mouths, the Inuit were ruthless in their choice of preserving the living and the useful. Without any thought of guilt, they would practise infanticide, and when food was scarce they would abandon old and sick people to die in the wilderness, as some of the northern Indians also did. Although there is no documentation to suggest that an Inuit ever murdered out of sexual jealousy, they would sometimes kill people they suspected of sorcery. When that happened, a blood-feud would follow, continuing for generations and involving the innocent as well as the guilty, for among Inuit as well as among most of the Indians of Canada, guilt settled not only on the actual perpetrator of a crime but on his relatives as well. Any member of a family could be killed to pay for the action of one of its members. According to the Judeo-Christian myth, Eden was the place where man first learned evil. The life of the Inuit as the white men found them, so gallant in the way it challenged an appalling environment, so lacking in the calculations of politics or commerce of social life, so devoid of envy or jealousy, so generous and genial, was also darkened by hatreds that were bred of the fears which flourished in a perilous land where half the year was night.

BELOW THE NORTHERN ARC occupied by the Inuit, there existed another great curve of territory. It was inhabited by people who lived precariously on the products of the northern forests. Although the life of these Indians was as harsh as that of the Inuit, the two groups sustained a mutual hostility that must have arisen four or five thousand years ago. This was when successive waves of Inuit began to penetrate the Arctic and must have pushed southward the Indians who originally wandered over those cold lands. On his journey to the Coppermine River in 1771 the English explorer Samuel Hearne had witnessed a dramatic instance of this hostility. He stood helplessly by while his Chipewyan travelling companions deliberately massacred the inhabitants of an Inuit fishing camp. And as late as the 1960s I remember talking with an old Indian hunter at Baker Lake, and arousing his contempt when I compared the Inuit way of life on the tundra with that of the northern Indians. To him the Indians were an inferior race. And in recent years the tenuous alliance of the peoples of the North — Inuit, Indians and Métis — seeking greater autonomy within the Northwest Territories, the only area of Canada where aboriginal peoples are still in the majority, has constantly been threatened by the resurgence of old animosities between the two earliest Canadian ethnic groups.

The northernmost Indian peoples lived in an area that stretched over nearly the entire width of Canada. This region extended from Labrador across the Laurentians and to the Canadian Shield, over to the sparse woodland that runs northwest along the Mackenzie valley's treeline and finally into the Yukon valley, across the Rockies and into northern and central British Columbia.

There were about twenty tribal groups in this area, belonging to two major language groups. The Algonkian speakers ranged from the Naskapi of Labrador and the Micmacs of Nova Scotia to the Woods Cree of what later became northern Manitoba, who inhabited the land south of Hudson Bay. Beyond Cree territory stretched the great triangle of territory inhabited by the Athapascan speakers. Among these were the Chipewyan, who lived north of the Churchill River in the east, the Kutchin in the Yukon valley and the Carrier and Chilcotin of the inland plateaus of British Columbia.

In spite of linguistic differences, the Algonkian and Athapascan speakers had similar environments and life patterns. They inhabited the least clement and the least fertile parts of Canada; theirs was a cold country with meagre forest cover and scarce game. A life of incessant wandering was necessary to ensure even an adequate food supply. Often the hunters failed to secure even this, and many accounts appear in fur traders' journals of Indian groups dying or almost dying of starvation as they made their way to posts like York Factory on the Churchill River.

The staple foods of these groups varied from area to area. The Naskapi in Labrador combined seal hunting and fishing with the pursuit of big game like moose, and, in season, caribou. The Cree tended to rely mainly on moose and deer, while the Chipewyan and other tribes bordering on the tundra were largely caribou hunters. The Beaver Indians in the foothills of the Rockies hunted moose and deer. But in most areas there would be times when big game was hard to find and the hunters had to live on hare and other small animals they caught in snares. The tribes living beside the Mackenzie and Yukon rivers combined large-scale fishing with hunting. The British Columbian tribes, like the Carrier, the Tahltan and the Tsetsaut, fished for the Pacific salmon that went far upriver into the interior to spawn.

Like the Inuit, these Indians had an intimate knowledge of their unfriendly environment, and they developed specialized skills to cope with it. Most of them lived in portable wigwams covered with caribou or moose skin or birchbark. They used birchbark canoes or dugouts, and in winter, they travelled by snowshoe. Some of the groups used primitive forms of weaving to make mats from reeds, baskets from twigs or roots and sometimes warm robes from strips of rabbit skin.

A few of these tribes learned less uncertain ways of life from their neighbours and abandoned woodland hunting. The Athapascan Sarcee and some of the Cree, for example, adopted the prairie way of life based on the bison hunt. The Ojibwa, influenced by the Iroquois, developed a rudimentary agriculture. But in general these forest peoples depended on game and fish (though the Cree despised fish and would eat it only as a last resort), and were vulnerable to the periodic shortages that sometimes turned into famine. The shortages were caused by over-hunting or cyclical variations in animal populations. Perhaps it was because of the chronic precariousness of their lives that the woodland peoples were most inclined to welcome the fur traders. From the early eighteenth century onward they depended on that commerce more than any other group of native peoples.

Apart from Athapascan tribes like the Tahltan and the Carriers of northwestern British Columbia, who imitated the ranking systems of the coastal tribes, the peoples of the woods had little more political and social organization than the Inuit. They travelled in bands, consisting of extended families, looking for food and abandoning an area as soon as the game had been hunted out. Older men might enjoy a degree of respect, and they were often regarded as chiefs by visiting Europeans who expected to find hierarchical patterns. They wielded little real authority, however, and the band seemed to operate mainly through consensus among the hunters. Since it was impossible to accumulate wealth, there was no division between rich and poor, and skills in survival rather than hereditary claims determined the esteem in which a man was held.

If there was any class division among the northern Indians, it was based on gender. Women enjoyed little of the freedom they possessed among the Inuit or of the influence they wielded among the Iroquois. The degree to which they were considered inferior varied from tribe to tribe, but all witnesses seem to agree that women had the worst position in the tribes that were most economically deprived. Chipewyan women had the lowest status. This "edge-of-the-woods" people lived precariously between the boreal woodland and the tundra, leading a life similar to that of their nearest neighbours, the Inuit of Keewatin, but with somewhat less efficiency.

Necessity seemed to encourage cruelty among the Chipewyan; they left their old people and their sick to starve to death, and in their disputes with other Indians or with the Inuit, mostly over hunting or fishing territories, they would massacre their rivals ruthlessly without regard for age or sex. The women, according to ethnologist Diamond Jenness,

> ranked lower than in any other tribe; separated from all boy companions at the age of eight or nine, married at adolescence, often to middle-aged men, and always subject to many restrictions, they were the first to perish in seasons of scarcity. In winter they were mere traction animals; unaided, they dragged the heavy toboggans. In summer they were pack animals, carrying all the household goods, food, and hides on

their backs . . . . A skilful hunter enjoyed great prestige and could maintain several wives; he needed
them to pack all his hides.[2]

One such famous Chipewyan hunter was Matonabbee, who acted as Samuel Hearne's guide on his journey
to the Coppermine River. Hearne had made two earlier,
unsuccessful attempts to cross the tundra with male
companions only, and Matonabbee lectured him on the
wisdom of including the other sex in his entourage:

> "Women," added he, "were made for labour; one of
> them can carry, or haul, as much as two men can do.
> They also pitch our tents, make and mend our cloth-
> ing, keep us warm at night; and, in fact, there is no
> such thing as travelling any considerable distance, or
> for any length of time, in this country, without their
> assistance. Women," he said again, "though they do
> everything, are maintained at trifling expense; for as
> they always stand cook, the very licking of their
> fingers, in scarce times, is sufficient for their
> subsistence."[3]

After this, one of the first great European travellers in
Canada reached his journey's end successfully thanks to
the ruthless exploitation by Chipewyan hunters of their
womenfolk, in this case Matonabbee's eight wives.

The woodland peoples seem to have been animists of
the simplest kind, living in a world of spirits rather than
of gods. Every being, whether human or animal, had its
appropriate spirit, and the placating of these beings to
ensure sufficient game and to avoid calamity was the
nearest thing they had to a religious life. The idea of a
deity such as the Great Spirit, which was developed by
some of the more sophisticated Indian peoples, played
no part in their view of the supernatural world. At the
same time they had concepts of human — and perhaps
animal — immortality which were expressed in a variety
of myths about life after death. Often these myths

included journeys by water to a kind of paradise where animals were abundant and — unlike the game of the real northern woodland — never failing.

BENEATH THE GREAT NORTHERN ARC of the Inuit people, with their remarkable adaptations to an extreme and rigorous climate, and below the lower arc of woodland Indian groups who survived precariously on the scanty food of an inhospitable zone, there extended across southern Canada a region where the peoples led a very different life. They took advantage of a more favourable climate and a more abundant environment and developed a number of specialized cultures.

To the east, along the banks of the St Lawrence and on the shores of the Great Lakes, lived various peoples of Iroquois stock who had not only developed a flourishing agriculture, but had built upon this economy of the fields a genuine polity. They had formed confederacies of tribes, in which political decisions were made with the widespread participation of the people. Farther west, a group of prairie tribes, supported in this case by the relatively reliable economy of the bison hunt, had created their own confederacy, made up of the Algonkian-speaking Blackfoot, the Piegan and Blood tribes, with the Athapascan-speaking Sarcee joining later. Once again a high degree of democratic decision making had developed in this confederacy.

Between these two great confederated groups, in the southern woodlands between Lake Superior and Lake Winnipeg, lived the Ojibwa, who had found their own ways of improving on the primitive forest economy. They not only borrowed the technique of corn cultivation from the Iroquois, but also harvested wild rice from the lakes of this region and learned to tap the maple trees for sugar. They were therefore able to add to the normal fish and game diet of the woodland people a considerable variety of vegetable foods. This helped to protect them from shortage. The Ojibwa remained politically unsophisticated, but they had created quasi-religious fraternities which seem to have led to a level of moral and spiritual development higher than that of the other woodland tribes.

Finally, far to the west and beyond the Rockies, the tribes of the Pacific coast had developed a flamboyant culture based on abundant fisheries. Social considerations became more important than political ones, and elaborate ranking systems and ritual fraternities with complicated ceremonials led to a flowering of art unrivalled among other Indian peoples north of the valley of Mexico and perhaps unrivalled among primitive peoples anywhere in the world.

WHEN JACQUES CARTIER FIRST REACHED the St Lawrence in 1535 he found Iroquois peoples, who were living in a large area that stretched from near the mouth of the Saguenay near the Gulf of St Lawrence to the Great Lakes. Their settlements, scattered along the Lower St Lawrence, consisted of bark-covered longhouses and resembled the prehistoric villages of the area. Around the longhouses were cultivated plots of corn, beans, squash and tobacco. On the island of Montreal stood Hochelaga, a palisaded village of about two thousand and the largest settlement in the area. Downriver there were seven unfortified villages, of which Stadacona, which stood near the site of Quebec City, was the most important. It was from the Stadaconans' word for "village" that Cartier derived the name of Canada, which was first applied by the French to their realm on the St Lawrence and later used to designate the whole of what became British North America. After the initial friendly encounters, the behaviour of the French, of which more will be said later, alienated the Stadaconans, and until at least the 1580s, they prevented Europeans from going upriver beyond Tadoussac at the mouth of the Saguenay.

By 1603, however, when Champlain arrived to do the first survey of the St Lawrence valley, he found that the Iroquois peoples had entirely vanished from the lower river and that grass had grown over the sites of their settlements. There is no clear record telling what happened to them, and even early seventeenth-century explanations varied considerably. Intermittent warfare with the Algonquin and Montagnais hunting peoples in the area had obviously gone on even before Cartier came, but the general view is that Hochelaga and Stadacona were destroyed by other Iroquoian peoples — either members of the league of Five Nations, who lived in what are now the states of New York and Vermont, or the Hurons from the Great Lakes area. The people of Hochelaga and Stadacona were not necessarily annihilated, however. It was the custom of the Iroquois to absorb large numbers of defeated peoples into their own tribal structures.

The Five Nations Iroquois were one of three Iroquoian-speaking confederacies that existed after the arrival of the Europeans. The other two were the Huron and the Neutral confederacies. The Huron, and the associated Petun tribe (the Tobacco Indians), lived in central Ontario, in the fertile lands south of the Shield. They numbered about fifty thousand by the end of the sixteenth century. The Atiwandaronks to the south of them, around the western end of Lake Ontario, were generally called the Neutrals, since they preferred peace and trade to warfare. A rather isolated group, who also spoke an Iroquois dialect but were not in any confederacy, were the Erie. They had settlements along the shores of the lake that now bears their name. The Neutrals, the Erie and the Petun all tried their best to keep out of the intermittent warfare which the two largest groups, the Huron and the Five Nations, seem to have carried on since prehistoric times. (At the end of the sixteenth century, the Five Nations were a slightly smaller group than the Huron, numbering about twenty thousand.) Generally speaking, the Huron traded with the Algonkian tribes to the north and east, and eventually the French, while the commerce of the Five Nations lay mostly to the south. They traded with the neighbouring Indian tribes and ultimately with the Dutch and then the British. Sometimes they also followed a trade route around the shores of Lake Ontario that kept them in touch with the Algonkian peoples who lived beyond the Hurons.

The Iroquois lived to the south of Lake Ontario, in territory that was lost to British North America after the creation of the United States. But they also played vital and violent roles in New France and in the Huron territories that later became Upper Canada. Eventually, after the American Revolution, large numbers of Iroquois migrated to both Upper and Lower Canada.

Of the Huron and the Neutral leagues' political organization we know very little, because they were destroyed in warfare with the Five Nations during the 1640s, and the Jesuit missionaries — the Europeans who had the closest contact with them — were too much concerned about converting them into French-speaking Christians to take time to study and record the political arrangements of what they hoped would soon become a pagan past. The Five Nations confederacy offers the most striking and best-documented example of Iroquoian political arrangements.

At the time of first contact with Europeans, the Iroquois league consisted of five tribes: from west to east they were the Seneca, the Cayuga, the Onondaga, the Oneida, and the Mohawk. In the early eighteenth century, the league would become known as the Six Nations because the Tuscaroras, an Iroquoian people who had been driven out of Carolina, were accepted into the league when they moved north.

The league was partly a forum where the representatives of the various tribes could meet together and discuss matters of common concern, and partly a kind of federal diplomatic service. To a great extent, it controlled the external relations of the tribes belonging to it. In domestic matters the tribes remained autonomous, though internally they were much more highly organized than the woodland peoples. Each tribe consisted of a number of clans and each clan was divided into two complementary phratries, whose functions seem to have been mainly ceremonial.

The clans were exogamous. That is, the men were required to marry wives outside the clan. And it was through the women that descent within the clans was reckoned, a fact which gave Iroquoian women a status that few other Indian women enjoyed. The children of a family inherited their mother's name, and the women were the custodians not only of the names but also of the traditions of the clans. Authority lay largely in the hands of female elders. Each longhouse — which might give shelter to as many as twenty families — would be ruled by an elderly woman. The whole group would really be a big matriarchal joint family, consisting of the old woman, her daughters and sons and the children of her daughters and granddaughters. After marriage the sons would go to live in the longhouses of their wives' families. A maternal joint family of this kind could consist of fifty to two hundred people.

The council of the league of Five Nations consisted only of men, however. Fifty chiefs, known as sachems, were selected from the joint families, on grounds of heredity and ability. A sachem had to belong to a lineage through which the rank descended, but he was personally selected by the house mothers after consultation with the other women of their clan; the men took no part in the process. Such nominations did have to be approved by the sachems of the phratry to which the nominee belonged, and finally by the whole federal council of the League at an intertribal festival during which the new sachems were installed. But the old women still had power to depose sachems who did not uphold their positions with sufficient ability and dignity. Tribal affairs were therefore under the constant supervision of women, and the important role they played in the political structure of the Iroquois was supported by their economic contribution to the tribe. They alone cultivated the fields, while the men engaged in hunting, fishing, trading and fighting. This meant that they provided the greater part of the food supply and gave the men the time to carry out their activities.

The sachems had no formal authority over the internal affairs of the specific tribes to which they belonged, though their views were heard with respect and they wielded a certain moral influence. This, however, was limited by a parallel and more informal system of authority, that of the war chiefs, who seem to have maintained their positions through their reputations for valour or cunning in warfare, rather than through formal election. Sachems were civil chiefs, and the war parties that played such a large role in Iroquois connections with the outside world seem largely to have been organized without their knowledge or consent. It was the unofficial war chiefs who instigated these campaigns to give the warriors a relief from idleness and to acquire merit within the tribe by bringing home a few scalps or some booty.

The political organization of the Five Nations did not imply a strong class structure. Although families did have hereditary rights to chieftainship, the individual chiefs owed their prestige to merit: valour and skill in warfare, dignity, and eloquence in the council, which was greatly valued. Otherwise there was no difference between a chief and any other man, and while there were limitations on those who might become sachems, there were no restrictions on those who might become war chiefs.

Like the abundant supplies of fish among the tribes of the Pacific coast, the large quantities of preservable food available to the peoples of the Five Nations allowed for a great deal of leisure during the winter. During that season war and trade, as well as farming, were largely discontinued, and the abundance of food and time were used to support a rich pattern of feasting and ceremonies. There were public festivals in which the whole of the tribe would participate, and the restricted and esoteric ceremonies of the medicine societies.

Many of the public festivals were really part of a fertility cult that was linked to the various stages in the yearly process of cultivation and growth. The first would take place when the corn was planted, the next when its green shoots were well above the ground and a third when it was harvested. Beans and wild fruits were connected with smaller festivals. On all such occasions the Great Spirit in his manifestation as Jouskeha, the sun god, would be celebrated by prayer, orations, dances and offerings, and so would the minor deities who ensured the abundance of specific crops like corn, beans and squash. Elected stewards would supervise the festivals, collecting food for the feasts and fixing the days for the ceremonies. At mid-winter the Iroquois would hold their own kind of Yule in a great festival celebrating the solstice. It would last for a week or more, with abundant meals and the sacrifice of a white dog. Like the great festivals of the ancient Greeks at Olympia and Delphi, it would end with several days of games. There was also an annual feast of the dead, though it seems to have been less elaborate among the Five Nations than it was among the Hurons, whose ceremonies greatly impressed observers. During that feast the bodies of the dead were exhumed and the cleaned bones were deposited in great tribal ossuaries.

The secrets of the medicine societies were well kept, but they seem to have played a very important role in Iroquois life. The most open society, which survived into the modern age, was the False Face Society. Each spring and fall, wearing grotesquely carved wooden masks, its members invaded the longhouses to drive away the spirits that cause sickness. Afterwards they gathered in the big council house that stood at the centre of every village to hold their dances. Other societies seem to have been more prestigious, and it is a further sign of the strength of female influence among the Iroquois that two of these, the Dark Dance Society and the Death Feast Society, were controlled by women, even though membership was open to both sexes.

The relentlessness and cunning of their warfare gave the Iroquois a bad name in their time and that reputation has persisted ever since. This is largely because their methods of warfare were based on elements of surprise and ruse, which could be used to great effect in the forests that covered the lands around the St Lawrence and the Great Lakes. Father Jérôme Lalemant, a Jesuit who was eventually to become one of their most celebrated victims, remarked: "They come like foxes through the woods. They attack like lions. They take flight like birds, disappearing before they have really appeared."

When the Huron nation was destroyed by the Iroquois in 1649, Lalemant and his missionary colleague, Jean de Brébeuf, were tortured to death at the hands of the conquerors. An image of Christian courage facing devilish savagery was to linger for generations in the minds of Canadians, and it inspired E. J. Pratt's flawed epic, *Brébeuf and His Brethren*. But in fairness to the Iroquois it must be said that they were in general a hospitable and even a charitable people in the classic sense. It was part of their unspoken moral code that the needy had first call on whatever food was brought into the village. They never abandoned their sick or old, as some other tribes did. And the killing of prisoners by extreme and ingenious torture was not nearly so widespread as legend has suggested, for the simple reason that the Iroquois, never a numerous people and often at war, suffered a perpetual manpower crisis. Most of the prisoners they took were in fact adopted into families. The captives were treated well, and, far from suffering the indignity of being enslaved, as happened to prisoners among the Pacific Coast tribes, they enjoyed from the beginning equal status among the members of the tribe into which they had been taken. This practice had become quite common by the middle of the seventeenth century when the effects of imported sickness had further reduced the strength of the tribes. Diamond Jenness gives the following description:

> In 1668 . . . Huron and Algonkian ex-captives made up two-thirds of the Oneida tribe; and about the same time the Seneca became a medley of Neutral, Erie, and Conestoga remnants with only a small inlying stratum of the original Iroquois. In the eighteenth century all five tribes absorbed an appreciable number of Europeans . . . .[4]

We are not even certain of the real reasons for which certain prisoners were tortured to death, but in an oblique way, respect seems to have entered into the situation. The man chosen for such a death was not likely to be the coward; he would be the warrior or the saint whom his torturers would expect to die without flinching, and so prove the courage which they valued in themselves. Similarly, the ritual cannibalism in which the Mohawks occasionally indulged may have arisen from the notion, widespread among primitive peoples, that to eat the flesh or drink the blood of a brave enemy would result in his courage being transferred to the partakers. The idea of the brave man ceremonially killed also fits in with the concept of the sacrificial king, whose death among agrarian peoples was thought to guarantee the continued fertility of the earth. In the case of the Iroquois, we cannot entirely discount the possibility that the occasional killing of brave captives may have been not only an atrocity of Indian warfare, but also a part of the fertility rites to which these tribes were so devoted.

The potency released by the sacrifice of shamans from another land like Lalament and Brébeuf may have seemed enormous to their killers.

ALTHOUGH HENRY KELSEY HAD ALREADY encountered the tribes of the prairies in the late seventeenth century, real and lasting contact between them and the Europeans was not established until the later part of the eighteenth century. Even then the plains peoples were probably the most resistant of all Canadian Indians to European penetration. When Anthony Henday tried in 1754 to persuade the Blackfoot chiefs to take furs to Hudson Bay for trading, he was proudly told that their hunting life gave them all they wanted, and that they felt no need to disrupt their way of life to please strangers.

The bison herds did in fact supply most of the needs of the plains Indians. They had created their own equivalent of the Iroquois winter larders of corn and beans: they preserved bison meat, sun-drying it and making it into that long-lasting, versatile food known as pemmican, made of powdered dried meat mixed with the animal's own fat in buffalo-skin bags. Their lodges, or teepees, were made from the bison's hide, and so were their clothes, sewn with the animal's sinews. "Buffalo robes" served as bedding, and the rawhide thonging known as shaganappi had a multitude of purposes. Once the horse was adopted by the prairie tribes, supplies of food became even more reliable and abundant and the tribes became more self-sufficient. Their weapons remained unsophisticated, however. Until the late eighteenth century, they hunted with stone-tipped arrows.

This self-sufficiency lasted only a short time. Before the first years of the nineteenth century the spread of firearms from the direction of Hudson Bay, obtained first by the Cree, was changing the balance of power in the prairies. To obtain the muskets and later the rifles necessary to preserve control of their hunting grounds, even the Blackfoot had to establish contact with the traders, at which point the rapid transformation of their culture began.

AT THE END OF THE EIGHTEENTH CENTURY the inhabitants of the plains belonged to two mutually hostile groups. Three associated tribes made up the Blackfoot nation: the Blackfoot, the Piegan and the Blood. According to their legends they always lived on the prairie, and archæological evidence suggests that they are indeed the descendants of the people who originally settled on the plains after the retreat of the great icefields. By the time the first Europeans wrote about them, these tribes were part of a close confederacy that must already have existed for a long time. It was evidently tightened, in self-defence, as new peoples moved into the plains from the surrounding woodlands.

The most important groups of intruders were the Assiniboine and the Cree. The Assiniboine were related to the Dakota Sioux, and may have been an offshoot of that tribe which moved northeastward into the western woodlands around Lake of the Woods. Early in the seventeenth century they began to move into the eastern prairies, establishing themselves mostly along what is now called the Assiniboine River. As they moved into the new territory, they adopted many of the customs and practices of the original plains peoples. The movement of the Assiniboine may have been accelerated in the eighteenth century when the Ojibwa obtained firearms and began to push both the Sioux and the Assiniboine westward. At about the same time bands of Cree in northern Manitoba and Saskatchewan started to move from the forest edge through the North Saskatchewan parklands, where they, like the Assiniboine, assimilated some of the culture of the plains tribes.

The mobility provided by the horse and the killing power of the firearms, accelerated not only hunting, but also warfare. Some large battles took place between rival

tribes, but more often warfare was carried on by raiding
parties which fled as quickly as they came, with the
horses they had stolen or the scalps they had seized.
Out of these conflicts two rival blocs of tribes emerged.
One was an alliance formed by the newcomers, the Assiniboine and Cree. The other was a league of the older
tribes who felt that the lands belonged to them by ancestral right. They were the peoples who became known
as the Blackfoot nation, and they set out resolutely to
defend the western plains, bounded by the Rocky
Mountains, against all comers. This meant they were
frequently at war not only with the Assiniboine and the
Cree, but also with tribes like the Kootenay and the
Shuswap, who came over the mountains from the valleys of British Columbia to hunt bison at certain seasons, and the Sioux, the Shoshone and sometimes the
Gros Ventres to the south. The only alien people against
whom their hands were not turned were the Sarcee, a
small group of Athapascan-speaking people who lived
in what is now northern Alberta. They had accepted the
prairie way of life and now fought beside the Blackfoot
in their wars against the Cree.

This constant warfare gave the Blackfoot a reputation
for bellicosity and made them feared throughout the
Northwest, yet if we could bring a good Blackfoot orator
back from the past, he would probably argue that they
were merely protecting their ancestral heartland from
outsiders who wished to exploit its wealth of bison and
that their attacks on their neighbours were merely extended measures of defence. However, he would certainly not wish to deny the joy his people gained from
the adventure of warfare.

The need for constant defensive vigilance united the
three peoples of the Blackfoot Confederacy and dictated
the league's form. It was a closer alliance than that of
the Assiniboine and Cree, but it was less structured
than the Five Nations of the Iroquois. Yet within the individual tribes of the confederacy a relatively elaborate

and active organization existed. It was dictated by the need for disciplined cooperation among relatively numerous groups of people at the time of the large bison hunts, in which hundreds of people would be involved. The remains of prehistoric pounds show that even before the horse created greater mobility, plains Indians would often carry on the hunt in large groups.

In historic times the Blackfoot moved about in bands composed of a number of families and often numbering several hundred people. Each band would have its council of wise elders and good hunters, and one of them would be picked to serve rather informally as a chief. Every summer the whole tribe would gather for several weeks, and then a head chief of the people would be selected. Often the three peoples — the Blackfoot, the Piegan and the Blood — would meet at the same spot. The tribes would arrange themselves into three separate groups, band by band, their lodges deployed in a large circle, with the high chief's teepee in the centre. The Blackfoot Confederacy had no formal high council like the Iroquois council of sachems, but their chiefs would meet together informally to discuss common interests whenever the three tribes were assembled. Their alliance against external enemies was also firm, even though Blackfoot bands would often fight against each other.

Differences in wealth existed among the Blackfoot, largely defined by the number of horses a family possessed. However, there was no class system as we understand it. Indeed, something near a real democracy seemed to flourish in this society where the structure of authority depended greatly on the support a chief might gain from his braves. Bishop Pierre-Jean de Smet, a Flemish missionary who lived on the prairies for a quarter of a century beginning in 1845, wrote about the role of the chief as he observed it in a period when Indian peoples were still effectively lords of the plains.

The power of a chief is sometimes merely nominal; sometimes, also, his authority is absolute, and his name, as well as his influence, extends beyond the limits of his own village, so that the whole tribe to which he belongs acknowledges him as their head . . . . Courage, address and an enterprising spirit may elevate every warrior to the highest honours, especially if his father or an uncle enjoyed the dignity of chief before him, and he has a numerous family ready to maintain his authority and avenge his quarrels. Yet when the seniors and warriors have installed him with all the requisite ceremonies, it must not be supposed that he, on this account, arrogates to himself the least exterior appearance of rank or dignity. He is too well aware that his rank hangs by a frail thread, which may quite easily be broken. He must gain the confidence of his uncertain subjects, or retain them by fear. A great many families in the village are better off than the chief, dress better, are richer in arms, horses and other possessions. Like the ancient German chiefs, he gains the confidence and attachment of his soldiers, first by his bravery, more frequently by presents, which only serve to impoverish him the more. If a chief does not succeed in gaining the love of his subjects, they will despise his authority and quit him at the slightest opposition on his part; for the customs of the Indians admit no conditions by which they may enforce respect from their subjects.[5]

Just as authority was tenuous among the prairie Indians, democracy was strong. Nowhere was this more evident than in the horizontal structure of the warrior fraternities, which were not restricted to any one band, but were spread through the whole tribe. There were ten or twelve of these societies in each tribe, roughly graded, so that every four or five years a man would enter a higher society. Many of the older men retained their memberships in the junior societies, however, presumably so that the young would not be deprived of the wisdom and experience of the old. These societies were quasi-ceremonial and quasi-religious in character, each having its own dance festivals, and all meeting for the annual Sun Dance in celebration of the Great Spirit in his solar manifestation. This was the festival at which warriors who had made vows would torture themselves by dancing in a gigantic lodge around the sacred central pole. They were attached to the pole by thongs threaded through their chest and shoulder muscles and they danced until the thongs tore through their flesh.

Apart from filling a ceremonial function, the warrior fraternities maintained the democratic disciplines of the tribes. The need for concerted action when bison were being driven into the pounds had already taught the plains Indians the importance of effective cooperation. With the advent of the horse, which allowed the bison to be hunted in a kind of coordinated cavalry charge, with the hunters riding through the herd and shooting the animals, regulation was all the more necessary. In such operations much depended on the animals not being frightened away before the charge was organized, and one of the duties of the warrior fraternities was to provide the necessary police to enforce the rules of the hunt. Bishop de Smet described the procedure used by the Assiniboine, which was virtually identical to the methods of the Blackfoot peoples.

> They first choose a band of warriors to hinder the hunters from leaving camp, either alone or in detached companies, lest the bison be disturbed and thus be driven away from the encampment. The law against this is extremely severe; not only all the Indians of the camp must conform to it, but it reaches to all travellers, even when they are ignorant of the encampment or do not know that there is a hunt in contemplation. Should they frighten the animals, they are also punishable; however, those of the camp are more rigorously chastised in case they transgress the regulation. Their guns, their bows and arrows are broken, their lodges cut to pieces, their dogs killed, all their

provisions and hides are taken away from them. If they are bold enough to resist this penalty, they are beaten with bows, sticks, and clubs, and this torment frequently terminates in the death of the unhappy aggressor. Anyone who should set fire to the prairie by accident or imprudence, or in any way frighten off the herd, would be sure to be well beaten.[6]

The leaders of the warrior societies sat in the tribal councils when the bands met together in the summer, and it was they who decided when and how the herds of bison were to be attacked. Their fraternities provided scouts when the bands were on the march and organized the pitching and policing of the camps. In fact they created the effective working infrastructure of a nomadic hunting society that was more complex in its organization and more collectively motivated in its actions than that of the woodland Indians. The societies seem to have been non-exclusive, and, rather like commissions in the eighteenth-century British army, society memberships could be obtained by purchase. A man bought into a society when another man, ascending to a higher fraternity, was willing to sell his regalia. There was no provision for blackballing a potential member and no mechanism for expulsion.

An exception to this easy democracy of attitude was the status of the women. Apparently a few fraternities did admit a limited number of women, but there was never a situation in which women controlled them as they did some of the medicine societies of the Iroquois. In their view of women, there were indeed considerable differences between the two great confederated groups. The Blackfoot tribes were patrilineal societies; lineage was reckoned through the male line. In their economies the men were the principal providers of food and of the materials for shelter. The women did process the material the men provided, preparing dried meat and pemmican and sewing hides into garments and lodge covers, but they were not major primary producers of food as the Iroquois women were. The tribal economy did not depend on them except in a secondary way, and so their influence was small.

Yet, in spite of their limitations, the social and political structures of the Blackfoot and other plains Indians — like those of the Iroquois — show how well so-called primitive people can organize their lives when, by effort or good fortune, they are able to secure enough food. Circumstances later changed, and external factors made obsolete their aboriginal ways of life. However, this does not diminish the capability with which they evolved political and social structures that encouraged cooperation and minimized dissension within their simple and not very populous societies.

THE BLACKFOOT AND THE IROQUOIS shared with all the other native peoples of Canada the animist belief that they lived in a world where everything was permeated by spirit. In one sense this was a positive belief, since it eliminated the possibility of people elevating themselves above other creatures, as people in Christian societies have done, on the assumption that human beings have souls and animals do not. If one believes, as the Indians and the Inuit did, that in spiritual terms human beings and animals and even plants are equal though different, then one does not assume that humanity has the privilege of dominating the world. Native groups in Canada have generally seen themselves — even if they never articulated the idea in the European way — as living in and on and with the environment. The intrusive Europeans, on the other hand, wished to live off the land, to dominate and exploit it.

But if an animist attitude leads to respect for other creatures and life forms in the natural world, it also opens the mind to fear and distrust of spiritual potencies in the environment. Since human fears demand reassurance and human ills demand cures, there inevitably emerges a class of people who claim to live in the interface between the natural and the supernatural, between the human and the extrahuman. These are the wizards, the medicine men, the shamans, who can move at will from the physical into the spiritual realm and who in the process can acquire superhuman powers that may be turned to good or to evil.

Every native group in Canada had its shamans or medicine men, who were credited with divinatory and curative powers, but, if they wished, could direct their powers in a negative way and become sorcerers, killing by magical means. The shamans were feared, since nobody knew which of them might have turned to sorcery, but also courted, since only a shaman could detect and counteract a sorcerer's work.

In some Indian societies the shamans tended to be solitary beings, often acquiring their powers through spirit encounters in the wilderness, transmitting them furtively to their apprentices, and appearing in public only when their powers were called upon. But among one Canadian people, the Ojibwa, the shamans became an important corporate entity, and their collective power assumed a spiritual rather than a political form.

The Ojibwa inhabited a wide strip of forest along what is now the southern boundary of most of Canada, extending north of Lake Huron and Lake Superior and as far as the Red River valley. They were a loosely organized woodland people who were divided into four groups hardly cohesive enough to be called tribes: the Ojibwa, or Saulteaux, the Mississauga, the Ottawa (also called the Traders because of their commercial activities) and the Potawatomi, who lived in what later became American territory on the Michigan side of Lake Huron. They moved around in small bands of two or three hundred people, divided into a number of exogamous clans. Each band had a chief, who was often also the leader in war, but none of the larger groups had what might be called a tribal chief. Certainly no individual ever appeared in history who might be considered the leader of an Ojibwa nation.

Yet there were, as among the prairie peoples, certain horizontal structures uniting the bands. Members of one clan, for example, could be found in a number of Ojibwa bands, and they considered each other relatives. The bands also shared friends and enemies. The Cree were generally seen as friends and the Sioux and the Iroquois as enemies. For a while the Ojibwa, the Ottawa and the Potawatomi maintained a loose defensive alliance and their chiefs would sometimes gather in what was called the Council of the Three Fires.

The Ojibwa were woodland nomads, but they lived in relatively productive terrain. They were much more prosperous than most forest tribes, and this may explain the relatively rich ceremonial life they developed, centred on an institution unique among Canadian native peoples. This was the Midewiwin, or Grand Medicine Society, in which the shamans ceased to be solitary wizards and became a semi-religious order wielding great influence.

The Midewiwin were men and women who went through long periods of initiation involving tranced experiences, in which they learned about practical herbal medicine. They also seem to have acquired hypnotic powers that enabled them to cure a variety of psychosomatic illnesses. Eventually, by gaining knowledge and by making suitable gifts, the members of the society could rise through its four grades, though the process of ascent was so expensive that few became initiates to the highest grade. The great annual festival of the Midewiwin was the Ojibwas' central ceremony and this society of mystics seems to have held the Ojibwa together as a people. This was particularly true after European penetration began to erode other aspects of tribal life; the Midewiwin became the remembrancers of the people, preserving its heritage of myth and tradition. Perhaps this is why even now, when their traditional life has

largely disintegrated in material ways, the Ojibwa seem
to have retained a more lasting sense of their identity
than the other western tribes.

LIKE THE WOODLAND HUNTERS, the tribes of the Pacific coast
developed little sense of political structure, though the
rich natural resources of their region gave them an even
higher standard of living than that of the Iroquois or the
tribes of the plains. They dwelt in a mild, equable climate, on seashores and beside great rivers which provided fish and shellfish. They learned to preserve these
harvests, so they were rarely short of food at any season
of the year. They varied their fish diet with land game
and with the flesh of sea mammals, with wildfowl and
berries, and with vegetable foods like seaweed, fern
roots and the bulbs of the blue-flowered camas that
grow in parts of the coastal area.

As they also lived on the edge of enormous rainfor-
ests, they learned how to utilize the gigantic red cedars
that grew there. With antler wedges, cedar logs could be
split into surprisingly regular planks. Using only stone-
bladed tools, they then constructed solid houses. When
Alexander Mackenzie came to the villages of the Bella
Coola in 1793, the first white man to visit them, he remarked that the boards of the houses were so neatly
jointed they seemed to be all of one piece. Captain Cook
was impressed by the size of the great gabled houses of
the Nootka on Vancouver Island in which he found
many families living in compartments divided off by
mats and planks. Captain John Meares claimed that in
1788 he saw one such gabled building that housed eight
hundred people. If this sounds like exaggeration, it
must be recorded that when Simon Fraser sailed down
the river that bears his name, he once meticulously
paced out a Salish longhouse near the present site of
Vancouver and found that it was ninety feet wide and
fifteen hundred feet long.

The peoples of this coast were divided by language into a number of sharply distinct groups. From the Tlingit in the north, who lived mostly in what is now the Alaskan panhandle, to the Salish in the south, who spilled over into what is now Washington state, they lived a relatively settled life, moving only from established winter villages to summer fishing sites and berry-picking grounds. They were really peoples rather than tribes, for in pre-European times they had no collective political organization that corresponded to their respective language groups. Each of their big houses was a clan dwelling, dominated by the hereditary chief of a family line, and housing the commoners related to him as well as his slaves. These last were mere chattels over whom the chief had power of life and death; they were usually captives from another tribe. A village would consist of a number of dwellings ranged along a beach or a river bank, and the chiefs of the two or three most powerful houses would exert a degree of domination over the village. But there was no political cohesion. Even villages speaking the same language would often fight with each other, and only rarely did two villages enter into more than a fleeting alliance; even then it was usually in order to carry out a raid.

But if politics were rudimentary in these societies of scattered wealthy villages and nobody held much effective power, the social pattern was elaborate. Everyone sought the prestige offered by an intricate system of ranks and titles. For the coastal peoples, the years were divided into two parts. The summer was active, with people working hard to gather food and turn it into disposable wealth by various means of preservation. In the winter the same people used their leisure to get rid of that wealth in great sprees of conspicuous consumption, and this earned them social merit and position.

There were essentially two kinds of winter festivals among the coastal peoples, the potlatch and the ceremonials of quasi-religious societies. Both encouraged the craftsmen of the region, unrivalled among the Indians of Canada, to produce their splendid artifacts. The main aim of the potlatch was to validate rank by speech making and elaborate giving to the people who witnessed its assumption. Every lineage possessed a number of ranks, crests, names, songs, dances and types of mask that were inherited but could be used only after they had been confirmed by a potlatch. Other actions involving claims to prestige also had to be confirmed by a potlatch. Among these were the raising of a so-called totem pole, carved with the crests and legends to which a chief laid claim and the setting up of a memorial post to a dead chief. Puberty and other important rites of passage could also be occasions for potlatches.

When such a feast took place the chief would call on his clan fellows to help him accumulate objects that could be given. These ranged from cedar-bark blankets to elaborately carved dugout canoes. The chief would then invite his fellow chiefs to a great feast. They would arrive standing in the bows of their canoes, masked and singing their own songs. They would enter the host's house clad in elaborate regalia, including carved diadems ornamented with abalone shell and ermine skins and blankets of intricately woven mountain goat wool. They proceeded to the seats appropriate to their respective ranks; to be placed below one's rank was a notable insult that might lead to a lasting feud.

At the feast the host chief would give lavishly, but what to the casual visitor might have appeared to be generosity was in fact competitiveness. Every gift would be calculated to exceed what the chief had received from a particular guest at the latter's own potlatch. In this way a curious debt-and-credit system was evolved by which a chief expected to receive back more than he had given and thus eventually recoup his gifts — until he beggared himself again at the next potlatch. Sometimes the desire to assert his superiority would lead a chief not only to give but also to destroy property, accompanying such acts by speeches boasting of the chief's own lavishness and mocking his rivals, who also happened to be his guests, for the meagreness of their feasts.

These bizarre and extravagant family feasts were paralleled by the winter ceremonials of a number of quasi-religious societies, of which the leading one was the Hamatsa Society. Its mythical patron was Cannibal from the North End of the World, and its members practised ritual cannibalism, eating — or pretending to eat — the flesh of corpses at their initiations. The gatherings of these societies were highly theatrical occasions, when supernatural happenings were simulated for the "edification" of the credulous. Elaborate masks and illusionist devices were devised for these occasions by the local craftsmen, and men and women performed their inherited personal dances, wearing their own masks. (Women were often admitted to the societies and, among the Tsimshian, could even be chiefs.) The whole tradition of Pacific coast art developed to be used at the potlatches and winter ceremonials and to memorialize the pretensions of the chiefs. It consisted mainly of painted sculptures in wood, but also included stone carvings, some of great antiquity. There is now no doubt that the sculpting tradition was an ancient one and that the lack of relics to memorialize its prehistoric periods can be attributed mainly to the fact that most of the work of its artists was carried out in perishable materials.

THESE ARE THE MOST STRIKING aspects of the native societies of Canada as they were first seen when the Europeans came. From the Norsemen who arrived on the east coast late in the ninth century to the Spanish and British whose naval vessels dropped anchor off the Pacific coast in the latter part of the eighteenth century, they encountered societies as diverse in character as those that made up the European continent. From this point on, the histories of the two currents of culture and life, aboriginal

and alien, run together. And it was from this time that
the native societies began to change and disintegrate —
in much the same way as the contents of a long-buried
tomb will crumble when modern air enters the ancient
stillness.

PART
II

CHAPTER
3

Men from the Sea

THE FIRST GREAT WAVE OF IMMIGRATION into Canada came
from Asia in the west, over the northern wastelands of
Siberia and Alaska. The second was also a northerly
one, but it came from the east, over the cold waters of
the Atlantic from Europe. Its advance guard arrived just
over a thousand years ago, for it was in A.D. 896 that the
Icelandic mariner Bjarni Herjolfsson was blown off
course on his way from Iceland to Greenland and first
sighted North America, probably the coast of Labrador.

The Norsemen were a questing people. They had established themselves in some surprising corners of Europe — Normandy, Sicily and inland Russia — and
shortly they would conquer England. In the ninth century they followed the ancient Celtic monks who had
gone north from Ireland in search of hermit retreats and
settled first on the Faroe Islands and then in Iceland.
Still restless, the Norsemen continued to venture and
explore, and in the 890s, only a few years before Herjolfsson's voyage, Eric the Red had travelled from Iceland to Greenland and established a settlement that
would continue to prosper and spread. In the twelfth

century there were more than three hundred farms and hamlets in two separate areas of Greenland, as well as churches, a cathedral, a monastery and a nunnery.

The early years of the Greenland settlement seem to have been the most enterprising ones, and these are particularly associated with Canada. Leif, the son of Eric the Red, made a voyage to the northwest from the Greenland settlements in A.D. 1000. On that trip he discovered the territory he called Helluland, then turned south and reached Markland, going from there to Vinland in the south. In Vinland he found timber, which his men felled for use in woodless Greenland, as well as grapes and salmon larger than the Norsemen had ever seen. According to the sagas, the pastures were so abundant "that it seemed as though cattle would need no winter fodder, since the grass hardly withered in winter, while the days and nights were more equally divided than in Greenland or Iceland." The identity of Vinland has long been debated, but it was most commonly thought to be Newfoundland, where the climate was considerably more clement at the beginning of the eleventh century than it is today. The 1961 discovery of the remains of a Norse settlement at L'Anse aux Meadows on Newfoundland established that this was the site of Leifsbudir, the short-lived outpost to which, according to the sagas, at least four voyages were made.

Leif's brother Thorvald and his half-sister Freydis were involved in later expeditions, on one of which the first recorded encounter between Norsemen and North American natives took place. Thorvald and his men were attacked by a people whom they called "the Skraelings" and described as "dark ugly men who wore their hair in an unpleasant fashion." The "Skraelings" came in skin boats and shot Thorvald with an arrow; he died of the wound. On two later expeditions to Leifsbudir there were other hostile encounters with the Skraelings, during one of which the natives were routed by Freydis who led her warriors like a Valkyrie, beating her bare breasts with the flat of her sword. Perhaps because of this hostile reception the place was soon abandoned. The remains at L'Anse aux Meadows suggest that this was a seasonal camp rather than a permanent settlement; there is no evidence of the cattle rearing that the sagas suggest was contemplated. The buildings included dwellings combined with workshops, used for carpentry and blacksmith's work, the latter consisting mainly of making iron rivets to repair the Norse longships.

To fire their smithies the Norsemen used wood from the large trees they found growing there. The settlement may also have been a kind of temporary logging camp where trees were felled and the logs loaded on ships to be taken to Greenland. There may have been other, unrecorded contacts with the native peoples of Canada, for the Nordic settlements on Greenland continued until the beginning of the fifteenth century, and smelted iron that may have been traded or stolen from Norse hunters has been found in the remains of Thule settlements on Baffin Island and as far away as the shores of Hudson Bay. There may have been encounters with the Inuit less belligerent than those with the Skraelings, and some travellers and historians in modern times have suggested that Norsemen from Greenland interbred with the Inuit. This would explain the occasional incidence of fair or red-haired Inuit in the eastern Arctic. Given the Inuit custom until very recent years of men offering their wives to visitors as a token of hospitality, this does not seem unlikely, even though there are no Norse records or Inuit traditions that seem to confirm it.

If interbreeding occurred, it is perhaps the only lasting legacy we have in Canada of the Nordic presence. There is no sign of any settlement other than short-lived Leifsbudir, and no evidence of any profound change in native ways of life that can be attributed to the Greenland settlements. The most one can say is that in a very significant way the Norsemen on Vinland anticipated the next wave of Europeans, which began at the end of the fifteenth century with the discovery of the cod fisheries on Newfoundland. So far as Vinland was concerned the Norsemen were seasonal visitors like the first cod fishers — nomads by other names.

In this as in other respects they resembled most of the aboriginal peoples of Canada. We are inclined to assume that there were fundamental differences between the native peoples and eleventh- or fifteenth- century European men, but the early European arrivals came from often quite backward pre-mechanical societies, where seasonal wandering in search of one's livelihood was as customary as it was among the Indians or the Inuit. The Icelanders especially were as accustomed as the native peoples to adapting to harsh living conditions with relatively primitive resources. It is true that they had different languages and different beliefs, though the fear of sorcery was equally widespread within both groups.

The most important differences were a few technological ones, and these helped to determine the eventual outcome of the relationship between the two groups. The Europeans had woven cloths that were greatly superior to animal skins for making clothing; they had metal tools and weapons and utensils; and most important, the men who came at the end of the fifteenth century had firearms (though the Norsemen did not share this advantage). In other ways, however, the native peoples were more sophisticated than the intruders, and the more practical of the Europeans would imitate Indian or Inuit ways of living off the land and use aboriginal means of transport and modes of warfare. If we sought to establish, as many earlier historians did, a clear line between the representatives of European civilization and those of aboriginal primitivism, we would be losing much of the significance and the tragedy of the encounter between the two cultures. Often the Europeans were a good deal less than civilized and the aboriginals were a good deal more than primitive in their intellectual, technological and artistic development.

IN THE PAST THE NORSE INTRUSION into the North American continent was often treated as an isolated incident, having no connection with the intercourse between the continents that began with Columbus's arrival in the Caribbean in 1492. But trade between Greenland and Europe had gone on for several centuries, and the exploits of its early explorers were not forgotten. In 1070 a north German priest, Adam of Bremen, wrote that he had been told by a Danish king of "a land, discovered by many in that ocean, called Vinland." Beyond Vinland King Harald the Ruthless of Norway had voyaged through "intolerable ice" and seen "the bounds of the north grow dark before his eyes." Harald the Ruthless was presumably Harald IV who reigned in the twelfth century, lived a violent life and spent some time in exile. Although I have found no other record of his having voyaged across the north Atlantic, the details of the story do suggest that whoever did sail in this way encountered the long Arctic night. The lore of Greenland and the islands beyond it obviously survived among the merchants of the Hansa trading towns of northern Germany, and perhaps among those of the English and northern French seaports as well. In the early 1490s a certain Martin Baheim made a note on a map at a point near the actual location of Baffin Island: "Here one catches white falcons," an accurate observation which suggests how well the Norse voyages to the shores of Canada were still remembered in northern European nautical circles.

Were there in fact any contacts between Europe and North America between the demise of the Greenland settlement at the end of the fourteenth century and John Cabot's sighting of Newfoundland in 1497? There is one intriguing piece of evidence which suggests that the first wave of regular European visits to Canadian waters may

have begun with the arrival of cod fishers even before
the accredited explorers arrived. Queen Elizabeth I's as-
trologer, Dr John Dee, one of the most learned men of
his time, noted on a chart that in about 1494 — three
years before Cabot's arrival — Newfoundland had been
discovered by two Bristol merchants, Thorn and Eliot. It
is possible that other fishermen also arrived there before
Cabot, for in the late Middle Ages the demand for fish
and the depletion of traditional grounds was already
sending European fishermen on lengthy voyages. During these trips they developed some of the techniques of
preservation later used in the Newfoundland fisheries.
Boats from East Anglian ports sailed as far as Iceland in
search of cod; Portuguese boats fished tuna off the
Azores and the northwest coast of Africa. The voyage to
Newfoundland was not much farther or more perilous,
and those who made it would have as much reason to
keep their discoveries secret as Cabot would have to
make his public.

Certainly, by the early years of the sixteenth century,
fishermen from France and Britain, from Portugal and
Spain, were appearing in considerable numbers off the
shores of Newfoundland and Labrador. By the time Cartier sailed for Canada he was able to find in St Malo
men who had worked on fishing boats that had sailed in
the Gulf of St Lawrence, though they had not entered
the actual river. These early fishermen included not only
those who went in relatively small boats in search of
cod, but also the Basque whalers who had exhausted
the harvest in the Bay of Biscay and now came in fairly
large boats of five to six hundred tons. At first they operated mostly off Belle Isle, but eventually they followed
the river as far as Tadoussac at the mouth of the Saguenay, where they established a depot. By the 1570s, according to one captain who had made several voyages,
there were almost four hundred ships fishing off Newfoundland, as well as twenty or more Basque whalers.
At this time the English, who would eventually control

Newfoundland, were still in the minority; Iberian and French ships dominated the scene. This situation would begin to change, however, as the Danes drove the English out of the Icelandic fisheries.

There was really a double traffic into Canadian waters during the sixteenth and early seventeenth centuries. While the fishermen and the merchants who employed them were seeking profits off the shore, mariners encouraged and often subsidized by European rulers were seeking ways across or around the barrier of the American continent so that they could reach Asia. Once they had found that trade route, they could tap the fabled riches of Cathay, as they called China, and could equal the achievements of the Spaniards in Mexico and Peru. Cartier sailed with instructions to discover a way through the continent that would provide an easy northern route to the Orient, and this continued to be the official policy for French explorers at least as late as the travels into the prairies of La Vérendrye and his sons in the 1730s. A series of mariners, mostly British, attempted to find the famous Northwest Passage (a fable that eventually turned out to be a fact) around the north end of the continent. Martin Frobisher found his way to Baffin Island in 1576 and was wounded in the rump by an Inuit arrow. Unlike Thorvald Erickson, he survived, and in 1585 John Davis discovered the strait that bears his name and through which later explorers found their way into Hudson Bay. By the 1630s this early spurt of activity had died down, and voyaging in the Arctic was confined until the early nineteenth century to the whalers who began to arrive in the late 1600s. They did not go much farther than Davis Strait.

These exploratory voyages, apart from Cartier's journeys up the St Lawrence to Stadacona and Hochelaga in 1534–36, had little effect on the social history of Canada. On the other hand, the arrival of the fishermen and the whalers had an almost immediate effect. They were essentially seasonal migrants; no real settlement was established either on Newfoundland or on the mainland until the seventeenth century. The cod fishery, which was the main imported industry of the time, was divided into two parts, the "wet" fishery and the "dry" fishery. The "wet" fishers did not establish any depots on land. They fished mostly on the Grand Banks, salting down the fish, also called "green" cod, in the holds of their ships and returning to sell their cargos quickly in the markets of northern Europe.

The in-shore fisheries were both older and more numerous. A ship would anchor or beach in one of the many harbours of these highly indented coasts, and its men would begin by assembling the light fishing boats called shallops that they had brought in sections. They would then build cabins to live in, wharves or "stages" where the shallops could unload their catches, and platforms or "flakes" where the fish would be dried. They would fish in-shore and at the end of each day bring back the catch for light salting and sun-drying. The shallops were large boats and could carry about five tons of cod, which were then so abundant that, in Cabot's words, they could be taken "not only with the net but in baskets let down with a stone." The dry cod was sold mostly in southern Europe, though in later years a market developed in the West Indies, where inferior fish was often bought cheaply to feed the slaves. With this trade a triangular pattern developed: the boats that carried the fish to the Caribbean would load up there with rum and other products to take back to England, so that the merchants made a double profit on their voyages.

ANOTHER TRADE WHICH BEGAN at this time was the trade in furs. It was to eclipse the cod fisheries as the staple industry of early Canada. Around the Gulf of St Lawrence, mariners and fishermen found that the Indians had pelts that could be sold in Europe for a large profit. The Indians, on their part, were eager for the iron knives, hatchets and cooking pots that lifted them immediately out of the stone age and they preferred the Europeans' cloth to the skins that the traders coveted. The benefits to the native people of more efficient tools and utensils were more than negated, however, by the ills that came in the wake of the new trading connection. The various Algonkian-speaking groups in what are now Labrador, Quebec, Nova Scotia and New Brunswick quickly disrupted their patterns of living and began to winter in the interior so that they could bring back furs in the spring to trade with the returning ships. As the fur-bearing animals became depleted, the various tribes and bands began to quarrel over hunting or trapping grounds, and Indian warfare increased. But even worse than the effect of endemic fighting was that of the diseases the Europeans brought with them and to which the aboriginals of North America were not immune.

Since at this time there were no men literate enough among European intruders to keep any kind of accurate records, we have no comparative figures to tell us clearly to what extent the population was reduced. The evidence gathered by later missionaries, however, suggests that the decline, doubtless aggravated by the introduction of alcoholic drinks, was rapid and drastic. Father Biard, the Jesuit who came to North America in the early seventeenth century, noted that the Micmac "often complain that since the French mingle and carry on trade with them they are dying fast and the population is thinning out . . . and one by one different coasts, as they have begun to traffic with us, have been more reduced by disease."[7]

Not all the native peoples were content to welcome the intruders. The Inuit in both Labrador and Newfoundland tried to fight off the aliens who were encroaching on their fishing grounds. In Newfoundland there also appears to have been little friendly intercourse at any time between the Beothuk and the whites. The Beothuk had little to offer in trade, so they began to steal what they coveted from the fishing camps; this was the beginning of a mutual hostility between the fisher-men and the Newfoundland tribe which forced the latter to retreat inland from its original coastal sites. Gradu-ally, the tribe was harried into extinction by a kind of in-formal alliance of white men and Micmac Indians, who eventually took the place of the Beothuk as the native tribe inhabiting parts of Newfoundland.

In considering such lamentable episodes as the de-struction of the Beothuk and their culture — even the memory of their culture — one has to bear in mind that this was a particularly violent age, the age of the reli-gious wars in France, of the Thirty Years' War in Central Europe and of Cromwell's exterminatory campaigns in Ireland. It was an age when hangings and even more cruel executions were public and enjoyed by the popu-lace and when sailors were often flogged to death for minor infringements of discipline. The men who sailed on the fishing boats often came from seaports where vi-olence, drunkenness and prostitution were features of everyday life, and when abroad they tended to behave as they did at home. That made them dangerous neigh-bours for defenceless peoples. Added to that, one has to remember the combination of racial and religious preju-dices that characterized the age. In the sixteenth century even Frenchmen massacred each other and Englishmen burned each other over religious differences, and non-Christians were automatically hated and despised at the same time. Even among the churchmen there was often a narrow line between the urge to convert and the urge to exterminate; the Dominicans were both active mis-sionaries and formidable inquisitors.

FOR MORE THAN A CENTURY after the first Europeans ar-rived in Canadian waters their presence was essentially nomadic. It is true that as early as 1502 a consortium of Bristol merchants, perhaps including Thorn and Eliot, obtained — under the title of the Company of Adven-turers to the New Found Land — a royal patent to establish a colony on the island. The Company is said to have landed settlers as early as 1503 and to have sustained the settlement until 1506, which would make it the earliest actual European community anywhere in the Americas. However, there are no records of the actual location of the colony, and it seems likely that the people left by the merchants were not real settlers but winterers — caretakers left to maintain the summer installations until the ships returned the following year.

Towards the end of the sixteenth century important changes in the cod trade took place, mostly because the Spanish and Portuguese fleets were much smaller after the disastrous venture of the Armada took its toll of manpower and ships. The Portuguese would eventually return, but only to fish on the banks; they never attempted to set up shore establishments. Effective control of the trade fell into the hands of the English and the French, who remained powerful rivals until the Treaty of Utrecht. Then the French acknowledged the English title to Newfoundland and restricted their own activities to the so-called French Shore at the west end of the island. Migrant French fishermen went there right into the present century.

It was during the period of French-English rivalry that the wintering settlements began to develop into permanent ones. The most famous case of wintering in early Canada occurred when Cartier and his men stayed near Stadacona in the winter of 1535–36. Twenty-one of his men died of scurvy that time, and the rest would have perished if the Indians had not taught them how to brew the spruce beer that counteracted the disease. The winterings on Newfoundland were somewhat less dramatic. The first "overwinterer" seems to have been one James Rut, who stayed with his ship in St John's harbour over the winter of 1527–28 and built the first shack on its shore. St John's soon became a regular calling place for the English ships, and Sir Humphrey Gilbert found a settlement consisting of a makeshift cluster of buildings there in 1583, though he did not make clear whether these were permanent or had been put up that season by the crews of the Devon fishing boats that were working the Newfoundland fisheries at the time.

Both English and French fishing activity eventually became concentrated in the southeastern Avalon Peninsula, which had many excellent protected harbours. In this region are found most of the places that became important in the early history of Newfoundland: St John's itself; the important English trading centre of Trinity; Ferryland, which for some time was used by pirate leaders as a base for their expeditions to the Spanish Main; the French centres of Trepassey and Placentia (originally Plaisance); and a number of places linked with the first abortive attempts at organized settlement by chartered companies of English merchants and aristocrats.

These were almost — but not quite — the first settlements in Canada. Pierre du Gua, Sieur de Monts, had actually led a group to Acadia in 1604 and in the following year had established Port Royal there. In 1608 Champlain had founded the *habitation* at Quebec, the first lasting European settlement on the St Lawrence. Two years later, in 1610, a group led by John Guy, representing the London and Bristol Company, set up a settlement at Cupers Cove (now called Cupids) on Conception Bay. A number of other attempts at settlement followed during the next two decades. One was organized by the English landowner George Calvert, who later became Lord Baltimore, and eventually left for Virginia, having found Newfoundland a "wofull country" with the "sadd face of wynter" upon it for more than half the year. And while Port Royal at this period saw the first French poems written on Canadian soil — by Marc Lescarbot — Robert Hayman, the friend of Ben Jonson, wrote the first English poems a few years later at the Newfoundland settlement of Harbour Grace. It had been founded by merchants from the west of England in 1617. Hayman offered a somewhat more

benign view of the island than Calvert's disillusioned
outburst:

> The Aire in Newfound-land is wholesome, good;
> The Fire, as sweet as any made of wood;
> The Waters, very rich, both salt and fresh;
> The Earth more rich, you know it is no lesse.
> Where all are good, *Fire, Water, Earth* and *Aire,*
> What man made of these foure would not live there?

All these settlements failed, and most of those who
participated in them dispersed, either returning to England or seeking more congenial surroundings in New
England or the seaboard colonies farther south. Calvert
became the father of Maryland, and its capital, Baltimore, would be named after him. But some remained to
fish on their own account, and these were probably the
first resident fishermen in Newfoundland, the true pioneers of settlement by virtue of their tenacity. Gradually, as the seventeenth century continued, both
settlement and wintering increased, though there was
considerable opposition among English merchants, who
did not want the competition of a resident industry that
might trade its fish to all comers.

The imperial authorities tended to be sympathetic to
the pleas of the powerful mercantile houses in the west
of England, particularly after the restoration of the
Stuarts in 1660, for this had been a loyal Cavalier area.
Moreover, the Admiralty regarded the Newfoundland
fishery as an excellent training ground for seamen, who
could be recruited or pressed into the navy in time of
war. Regulations were imposed under Charles II, forbidding anyone to settle within six miles of the coast, and
requiring captains to bring their seamen back to England. But such official attempts were largely disre-
garded, and "planters," or small entrepreneurs who
owned a few shallops and traded their dried cod to visiting ships, began to settle in the coves along the coast-

line of the island. Their establishments became the nuclei of the famous Newfoundland outports. When, in the
1650s, the French established a colony on the side of the
Avalon peninsula opposite to St John's, the authorities
in Britain began to turn a blind eye to English settlement
on the island. By the end of the seventeenth century
there were about forty places on the Avalon peninsula
inhabited by English planters, and St John's was a substantial village with thirty families. Plaisance, where the
French colony had its civil administrator and garrison,
was also growing apace.

The English merchants were given a certain advantage in that the imperial government was unwilling to
establish its authority over Newfoundland's highly vola-
tile society. By custom, at each harbour where ships
gathered during the season, the captain of the first boat
to arrive became the "fishing admiral," who wielded ar-
bitrary power not only over the fishermen of the fleet
but also over the people living on the coast. The coast
dwellers sometimes fled into the interior to escape these
petty despots, and there became members of that anarchic movement about which history tells us tantalisingly
little, the Masterless Men.

IN 1699 THE IMPERIAL GOVERNMENT brought a semblance of
order into the situation by acknowledging the settlers'
property rights and by instituting a right of appeal to
the commanders of the naval convoys. But the naval
men tended to sympathize with the "fishing admirals,"
and it was not until a governor was appointed in 1729
and local magistrates were named that the tyranny of
the merchants began to abate somewhat. Something resembling a stable society then began to emerge.

Yet right to the end of the eighteenth century the actual settlers who became permanent inhabitants of Newfoundland were distinct from the overwinterers. It has
been estimated that the summer population of Newfoundland in the 1790s was about twenty-five thousand,

of whom five thousand would be seasonal workers who would depart in the autumn. Of the winter population of twenty thousand or so, only about ten thousand would be long-term residents. The rest were overwinterers usually employed under indenture by merchants for fixed periods. Through an infamous truck system by which they took their pay in goods provided by the merchants at inflated prices, they were usually in debt — as were many of the permanent residents. Sir Hugh Palliser, governor of the island in the 1760s, remarked that these people were "no better than the property or Slaves of the Merchant Supplyers to whom by exorbitant high Prices on their Goods they are all largely in Debt, more than they can work out during life." Like many impermanent societies of its kind, it was largely male, for even among the residents there were at least four men to every woman, and none of the overwinterers brought female companions with them.

By this time the shifting population of winterers and summer arrivals had become largely Irish, and the Irish were more inclined to stay when their indentures came to an end, since life on Newfoundland was not much worse than life in nineteenth-century Ireland. At least there was plenty of fish to go with the potatoes that could be grown in the pockets of soil in the rocky terrain. Some settlements, like St John's, became predominantly Irish. But no matter what their origins, the people who spent the winter together on Newfoundland were poor, deprived and, perhaps inevitably, given to drunkenness and riotousness. Those who had something to go back to returned after their indenture periods, and many escaped, if they had a chance, to the colonies of the American seaboard. The unstable, seminomadic character of Newfoundland society persisted until the Napoleonic Wars, which disrupted commercial activity and resulted in a decrease in the ships and manpower available to sustain the old sea trade. Out of that critical period Newfoundland would emerge in the early nineteenth century with a settled population, a poor man's culture of considerable vigour (of which more will be said later), and a fishing industry now dominated by locally established merchants, mainly in St John's. Though they were no longer predominant, foreign fishermen, like the White Fleet from Portugal still came each year to fish in international waters on the Grand Banks and to call in at the ports of Newfoundland.

So long balanced between marine nomadism and land settlement, Newfoundland was the site of Canada's first great primary industry — cod fishing. Its major lasting contribution, apart from the eventual settlement of Newfoundland, was the establishment of the sea routes to Canada. The fishermen who found their way across the Atlantic went on to explore the Gulf of St Lawrence. They made the first entries into the mass of the Canadian land and became precursors of the peoples of Europe who came to Canada in wave after wave, eventually dominating its life.

CHAPTER

4

Trade in the Wilderness

If THE COD FISHERS ESTABLISHED THE SEA ROUTES from Europe into the Canadian land, it was the fur traders who, from the seventeenth century onwards, established the land routes that led across the continent from the Atlantic to the Pacific coast and north to the Arctic sea. Like the fishery, this second great primary industry was essentially nomadic in its beginnings, depending, until it began to decline in the third quarter of the nineteenth century, on the constant movement of men and materials from one end of the country to the other. In accepting many of the features of native nomadism, the fur traders seemed to regress towards the neolithic past. They adopted the modes of travel used by the Indians and the Inuit and for several generations even abandoned that basic transportational tool of Old World civilizations, the wheel, relying instead on water transport or on the backs of animals and men.

Yet at the same time, just as the fishermen prepared the way for settlement on the eastern seaboard, so the fur traders prepared the way for settlement across Canada. Many a great Canadian city was to originate as a fur-trading post. This fact points up the great difference between the aboriginal nomads and the Europeans who adopted a nomadic life for the sake of trade. Aboriginal nomadism was a manifestation of cultures that had existed and developed in Canada ever since the human species crossed from Asia into the Americas. In fact, it was the necessary condition of those cultures' existence, for they depended on fluctuating and wandering animal resources. Immigrant nomadism was a temporary and expedient adaptation to North American aboriginal conditions on the part of intruders who represented the commercial interests of settled society. They retained their links to that society, to which most of them hoped to return if they survived the wilderness. They ultimately deferred to its values and, whatever the mode of life they adopted in the *pays d'en haut*, as the French traders called the forest land of the northwest, they could not avoid being the forerunners of settlement. Nevertheless, they moved across the continent as unsettled men, and it is significant that so many of the traders and their employees came from the margins of the settled world: from the crofts of the Hebrides and Orkneys off the northwest coast of Scotland, from the slum rookeries of English seventeenth- and eighteenth-century cities, from the marginal farms of the St Lawrence. They were men between two worlds, not completely civilized yet no longer primitive, and it is perhaps appropriate that the paths that opened the primitive and nomadic realm of Canada to the invasion of the civilized and settled world should first have been established and traversed by these marginal and restless men.

THE FIRST FUR TRADERS WERE THE FRENCH fishermen and the Basque whalers who found their way into the Gulf of St Lawrence from the very beginning of the sixteenth century. They were concerned primarily with commerce, but in the end, their activities resulted in Old World

authorities taking a political interest in the area. News of
the virgin territory quickly reached the ears of two
groups of people whose interests were somewhat different from those of humble fishermen or simple money-
minded merchants in St Malo and Honfleur. These were
the kings and courtiers, and the churchmen.

To the French court the almost furtive explorations
undertaken by Breton and Norman seamen gave the
promise — or at least the expectation — not only of
finding a way to China, but also of establishing dominions overseas that might rival those of the kings of
Spain and Portugal. Francis I, under whose instructions
Cartier sailed on all his voyages, was in fact the lifelong
rival of Charles V, King of Spain and Holy Roman Emperor, during whose reign Spain acquired the golden
kingdoms of Mexico and Peru. Henry IV, under whom
Samuel de Champlain founded Quebec and firmly established the early fur trade on the St Lawrence, was the
founder of the Bourbon dynasty, and reunited France
after the religious wars of the late sixteenth century. By
the time he became interested in Canada he had fought
his own wars with the Spaniards. For these French rulers a New France was at least a symbolic counterweight
to the New Spain the Habsburg kings of Spain were establishing on the ruins of the Aztec empire. Besides,
there was always the hope that the rivers of Canada
would not only lead to the Orient but would also yield
their own riches. This hope was fleetingly built up when
Cartier returned in 1542 from his last voyage with a
cargo of what he believed to be gold and diamonds.
They turned out to be iron pyrites and quartz crystals.
From this revelation arose the saying in France that first
brought the name of Canada into common parlance:
"Faux comme les diamants de Canada." (Ironically, the
place from which the false diamonds were quarried is
still called Cap aux Diamants, as Cartier named it.)

At the same time, regenerated by the Counter-Refor-
mation, the priesthood of a reinvigorated French church

was eager to enter the new mission field which they saw broadening before them. They were also moved to emulate the great conversions carried out by the Spanish clergy in Central and South America.

In the beginning, the fur trade seemed to create a point of entry for both state and church, for it had already been the means by which contact was established and sustained with the Indians of the Gulf of St Lawrence. Relations with the St Lawrence Iroquois, at first friendly, had been spoiled in 1536 when Cartier seized Donnacona, the chief of Stadacona, and nine of his fellow tribesmen, including two of his sons, and took them away to be presented before Francis I. None of them survived to return with Cartier, and when he went back to the St Lawrence in 1541 without them, he found, not surprisingly, that the Indians were hostile. Neither he nor de Roberval who followed him the next year, was able to establish the colony they had been instructed to found and of which de Roberval was to be the viceroy.

Later, in the 1580s, after the Iroquois had vanished from the river, Breton ships sailed up the St Lawrence and traded with the Algonquins and the Montagnais as far as the Lachine rapids, though they did not venture inland. Royal interest in furs and territory was aroused once again, and various grants were made to individuals who undertook both to trade and to establish colonies. Nothing much resulted from them until 1602 when Aymar de Chaste received a trading monopoly from Henry IV on condition that he report on the suitability of the St Lawrence valley for settlement.

It was a period when the actors changed quickly on the North American scene, and by 1603 Chaste had been replaced as owner of the monopoly and of the post that had been set up at Tadoussac by the Sieur de Monts, who employed Samuel de Champlain to carry out his survey. This journey, which Champlain undertook in the summer of 1603 in the company of François Gravé Du Pont, was the explorer's introduction to

Canada. He published an account of his visit, the first description of the St Lawrence and its valley to appear since the accounts of Jacques Cartier's voyages. He returned to France and in the following year sailed to Acadia, where he helped de Monts establish the abortive settlements of Ste Croix and Port Royal.

In 1608 Champlain returned to the St Lawrence, and established the *habitation* at Quebec. This represented the beginning of continuous settlement and of an organized fur trade in Canada. For the time being, and for some years ahead, settlement lagged, and Quebec began to serve as the inland *entrepôt* of the fur trade. It retained this role until Montreal was founded near the site of Hochelaga in the middle of the seventeenth century and gradually became the starting point for the journeys to the *pays d'en haut*.

It was Champlain who organized and rationalized the fur trade, hitherto a haphazard pattern of trafficking between ships' masters and the Indians they happened to encounter. He understood that in order to trade on a large scale one must establish relationships with the tribes who had access to the areas from which furs could be obtained. He also concluded that in order for those relations to be productive it might be necessary to enter into alliances. In this way he was drawn into the Indian rivalries and made decisions that would profoundly influence the development of New France. In the long run the alliances would disrupt completely the Indian societies of the St Lawrence and Great Lakes area.

Since the Iroquois had by now departed from the banks of the St Lawrence, and the sites of Stadacona and Hochelaga were grass-covered spaces, the Indian peoples with whom Champlain made immediate contact were the Montagnais and the Algonquin. They were enemies of the Five Nations Iroquois, and in 1609, to prove the good faith of the French towards the people who were his immediate neighbours, Champlain accompanied a war party of Montagnais, Algonquin and Huron up the Richelieu valley to raid the Mohawk villages there. Wielding his arquebus, he actually took part in the fight. This was interpreted by the Iroquois, with some justification, as an act of aggression on the part of the French, and it initiated a hostility on the part of the Five Nations that would have long-lasting consequences. At the same time, it placed Champlain in the good graces of the Algonquins and the Hurons, and after he had taken part in a second battle in 1610, an exchange of symbolic gestures cemented the alliance. A French youth, Étienne Brûlé, was adopted temporarily by the Huron, and a Huron boy came to live among the French, the idea being that they should learn each other's customs and in this way develop understanding and friendship.

The Huron and the Algonquin wanted allies to promote their wars; and Champlain and the French wanted furs. For the time being both their needs were met. In 1615, guided by Brûlé, who had already reached Lake Ontario, Champlain made his first trip to the *pays d'en haut*, the future Upper Canada, visiting the Huron with a small band of soldiers and Joseph le Caron, a Récollet priest and the first missionary to penetrate into the Indian country. Here he joined the Huron in an attack on another Iroquois tribe, the Oneida, and, though the allies failed to take any of the Iroquois villages and Champlain was wounded, he had succeeded in confirming the French bond with the Huron and pushing the fur trade into the area of the eastern Great Lakes. The fur trade had thus begun its steady, though often interrupted, western progress.

Some of the interruptions came from the Indians themselves, even those who were Champlain's allies, for the Huron contrived to prevent other Indian groups around them from making direct contact with the French and so established a temporary middleman monopoly. By this means a fair quantity of furs, including about fifteen thousand beaver pelts to be used in the hat trade, reached Quebec every year.

BUT THE TRADE DID NOT ENCOURAGE SETTLEMENT, and here, at the very beginning, arose what would become a perennial conflict. The acquisition of furs has always depended on an unspoiled wilderness, where fur-bearing animals can be found, and on a nomadic populace who will wander in search of them. Settlement has always been inimical to both these aims, and in a colony that began by concentrating on gathering the pelts of beaver and other creatures, settlement and conversion were at first neglected and even discouraged.

The two Roman Catholic orders represented on the St Lawrence — the Récollets (reformed Franciscans), who arrived from France in 1615, and the more highly organized Jesuits, who arrived in 1625 — raised their voices in a joint chorus of protest. They could not have chosen a better time, for in 1624 Louis XIII had appointed Cardinal Richelieu secretary of state for marine and commerce, which included colonies, and in 1627 Richelieu created the Compagnie des Cent-Associés (Company of a Hundred Associates), which undertook in return for a trading monopoly to settle four thousand French people in Canada over fifteen years and to promote the missions.

At this point a third interruption appeared, in the form of the English. News of the discovery of the St Lawrence had reached London and aroused ambitions to add this region to the existing North American colonies. Charles I organized merchants from London and Scotland and financed an expedition which captured the first flotilla of four ships sent out in 1628 by the Compagnie. In 1629 Champlain was starved into submission in the *habitation*. The first British conquest of Quebec lasted for three years; it was returned to France in 1632 under the Treaty of St Germain. During that period the English and Scottish merchants maintained an establishment of two hundred men and continued with considerable profit the trade Champlain had begun.

After the British had departed, the fur trade with the Huron middlemen was resumed, but it suffered from the devastating effects of European sicknesses, which reached the tribes of the Great Lakes during the 1630s. It was also undermined by disagreements among the Hurons themselves between those whom the active Jesuit missions were converting to Christianity and the pagan traditionalists. Intermittent raids by the Iroquois on the convoys of canoes carrying the furs to the St Lawrence did nothing to improve the situation. These raids were inspired partly by traditional enmities, which now involved the French as much as the Huron and the Algonkian tribes, partly by the need young warriors felt to prove themselves in raids, and partly, as we gather from the accounts of some of the Jesuit missionaries, by a kind of nascent nationalism among the tribes of the Five Nations, who wished to unite all those who spoke Iroquoian dialects, including Huron and Neutrals, into a single powerful confederation. There were truces and treaties between the French and the Iroquois which temporarily encouraged the fur trade, but in 1648 the Dutch on the Hudson River, concerned with commercial rather than territorial expansion, began to sell firearms in considerable numbers to the Iroquois. Attacks on the tribes allied to the French began immediately. The French — who had been largely responsible for the escalation of warfare through Champlain's involvement in Huron and Algonquin war parties — neither provided their allies with the firearms they needed to resist the Iroquois nor went to their aid with military forces.

The consequence was that all the Huron villages (and the Jesuit missions established among them) were destroyed and all the Iroquois tribes outside the Five Nations — the Huron and the Erie, the Neutrals and the Tobacco Indians — were dispersed. Many were killed, and most of those who survived were absorbed into the

victor tribes of the Five Nations. A tiny remnant of a
few hundred converted Hurons went to live under
French protection at Lorette near Quebec. Thus, one of
the early effects of the intrusion of Europeans into the
valley of the St Lawrence and the regions beyond it was
a major dislocation of tribal territorial patterns in what is
now southern Ontario. Two of the three original Iroquois confederacies were virtually eliminated. This left
the Five Nations, which would shortly become the Six,
unchallenged except by their European enemies. At the
same time, the area bounded by Lakes Erie, Ontario and
Huron was for a long time hardly populated at all.

The effect of these events on the fur trade was to
transform it from an industry which the French authorities had attempted to control from the homeland into a
locally based industry. The Compagnie des Cent-
Associés, having incurred heavy financial losses, abandoned the scene and turned its monopoly over to a
group of merchants who had already established themselves in Quebec. They stressed their local character by
calling themselves the Compagnie des Habitants.

This was the real beginning of the fur trade as a major force in Canadian history. During lulls in the intermittent fighting with the Iroquois, traders subsidized by
the Quebec merchants began to move westward into the
country of the Great Lakes, where, now that the Huron
power was destroyed, they could trade more directly
with the Indian groups farther west. And so there
emerged the class of men known as the *coureurs de bois*.

The *coureurs* were successful in penetrating the wilderness because, following the example of Étienne Brûlé
who had become half Indian during his period of residence with the Huron, they were willing to learn and
adapt for their own use the survival techniques of the
native peoples. Instead of moving through the forest
like soldiers in large groups, taking their European
equipment with them, they went singly and in small
parties, adapting their dress and their food requirements

to what the forest could give them. They travelled in light and easily portable birchbark canoes to thread their way through the intricate networks of lakes and rivers that stretched west from the St Lawrence waterway into the Canadian Shield. In winter they adopted snowshoes and sleighs. They learned Indian languages and if they stayed long enough in the forest, they took Indian wives *à la façon du pays*. Thus, a new racial element came into existence in Canada: the people of mixed blood whom the French called Métis and the English called half-breeds and who were destined to play a dramatic role in the country's history, far out of proportion to their numbers.

THE FIRST OF THE *COUREURS* must have been men from France who went native. However, from the mid-seventeenth century onward, the number of settlers increased and a population of French descent began to take root in the St Lawrence valley. They called themselves *canadiens* to distinguish themselves from the metropolitan-born official class, and the *coureurs* were recruited from among these *habitants* and their sons. Many such men spent part of their lives in the fur trade, and it has been estimated that during the seventeenth and eighteenth centuries no less than fifteen thousand men set out from Quebec and later from Montreal for the *pays d'en haut*. The custom continued after the British conquest of Quebec in 1759-60 and well into the nineteenth century, with men from the St Lawrence, later called *voyageurs*, becoming the crews of the fur traders' great canoes.

Most of the *canadiens* who went into the hinterland returned to their life of subsistence farming beside the St Lawrence. It was not greatly superior in terms of either comfort or security to that of agrarian tribes such as the Iroquois, for the *canadiens*, like the Indians, had to supplement their field produce by hunting and fishing and using wild vegetable products like maple sugar and syrup. Even at home they were at least in part men of the wilds, gathering food in the forests like their native neighbours. Some became lifelong voyageurs, attracted by the freedom of the life they could live in the forest. The settled existence beside the St Lawrence had many restrictions, as the French authorities were trying somewhat unsuccessfully to recreate on American soil a replica of the *ancien régime* at home, with all its ranks and privileges. After the Conquest, different kinds of restrictions were put in place as the British imposed a conqueror's rule. Something of the spirit that must have inspired the old *coureurs de bois* was caught by the fur trader Alexander Ross when, in his classic book on the Red River Colony, he described a conversation with an old voyageur he had had during the early nineteenth century. The old man told Ross:

> I have now been forty-two years in this country. For twenty-two I was a light canoeman. No portage was too long for me; all portages were alike. Fifty songs a day were nothing to me. I could carry, paddle, walk and sing with any man I ever saw. No water, no weather, ever stopped the paddle or the song. I have had twelve wives in the country and was once possessed of fifty horses and six running dogs. I beat all Indians at a race, and no white man passed me in the chase. I wanted for nothing. Five hundred pounds twice told have passed through my hands, although now I have not a spare shirt to my back nor a penny to buy one. Yet were I young I should glory in commencing the same career again. There is no life so happy as a *voyageur's* life; none so independent; no place where a man enjoys so much variety and freedom as in the Indian country. *Huzza, huzza pour le pays sauvage!*[8]

WHILE BRITISH GOVERNMENTS, UP TO the nineteenth century, were inclined to leave commercial trading companies both unregulated and unassisted once their founding charters had been granted, the French were more bureaucratically inclined. The authorities were therefore not too happy to see something resembling free trading developing in the Indian country. Until the 1680s, and particularly after Jean-Baptiste Colbert took responsibility under Louis XIV for the affairs of New France, the official policy was for posts to remain on the St Lawrence and the Indians to bring their furs to them. In this way it was hoped that there would be less possibility of Frenchmen becoming involved in the endemic warfare between the Indian tribes. There would be other benefits as well: the Jesuits would not have to fear that their potential converts might be corrupted by secular contact with Europeans, and the settlers would stay at home beside the St Lawrence, cultivating their lands. A series of decrees were promulgated forbidding Frenchmen to travel to the hinterland without permission, and permission was rarely given.

In defiance of these prohibitions, the merchants who had now established themselves in Montreal encouraged illegal traders to find their way into the *pays d'en haut* where, beside the lakes and rivers, they would build temporary cabins which served as moveable trading posts. It has been estimated that as early as the 1660s about two hundred *coureurs* were operating in the interior, and their numbers steadily increased. In the process, the exploration of the hinterland proceeded apace, as these small traders pioneered what would later become a historic route to the west, up the Ottawa River, across Lake Nipissing, and along the north shore of Lake Huron to Sault Ste Marie and Lake Superior.

Two of the illegal *coureurs* became the centre of an incident that radically changed the fur trade in Canada. They were Pierre-Esprit Radisson and Médard Chouart, known more commonly as the Sieur Des Groseilliers and later on referred to by the English as Mr Gooseberry. Radisson and Groseilliers had been trading sporadically in the west since the early 1650s and in 1659 they went on an expedition that took them not only to the familiar southern shores of Lake Superior, but to the northern shore as well, where they were the first traders to encounter the Cree. By now it was the spring of 1660, and what happened during the following summer is uncertain.

Nine years later, writing his boastful narrative of the journey, Radisson claimed that the two men had gone with the Indians by canoe and portage as far as Hudson Bay, but his account of the wonders seen there — such as eggs baking on the sun-heated sands beside the Bay — and the fact that they were back in Montreal, according to the Jesuit records, by August 19th, suggests that this part of the story which Radisson wrote for the eyes of King Charles II of England was a fabrication. What we do know is that in defiance of the authorities Groseilliers and Radisson did set out for the west in 1659 with a party of returning Mississauga, and they came back to Montreal in 1660, with sixty canoes manned by more than three hundred Indians, and an immense quantity of furs, whose value was variously reported at between 140,000 and 300,000 livres. The famous nun, Marie de l'Incarnation, remarked in one of her letters that their arrival compensated the local merchants for their losses in recent Iroquois raids, and she added shrewdly that "without commerce the country is worthless." But Governor d'Argenson was still angry at their defiance; he fined them heavily, imprisoned Groseilliers briefly and confiscated their furs. It seems likely that they had heard from the Cree about Hudson Bay but had not gone there themselves.

Groseilliers went to France in November 1660 to seek redress from the king, but he was put off with "fair words and promises," and now decided to try his luck with the traditional enemies of France. First he went to New England, where the Boston merchants were interested enough in what he had to say to finance a voyage to the Bay. They found a ship and set sail, but when they reached Hudson Strait the captain was scared by the icebergs and insisted on turning back. After a series of further disappointments, the two men encountered the commissioners whom Charles II had sent out to supervise the transfer of New Amsterdam from Dutch to British hands; it would be renamed New York after James, Duke of York, who was granted the right to develop the colony. Persuaded by the Englishmen, Radisson and Groseilliers accompanied Colonel George Cartwright when he returned to England and in the early winter of 1665 they had their first meeting with King Charles.

Shortly afterwards, with the king's consent, a consortium of private adventurers put together the money to finance an exploratory expedition, and in 1668 two tiny ships set out for Hudson Bay, the fifty-four ton *Eaglet* and the forty-three ton *Nonsuch*. The *Eaglet* was dismasted by storms and turned back, so it was the *Nonsuch* alone that sailed down Hudson Bay and eventually anchored in James Bay at its southern extremity. There its crew wintered and traded for the thick furs of the north in a log-built post they called Fort Charles. It would later be renamed Rupert's House, and the Hudson's Bay Company still trades from the spot.

The Company itself was chartered by the king on May 2, 1670, as the "Company of Adventurers of England Tradeing into Hudson's Bay." It was headed by the king's scientifically minded uncle, Prince Rupert, and the land over which the charter gave the company rights amounting to suzerainty was later called Rupert's Land. It consisted of the whole drainage basin of Hudson Bay, almost a million and a half square miles in area. That year the new Company sent out its first ships, much larger ones than the pioneer *Nonsuch*, and began the construction of permanent posts on the Bay.

MEANWHILE AMONG THE FRENCH a quiet conflict had begun between Colbert at home and the Intendant Jean Talon, the principal civilian official in New France. Wishing to

promote settlement on the St Lawrence and to avoid unnecessary conflict with the Iroquois, Colbert forbade the
establishment of posts and direct trading in the interior.
As an evasive tactic, Talon sent expeditions to "explore"
the hinterland, which in fact established a network of
trading contacts. One of the most important expeditions
was that of the Chevalier de La Salle, who was given
permission to find a way to the Gulf of Mexico and in
the process set up a series of posts south of the Great
Lakes and engaged actively in the fur trade. Hencefor-
ward the French fur trade became intimately linked with
the attempt to gain more knowledge of the interior and
to revive the old dream of finding an easy route to
China. These expeditions culminated in the great journeys of the 1730s by which Pierre Gaultier de Varennes,
Sieur de La Vérendrye reached the prairies accompanied
by his sons in the 1730s.

During the 1670s the fur trade out of Montreal was
caught between the pincers of British penetration from
two sides. To the north the posts established on James
Bay and Hudson Bay attracted the Cree from the region
north of Lake Superior. To the south, along the Hudson
River, the British had replaced the Dutch and were
proving more aggressive both in trading and in inciting
the Iroquois to attack the tribes with whom the French
were trading from Montreal.

Even Colbert eventually began to realize that maintaining the French position on the St Lawrence required
a more active policy in the hinterland. In 1681 he reversed his position, pardoned the *coureurs de bois* whose
status had become that of outlaws, and instituted a system of permits and licences which had one interesting
effect on the transportation system evolving in the *pays
d'en haut*. The quantities of furs authorized under licences were measured in canoe-loads, and this induced
the voyageurs to experiment with the construction of
larger freight canoes. Eventually the small craft that
originally carried about three-quarters of a ton were

replaced by the big *canots de maître*, which were more than thirty feet long, were paddled by eight men and carried three or more tons of cargo.

But more drastic action was needed to save New France from the British double threat, and in 1685 a new governor, Jacques-René de Brisay de Denonville, arrived with a contingent of soldiers. In the following year Pierre de Troyes led part of this contingent on an overland march north from Lake Superior. He surprised and seized the Hudson's Bay Company posts Moose Factory, Fort Rupert and Fort Albany, as well as a great loot of beaver pelts. The British recaptured Fort Albany in 1693, but it was not until the signing of the Treaty of Utrecht in 1713 when all the Hudson's Bay Company posts were returned to them and their rights over Hudson Bay were recognized that the Company could resume full-scale trading again.

Right up to the Conquest, the fur trade remained essential to the existence of New France, influencing the policies of both metropolitan and local governments and deeply affecting relations not only with the Indian peoples but also with the British, now the only European neighbours of the French in North America. By the end of the seventeenth century a precarious truce had been reached with the British after destructive raids and counter-raids across the New England borders, and the Iroquois had been effectively neutralized because of the heavy losses inflicted on their fighting men by mixed forces of the French and their allies. In 1701 the Iroquois entered into a non-aggression treaty with the French and a group of Algonkian tribes, and from this point on they ceased to be a significant independent force in North American affairs. At times, however, particularly during the American Revolution, they still played a role as allies of the British.

By this time the French fur trade had prospered so greatly that, largely because of the quantity of pelts traded at the captured Hudson's Bay Company posts on

James Bay, there was a glut of beaver in Montreal. Many of the pelts eventually rotted before buyers could be found in Europe, and the Jesuits used this opportunity to persuade the government to suspend the issuing of permits. Once again, the only approved trade was that carried on with natives who brought their pelts to Montreal. However, most of the *coureurs* remained in the woods, trading illegally and taking much of the fur they gathered to the English traders who were moving into the Ohio country from New York. The Treaty of Utrecht, which led to more than thirty years of peace between the British and the French, resulted in a major rationalization of the fur trade and a consolidation of territories. Having regained its posts on James Bay, the Hudson's Bay Company reasserted itself in the north. To the south the situation remained uncertain because the commission which under the Treaty of Utrecht was expected to establish a boundary between British and French hinterland territories never reached any conclusions. Indeed, when the situation was finally solved under the Treaty of Paris in 1763, after the Conquest of Quebec, the whole territory was lost as far as France was concerned. But after Utrecht the French were still pushing actively into the western and southwestern interior, which was still an uncharted no-man's-land.

Detroit, which had been founded in 1701, and Michilimackinac, which the *coureurs de bois* had already been using as a gathering point, now developed into major centres where merchants established themselves and from which their agents went out to found smaller posts in the wilderness. This practice virtually eliminated the Indian middlemen. Scattered over the whole area of the Great Lakes, there were establishments — often wretched log shacks — to which native hunters could easily find their way and gain the advantage of direct trading. This was a further stage in the disintegration of the structure of native societies in eastern Canada. Having lost their military power through attrition by war and sickness, the leading tribes were now losing the economic power which was formerly theirs by virtue of the trade routes. By the 1720s further social debilitation occurred when the French posts began to sell brandy to the Indians in order to keep them from frequenting the English posts on the southern shores of Lake Ontario where rum was readily obtainable. By the 1730s the French seemed to be gaining the upper hand in the fur trade, supported as they were by a series of military posts that extended as far west as La Vérendrye's Fort Bourbon on Lake Winnipeg and the other establishments he set up on the Assiniboine River. The rats had eaten up the surplus furs from the glut of the 1690s, and wider markets for beaver and other furs had opened up.

UNTIL THE CONQUEST OF QUEBEC IN 1760, the fur trade in Canada was really of two kinds: the static trade of the Hudson's Bay Company, and the dynamic trade carried on by the French. The Hudson's Bay Company was developed from the beginning as a hierarchical corporation, with a governor and a committee of merchants and other investors in London. Even in the field sharp distinctions were drawn between the "gentlemen," who headed the posts and acted as clerks on their way up the ladder of promotion, and the employees — craftsmen, sailors and labourers, who often came from the poorer quarters of the English cities. In the beginning, at least, few of these employees could speak any of the Indian languages, and for a number of reasons, including security and puritan morality, the Company discouraged any intercourse other than trading between its people and the natives. This, in spite of the fact that the presence of Indians, and particularly of Indian women, was quickly found to be necessary for carrying out a variety of important tasks, such as the cleaning and dressing of pelts, the cutting of shaganappi — that all-purpose rawhide cordage of the Northwest — and the making of moccasins and snowshoes.

As a result of this policy, most of the Company's employees and even its officers knew nothing of the country beyond the immediate shores of the Bay and little about its inhabitants apart from the travel-worn families who brought their year's catch of furs in for sale. Trading was done entirely at the Company's posts. Employees like Henry Kelsey and Anthony Henday, who occasionally went on expeditions into the hinterland and brought back the first observations of the Barren Ground and its inhabitants, were not sent out as itinerant traders with supplies of goods for trafficking. They were observers-cum-envoys, expected to acquaint themselves with the interior tribes in order to assess the possibility of trade, and also to persuade the outlying peoples to come to the Company's posts on the Bay. Not until quite late in the eighteenth century were posts built inland from the shore of the Bay.

The French fur trade was a much less rigidly organized affair. During the whole history of New France no large company successfully controlled the trade, and attempts to create monopolies were always short-lived. The pattern was essentially one of a swarm of individual traders, the *coureurs*, radiating over the *pays d'en haut* wherever it was safe for them to operate and bringing their furs to *entrepôts* like Montreal on the St Lawrence, and Detroit and Michilimackinac in the interior. There they would trade their goods to individual merchants who cooperated with each other only haphazardly and intermittently. The state would occasionally make a dramatic attempt at autocratic interference and try to control and limit the trade, but New France was not Old France. The *canadiens* had developed an independence of spirit that encouraged evasion and defiance of the law, and the paths through the forest into the interior were impossible to police effectively.

The French traders gained another great advantage from the fact that they mingled freely with the Indians, and, being themselves men of the wood and the river, between which their small farms lay, they had much more in common with them from the beginning than a man from a working-class district of London or Bristol could possibly have. The *coureurs de bois* learned the Indian languages, adopted the lifestyles of the natives, travelled like them and with them, and entered into temporary and sometimes permanent unions with their women *à la façon du pays*. In this way they were able to work their way into the hinterland around Hudson Bay, gaining control of the headwaters of the rivers by which the Indians took their furs to the Bay, and thus often effectively cutting off the flow of trade. Though York Factory, farther up the Bay, was little affected, the posts around James Bay were showing steadily smaller returns of fur, and it may well have been the British invasion of Quebec in 1760 that saved the Company from complete collapse, for many of the French traders went back at this time to help defend the settlements of the St Lawrence.

By the time of the Conquest the fur trade had already pioneered routes into the wilderness, had established the nuclei of later towns and had planted a French population in the *pays d'en haut*. There were perhaps two thousand or three thousand French inhabitants beyond the settled valley of the St Lawrence — traders, missionaries, soldiers — but despite losses resulting from warfare and sickness, the Indians of the region still outnumbered them twenty to one. This was the springboard from which, in the half-century or so that followed, the fur trade would overleap the continent as the harbinger of the invading European civilization.

IMMEDIATELY AFTER THE CONQUEST there was a scramble for control of the now vulnerable French trade. Traders from the Hudson River and the Ohio country — English, Scots, New Englanders — hastened into the country of the Great Lakes to fill the vacuum created by the withdrawal of traders from the St Lawrence; they arrived even before the British soldiers. The more prosperous and powerful merchants, most of them of Scottish extraction, made their way to Montreal and immediately began to take over the trade there. Temporary interruptions occurred, like the Indian revolt of 1763 which resulted from British attempts to impose a tighter military control over the Indian country around the Great Lakes. Led by the Ottawa chief Pontiac, it included Ojibwa, Potawatomi and even remnant Huron bands. For a while the whole of the *pays d'en haut* was in a state of war, as Michilimackinac and three other forts held by the British were captured and many whites were slaughtered. At the same time Detroit was besieged and a relief column headed for it was ambushed and defeated at Bloody Run in what is now Michigan. But British weapons eventually proved superior to the bows and trade muskets the Indians used, and in 1765 a peace was made that allowed the fur trade to resume and the new merchants of Montreal to establish their control over it.

A different situation now emerged from that which had existed in the days of New France, when the state tried rather ineffectually to control what was in fact a highly individualistic and fragmented trading pattern. By this time the English were no longer mercantilists like the French. While it is true that Adam Smith did not publish until 1776 his great anti-mercantilist work, *The Wealth of Nations*, his *laissez-faire* doctrine of free markets within freely operating societies had already been in the air for a long time. And so the prevalent atmosphere in Canada after it fell under the control of the British not only encouraged the individualist spirit that had formerly been associated with the *coureurs de bois*, but also, paradoxically, fostered powerful economic corporations that grew up parallel with the state.

The result was a radical reconstruction of the fur trade. Two gigantic companies engaged in a rivalry that dominated the whole area west of the St Lawrence valley as far as the Pacific Ocean until they were finally united in 1821 into a single monopoly. That institution, the reconstituted Hudson's Bay Company, controlled for another half-century the greater part of the vast territory that eventually became Canada. In the years immediately after the Conquest, the new traders, who were largely Scots and New Englanders, competed with the local merchants who had not chosen to return to France. Most of them were *canadiens* by birth. Gradually, through better organization, the English-speaking merchants gained ascendancy. Most of the voyageurs, however, on whose experience and energy the trade depended, were still *canadiens* from the St Lawrence valley until, a third of the way into the nineteenth century, the French-speaking Métis began to take their place.

Towards the end of the eighteenth century two events decisively affected the trade. One was the end of the American Revolution in 1783, which resulted in an influx of enterprising Scots and American-born Loyalists who had fought in the war and were now willing to put their energy and aggressiveness at the service of the fur trade. At the same time, a boundary between British North America and the United States had been agreed on tentatively, following a line through the Great Lakes and then continuing west of Lake Superior along the forty-ninth parallel. This meant that the important French posts of Michilimackinac and Detroit would fall into American hands. For a decade the traders from Montreal still probed southward and southwestward, as their predecessors had done, into the Ohio country and the headwater region of the Missouri, but this came to an end when Jay's Treaty of 1794 made the boundary definite. After this the Canadian fur trade was channelled northwestward into unknown territory rather than southwestward into the known territory that was now south of the new international boundary.

Once the state abandoned the role it had assumed in New France of controlling and occasionally restricting

the fur trade, competitive forces began to gain control.
The individualism of the old trade gradually disappeared on the upper levels, where the merchants began
to enter into partnerships and companies of varying
strength that competed for dominance of the Montreal
trade. The most energetic and durable of these groups
was the expansive and loosely organized partnership
known as the North West Company. Founded in 1779,
it survived struggles against several other competing
groups, the most formidable of which was the XY Company, founded by the great explorer Alexander Mackenzie in 1800. After a few years of bitter rivalry, in which
the Nor'Westers outbid their rivals, the two groups
amalgamated in 1804, and the North West Company,
having absorbed the XY, enjoyed a monopoly of the fur
trade out of Montreal until its eventual union with the
Hudson's Bay Company in 1821.

DURING THESE YEARS OF COMPETITIVE EXPANSION great explorations of Canadian territory took place as the trading
companies searched for new fur-bearing regions. The
routes the explorers opened up became the main routes
along which transport and communications would develop across Canada until recent times. Competition and
expansion also led to a structuring of the fur trade that
established within a still essentially nomadic world the
skeleton outline of an urban society.

A growing demand for furs and beaver hats in Europe led the traders of Montreal, even before the successful foundation of the North West Company, to press
farther into the west and northwest than their predecessors. Before the Conquest, the French were already trading as far west as the forks of the North and South
Saskatchewan rivers, and by the 1770s their successors,
skirting the south of the territory served by York Factory
on Hudson Bay, had reached the Upper Churchill River.
They were trading with the Chipewyan, who had formerly traded only to the Bay.

By 1778 Peter Pond, a New Englander of dubious reputation somewhat mysteriously involved in at least two murders, followed an Indian route through the Methy Portage. This land route led across the height of land between the Saskatchewan River system, which drains into the Hudson Bay, and the Mackenzie River system, which drains into the Arctic Ocean. Establishing a trading post on Lake Athabasca, he opened the door to the richest of all fur-bearing regions, in which the Nor'Westers quickly established themselves. Pond became entranced by the dream that had already attracted Cartier and La Vérendrye in the past — that of finding a way across the continent to the Pacific. At Lake Athabasca he gathered information from Indians about the river systems of the Northwest which made him believe he might have discovered the way. He drew a map illustrating his conclusions and showed it to Alexander Mackenzie, pointing to the river flowing out of Great Slave Lake that he believed must continue into the western ocean.

It was with Pond's hunch in mind that Alexander Mackenzie set out in 1789 on his voyage down that river. But instead of leading him to the Pacific, it took him north to the vast delta where he saw the tide throbbing and realized he had not reached the Pacific but the Arctic Ocean. Though he could not have known it, his arrival coincided with the historic day when the Bastille fell in Paris. On this desolate northern shore Mackenzie felt the reverse of exaltation, and before he set out against the stream on his way back to the Athabasca country, he named it the River of Disappointment. In his honour later generations would name this greatest of all the rivers of the north the Mackenzie.

But the route to the great Mer de l'Ouest, which had also lured the French explorers, remained a goal fixed in Mackenzie's mind. The Pacific coast of North America had become known to the world since the publication in 1784 of the official account of James Cook's expeditions,

A Voyage to the Pacific Ocean . . ., and some of the Nor'-Westers were convinced that land access to the western sea would counter the advantage the Hudson's Bay Company enjoyed of having their ships sail into the heart of the continent at York Factory and James Bay. The Nor'Westers had to carry their trade goods westward and their furs eastward along the long, complex and costly route that began in Montreal.

Starting again in 1793 from Fort Chipewyan on Lake Athabasca, Mackenzie reached the Peace River. From there he crossed the Rockies to the headwaters of the Fraser. Relying on the accounts of Indians he met on the way, he left that river and travelled through the Chilcotin country to the coastal mountains where he reached the source of the Bella Coola. Travelling downstream, he rested in the hospitable villages of the Bella Coola Indians, with their commodious cedar houses, and eventually arrived at salt water on Dean Channel. The Bella Bella he encountered there told him that white-sailed ships had recently visited their waters; he had arrived just after a marine explorer unconnected with the fur trade, Captain George Vancouver. That British explorer was now carrying out his great survey of the coastal waters of what are now British Columbia and the American state of Washington. The Bella Bella were hostile, and Mackenzie did not linger beside the sea, but before he departed on his journey back over the mountains he took care to leave a record of his visit.

> I now mixed some vermilion in melted grease, and inscribed in large characters, on the South-East face of the rock on which we had slept last night this brief memorial — "Alexander Mackenzie, from Canada, by land, the twenty-second of July, one thousand seven hundred and ninety-three."[9]

Mackenzie had reached the Pacific, but the route he had taken was far too arduous for the transportation of furs. His successors realized that a trade could be established in the fur-rich areas west of the Rockies only if practicable routes were found to carry goods through the series of great mountain ranges between the Rockies and the sea. Early in the nineteenth century the traders began to move over the fairly low passes from the Peace River country, and between 1804 and 1807 Simon Fraser established a series of posts — Fort McLeod, Fort St James and Fort George — in the thinly populated region (now northern British Columbia), which the Scottish traders named New Caledonia, after their native land. Fraser formed the opinion that the river which ran past Fort George, and which we now call the Fraser, was in fact the Columbia, whose estuary had been discovered in 1792 by the American captain, Robert Gray. By the time he had reached salt water near the present city of Vancouver, he realized that he, too, had been following a "river of disappointment," for it flowed into the Strait of Georgia well north of the Columbia estuary. Once again the route he had taken was far too perilous to be of any use to the trade.

Fraser's story of descending the Fraser Canyon is one of the epic tales of Canadian travel. He and his twenty-three men did so partly by land — or rather by cliff-face — and partly by water. He himself remarked that nowhere in his travels through the Cordillera had he encountered such difficult journeying, though he was following ancient Indian routes.

> We had to pass where no human being should venture. Yet in those places there is a regular footpath impressed, or rather indented, by frequent travelling upon the very rocks. And besides this, steps which are formed like a ladder, or the shrouds of a ship, by poles hanging to one another and crossed at certain distances with twigs and withes, suspended from the top to the foot of the precipices, and fastened at both ends to stones and trees, furnished a safe and

convenient passage to the Natives — but we, who
had not the advantage of their experience, were often
in imminent danger, when obliged to follow their
example.[10]

Sometimes Fraser chose to risk the water rather than the
precipices, and that involved the most consummate ca-
noemanship, to keep "clear of the precipice on one side,
and of the gulphs formed by the waves on the other."
Fraser found the Salish Indians, whose descendants still
live at Musqueam near Vancouver, as hostile as Mackenzie had found the Bella Bella. So he retreated by the
way he had come.

The third of the great explorer-traders of the North
West Company was David Thompson, a fine surveyor
as well as a resolute traveller. It was Thompson who
first established effective trade routes through the southern mountains of British Columbia. In the process he
finally identified the headwaters of the Columbia and
explored its relatively easy course to the ocean, intend-
ing to build at its mouth a post that would establish his
company on the Pacific. He reached the estuary in July
1811, four months too late; the traders of John Jacob
Astor's American Fur Company had already arrived by
sea the preceding March and they had established Fort
Astoria. But that single failure did little to detract from
Thompson's great achievements in a career lasting from
1784 to 1812. After his retirement from the fur trade he
embodied in a vivid narrative and in the first reliable
maps of Canada all his discoveries, and when all this
great work of charting and describing was finished, he
made a justified boast: "Thus I have fully completed the
survey of this part of North America from sea to sea,
and by almost innumerable Astronomical Observations
have determined the positions of the Mountains, Lakes
and Rivers, and other remarkable places on the northern
part of this Continent, the Maps of all of which have

been drawn and laid down in geographical position, being now the work of twenty-seven years."

By daringly penetrating the barriers of the Rockies and the Selkirks and exploring the great rivers of the west — the Mackenzie, the Fraser and the Columbia — the Nor'Westers completed the explorations begun by the early eighteenth-century French travellers and traders who had found their way to the eastern prairies. They established once and for all the great trade and transportation routes that in later generations would unite the various regions of Canada and make the country into a viable society rather than just a political abstraction.

But these more spectacular achievements of the Nor'-Westers should not obscure the genuine accomplishments of the Hudson's Bay Company's servants in this field. Its men were not merely the first in the prairies (Kelsey) and the first to see the Rockies (Henday). Hudson's Bay men like Samuel Hearne and Matthew Cocking carried out the first explorations of the great expanse of tundra known as the Barren Ground, and Hearne was the first European to reach the Arctic Ocean by land. In the nineteenth century the land-based explorations of Hudson's Bay traders like Dr John Rae did as much to establish the coastlines of the Arctic territories as the marine expeditions sent out by the Lords of the Admiralty in London. Rae and adventurers like him learned to explore economically and safely by acquiring the Indian and Inuit skills of living off the land. The success of their expeditions, on which few men ever died, contrasted strikingly with such grand and tragic failures as the heavily equipped and provisioned marine expedition sent out by the Admiralty under the command of Sir John Franklin in 1845. Ironically, it was Rae, travelling by sleigh with a few companions and living mainly on game and fish caught on the way, who discovered the grisly truth about Franklin's fate and the wretched death of his men from starvation and scurvy.

To such men, and to the less celebrated Hudson's Bay Company surveyors like Philip Turnor and Peter Fidler, we owe the early mapping and description of the country between the great trade routes. And to their narratives we owe some of the earliest images we have of the country westward from the Shield to the Pacific Ocean and northward to the shore of the Arctic Ocean. Yet though these men moved through the land with their instruments and equipment and made exact chartings of rivers and lakes and other natural features of the landscape, they all depended in the beginning on the accumulation of native knowledge. The fur traders provided the initiative, the means of travelling far, the vision of a whole continent that no Indian of that period possessed. But they still relied on native guides and on their intimate familiarity with terrain unknown to Europeans. Often they made extensive use of sketch maps which the Indians would draw on bits of birchbark or paper. Some of these maps that have survived are remarkably accurate in their sense of the directions of rivers, in their awareness of the spatial relationships between geographical features, and in their knowledge of the natural resources of a region — fishing spots, woodland areas, berry grounds. Often the Indians who guided the European traders were drawing on their own experiences as native traders in the era before the fur companies began trading directly in the Northwest. Their contribution to early Canadian exploration was considerable and should not be forgotten, even if for the most part they will always remain anonymous.

THE AREAS IN WHICH THE NORTH WEST and the Hudson's Bay companies operated in the early years of the nineteenth century consisted of the whole of Canada as we now know it, with the exception of the Maritime provinces, southern Quebec and southern Ontario. They also entered the no-man's-land of the lower Columbia River region — an area covering the present state of Washington and parts of Oregon, Idaho and Montana. The Hudson's Bay Company had charter rights over Rupert's Land, the vast drainage basin of Hudson Bay. The North West Company had no charter, and in theory its traders were trespassers on the prairies and in the Churchill River system, which were parts of Rupert's Land. In practice they disputed these areas with the English company. For a long time the Nor'Westers retained complete trading control of the Athabasca country, including the environs of Athabasca Lake, Great Slave Lake and the Mackenzie River. Beyond the mountains, in New Caledonia and the Columbia valley, which collectively they called the District of Columbia, they were unchallenged except by individual American sea traders — the so-called Boston Men — until the union of the two companies in 1821.

Neither company attempted to set up a government of any kind in the Northwest, apart from the Red River settlement, which was founded in 1812 under Lord Selkirk's patronage as a refuge for evicted Scottish crofters. Many of the fur traders regarded the colony with hostility, and it was destroyed by the Nor'Westers in 1816. After the settlement was re-established, a Council of Assiniboia was set up to create some semblance of an administration in this small farming area.

In the Far West, the area between the forty-ninth parallel and the Columbia River was lost to American administration as a result of the Oregon Boundary Treaty of 1846, when the British government somewhat pusillanimously gave in to American bellicosity. It surrendered a territory that by all the accepted rights of discovery (Captain Vancouver's surveys in the 1790s) and occupation (the North West Company from Thompson's journeys in 1811) was part of British North America and should have become part of Canada when British Columbia entered the Dominion in 1871. To the north of the Oregon Territory, British Columbia itself (all the land west of the Rockies and south of Alaska) was given

a colonial government as a result of the Fraser valley
Gold Rush of 1858. This meant that the Hudson's Bay
Company no longer had jurisdiction in that region. But
until the purchase of Rupert's Land by the Dominion of
Canada in 1870, the Company remained the sole legal
authority in the whole of the Northwest up to the Rocky
Mountains.

It was an authority lightly used, for the fur companies remained to the end trading enterprises, generally
opposed to settlement and uninterested in any kind of
administration not connected with the efficient gathering
of furs. They were interested in the Indians of the region only as providers of furs, and they interfered in native affairs only insofar as it was necessary to protect
their forts, their personnel and their transportation arrangements. Any Indian bands that were dependent on
the companies — such as the Crees around Hudson Bay
— were dependent economically, not politically. The
plains tribes, and especially the Blackfoot Confederacy,
which had turned into a formidable irregular cavalry
with horses and firearms, were treated with somewhat
fearful respect by any whites who entered the region. In
the mid-nineteenth century their only rivals on the prairies were the Métis hunters, who competed with them
for the bison herds. They held sway until the treaties of
the 1870s were signed and the bison herds were destroyed. After this their energies and their pride were
curbed.

The real structure of the fur-trading empire at its
peak was a unique mixture of nomadism and settlement. It derived much more from the dynamic model of
the French trade than from the static one of the Hudson's Bay Company, which did not move from the
shores of its inland sea until the last third of the eighteenth century. At that point it was forced into activity
by the active infiltration of its hinterland territory by the
traders from Montreal. Cumberland House, built in 1774
on the Saskatchewan River some five hundred miles

inland from the Bay, was the first of the HBC's inland posts.

Once the Company had abandoned the century-old "sleep at the edge of a frozen sea" of which its critics had accused it, a pattern common to both companies emerged. A series of inland posts, serving as trading centres, or sometimes as provisioning centres, were connected by the water routes followed by the fur brigades that set out from Montreal or the Bay each spring and returned before the winter freeze-up. The posts, some of which were substantial enough to be dignified by the name of forts, varied greatly in number according to whether the situation was one of intense competition or of total or partial monopoly. A few of the forts — such as Fort Garry, Fort Edmonton and Fort George — were permanent enough to become the nuclei of modern cities. The vast majority, however, were created either to drain trade away from the nearby fort of a rival company, or to exploit a new region. After these purposes had been accomplished, the establishment would be closed down.

Two key dates outside the era of intense competition bracket, as it were, the periods of intense competition and prodigious post-building. In 1774, when Cumberland House was built, there was a total of seventeen posts in the Northwest, seven belonging to the Hudson's Bay Company and ten to various traders from Montreal, who were not yet part of a company. In 1825, after the two great companies were united, the number of posts across the country from Montreal to the Pacific was reduced to fifty-two.

Between these two dates an intense three-way competition took place between the Hudson's Bay Company, the XY Company and the North West Company. Hundreds of posts — almost four hundred — were built to capture even small quantities of trade. Some of them were shacks run up to shelter a single trader over winter in the locality of an Indian encampment, and these represented the lingering nomadism of the trade. The competition led to the depletion of the beaver, so the smaller posts did not operate for long. Once the XY Company was eliminated, the number of establishments fell dramatically, though continued competition between the Hudson's Bay Company and the North West Company still kept it at an artificially high level. In 1814 there were more than a hundred posts, fifty-nine of them operated by the North West Company and forty-three by the Hudson's Bay Company.

By this time the competition between the two near-monopolistic groups had become intense, leading often to violence, particularly on the part of the more energetic Nor'Westers. It grew even more ferocious when the Hudson's Bay Company finally pushed its way over the divide into the Athabasca country, using voyageurs recruited in Montreal and tough former North West traders like Colin Robertson. The HBC finally broke the monopoly of its rivals there. During the peak of the struggle between 1815 and 1821 many new and unprofitable posts were again built, and competition reached the state of unofficial warfare. The Nor'Westers incited a company of Métis to attack the Red River settlement in 1816. They killed its governor, Robert Semple, as well as twenty-one of the settlers; in retaliation, Lord Selkirk hired Swiss mercenaries to capture Fort William, the Nor'Westers' headquarters in the *pays d'en haut*, taking prisoner many of the Company's chief traders.

Other skirmishes, ambushes and murders followed until, alarmed by the level of violence in the Northwest and fearing the total ruin of the fur trade, the British government put pressure on the competitors to reach an agreement, which they did in 1821. The result was a revived Hudson's Bay Company, embracing the personnel and posts of the North West Company, retaining its original chartered control over Rupert's Land, and gaining a monopoly of trade with the Indians in the area west of the Rockies and in Ungava. And it was after this that a great rationalization of the trade took place under the long governorship of George Simpson, whose associates called him "the little Emperor" for his dictatorial methods. Once competition had been eliminated, utility and profit were all that counted, and the fifty-two posts that remained a few years after the union of the companies were those considered essential for gathering in the trade of the various localities and for provisioning the fur brigades.

THE FORTS AND THEIR FUNCTION increased in complexity as the fur trade developed. Under the French, unless it was a military post with a small garrison, a fur-trading fort was usually a simple assemblage of a few log houses and stores within a palisade. The forest was cleared away to musket range to offer a degree of protection from unexpected Indian attack. Detroit was quite exceptional in that it had a settlement of *habitants* outside its palisades (protected by a considerable garrison), which supplied food to the soldiers and the fur traders.

During the period of competition between the Hudson's Bay and North West companies a wide variety of posts appeared. The simplest were the so-called hog-styes, double lean-tos that looked like roofs without walls and were used only for a season, then deserted and allowed to rot. A smaller permanent post, like the Hudson's Bay Company's Cumberland House, would have several dwellings and stores within its compound, together with a canoe shed that was also used for drying fish. Since the forts had to produce their own fresh food, Cumberland House had a garden as well as a fishery.

At the other end of the scale were the major posts like York Factory on Hudson Bay, Fort Albany on James Bay, and the North West Company's Fort William on Lake Superior. These were mainly trans-shipment points and administrative centres, where trading was only a minor function. At Fort William there were not only

warehouses and dwellings, but the Great Hall where
David Thompson's immense map hung on the wall and
where the wintering partners coming down from the inland forts would meet the Montreal partners each summer to conduct the Company's business. There were
workshops of various kinds, including a smithy, a tin-
smith's shop, a cooperage and a canoe-building yard, as
well as barns to shelter the fort's herd of cows and its
flock of sheep. There was also a hospital and even a jail.

York Factory had a similar range of industries, as
well as a distillery. The climate of the bayshore did not
encourage cattle rearing and limited the range of vegetables that could be grown, though it is said that the dan-
delions which now flourish all over Canada are
descended from those whose seeds were sown in the
early days at the forts around the Bay to provide the
Company's servants with salads. But these establishments were most important in their function as ports.
Those on Hudson Bay had facilities for loading and unloading the ships that came each summer from England
to bring trade goods and carry away the furs. These vessels could carry anywhere from six hundred to a thousand tons' burden. Fort William had facilities for
unloading the *canots de maître* that travelled from Montreal through the Great Lakes and transferring their contents to the smaller *canots du nord*, which took them
westward.

The gathering of local foods that could be preserved
and used to feed both fort employees and the voyageurs
in the fur brigades was another important function in
many of the forts, particularly in the Saskatchewan region. Fear of the plains tribes and particularly of the
Blackfoot prevented many forts from being built on the
prairie itself; they were more likely to be built in the
strip of parkland to the north which was dominated by
the friendlier Cree. In fact, the links between the fur
traders and the Cree, both at Hudson Bay and in the
west were so close that their language became the *lingua*

franca of the fur trade in the prairies and their women often entered into marriages *à la façon du pays* from which were born most of the originators of the Métis people.

Some of the Métis entered the Company's service, but many of them preferred to become "freemen," independent hunters who supplied the parkland posts with the bison meat from which pemmican could be made and buffalo robes for sale in the trade. In such parkland posts, with their gardens and cattle herds, a kind of backwoods lavishness could prevail, as the artist Paul Kane recorded in his description of a Christmas dinner at Fort Edmonton in 1846.

> At the head, before Mr. Harriett, was a large dish of boiled buffalo hump; at the foot smoked a boiled buffalo calf. Start not, gentle reader, the calf is very small, and is taken from the cow by the Caesarean operation long before it attains its full growth. This, boiled whole, is one of the most esteemed dishes among the epicures of the interior. My pleasing duty was to help a dish of mouffle, or dried moose nose; the gentleman on my left distributed, with graceful impartiality, the whitefish, delicately browned in buffalo marrow. The worthy priest helped the buffalo tongue, while Mr. Rundell cut up the beaver's tails. Nor was the other gentleman left unoccupied, as all his spare time was occupied in dissecting a roast wild goose. The centre of the table was graced with piles of potatoes, turnips, and bread conveniently placed, so that each could help himself without interrupting the labours of his companions. Such was our jolly Christmas dinner at Edmonton; and long will it remain in my memory, although no pies, or puddings, or blanc manges, shed their fragrance over the scene.[11]

AT THE PACIFIC COAST FORTS, a fledgling fish-exporting industry was carried on. Fort Langley in the Fraser valley developed a considerable trade in salted salmon with other forts in the region and with markets as far distant as Hawaii and San Francisco. Agricultural operations on the clement west coast became so extensive, that eventually a separate organization, the Puget Sound Agricultural Company, was established to handle them.

Yet while there was an abundance of food in many of the posts, others in remoter areas still suffered from shortage and monotony of diet. This was particularly the case in the remote posts of New Caledonia where game was scarce and the men complained about the fact that the only variation they ever had from dried fish and potatoes was an occasional roast dog.

This network of posts, each with its local function as well as the overriding purpose of gathering beaver pelts for European hatters and marten and otter furs for European furriers, was united by the vital transportation routes. Those used by the Nor'Westers were served by voyageurs from the St Lawrence, and later by their Métis sons as well. Every year from the 1770s to 1821, the fleet of *canots de maître*, each carrying up to four tons of trade goods, would set off from Montreal. Singing their boat songs, the voyageurs paddled along the Ottawa River, Lake Nipissing and the French River, making portages on the way until they reached Georgian Bay. From there they skirted the northern shores of Lake Huron to Sault Ste Marie. Then they crossed Lake Superior, first to Grand Portage and later, after that destination fell into American territory, to Kaministiquia in British territory. This is where Fort William was later built as the Nor'Westers' upcountry headquarters.

The men who paddled the *canots de maître* were called *mangeurs de lard*, because their basic diet (supplemented by whatever fish or game they caught on the way) consisted of corn or wild rice with fat — sometimes pork, but often bear fat. They were regarded with a certain condescension by the tough, pemmican-fed "northmen" who came down from the interior in their smaller *canots du nord*, headed by the wintering partners,

North West Company officers who shared the Company's profits. The furs that the northmen brought down were loaded into the *canots de maître* which, after riotous celebrations — and serious conferences among the partners — set off on the return voyage to Montreal. The smaller canoes of the northmen turned back on their long journeys through the intricate waterways to the Athabasca country. This procedure consumed the entire navigation season, and often the canoemen had to hurry to reach the remoter parts before the freeze-up closed the waterways.

At first the Hudson's Bay Company was at a disadvantage in its inland operations because the large birches from whose bark the great canoes were made grew only in the territory traversed by the Nor'Westers. The canoes used by the Indians on the rivers that ran into the Bay were much smaller, and at first this prevented an effective flow of trade into the area the Company controlled. However, once inland posts were established, the Company's shipwrights devised an adequate substitute for the *canots de maître*. It was the York boat, which was modelled on a kind of shallop used by fishermen in the Orkney Islands off Scotland. This flat-bottomed craft was made of spruce planking, rowed by eight men with long oars and directed by a steersman with a sweep and a bowman with a pole to push the easily sloping prow away from rocks or deadheads. It was less easily damaged and more durable than the birchbark canoes, and it carried almost twice as much cargo as a *canot de maître*. Eventually, after the union of the companies, when the pivotal centre of the trade moved from Montreal to York Factory, the canoe brigades were replaced on the larger waterways by the brigades of slower York boats. Canoes were still used on the smaller rivers, however, and on the routes where there were long portages, for which the York boats were too heavy. From this time until steamboats began to appear on the rivers of the West in the 1860s, the York boat was the principal means of water transport.

In the end the Company took to land as well as to water, for in the mountainous regions of the Far West, brigades of pack horses proved more practical in difficult terrain than boats of any kind. On the prairies, from the 1840s and on, the fur traders finally took to the wheel, and much of the heavier freight transported by the Hudson's Bay Company was carried from Red River over the Carlton Trail by slow-moving Red River carts, vehicles made entirely of wood and shaganappi by the Métis hunters. They were well adapted to the rough trails and ferry-less water crossings of the primitive prairie. Because of its large wheels, a Red River cart could cross with ease stretches of prairie pitted by gopher or prairie dog burrows, and when a river was reached it could be taken apart, transformed into a raft and floated to the opposite bank.

This pattern of posts and transportation routes which spread like a net over the wilderness beyond the settled areas of Lower and Upper Canada was operated by corporations in whose service hierarchy and discipline were supreme. They were regarded as necessary not only for the proper functioning of the fur trade, but also to ensure mere survival at a time when there were never many more than three thousand white men — and after 1821 hardly more than two thousand. Even after the smallpox epidemics that devastated the western tribes at the end of the eighteenth century, the Indians were still many times more numerous than the fur traders and their servants.

THE ORGANIZATION OF THE HUDSON'S BAY COMPANY in its original Bayside form was far more rigid than that of the North West Company. At the head of the pyramid were the governor and his committee of businessmen in London. In the Bay the structure was topped by the governor of the Bay and his deputy, who were located at

York Factory. It was both the North American headquarters of the Company and its largest fort. Only the captains of the Company's ships were regarded as the governors' equals. The other posts, according to their importance, were presided over by chief factors or chief traders. Surgeons were regarded as holding approximately the same rank as chief traders and chief factors, and often, as did Dr John McLoughlin and Dr John Rae, they transferred into those positions. The class of gentlemen was completed by the clerks and accountants. A clerk would sometimes manage a small post as a step towards higher rank. Among the servants there was a parallel hierarchy. In the forts on the Bay the artisans — gunsmiths, blacksmiths and shipwrights — held the highest ranks; inland, guides and interpreters might be just as important. Carpenters and cooks ranked next, and at the bottom were the labourers, hired on five-year indentures. Since there was no real escape from the Bay, they were really serfs for that period.

The difference between officers and men was emphasized by their divergent lifestyles. The governor might live in a primitive log building caulked with oakum, but he slept in a canopied bed, dined at an oak table, and ate off pewter plates, waited on by his own servant and attended by his secretary. He was allowed preserves and other dainties to vary the monotony of the diet, and the Company's papers repeatedly mention presents of wine — a cask of Canary to Governor Nixon, eight dozen bottles of fine red wine to Governor Knight.

Yet officers and men alike had to put up with the rigours of the Hudson Bay winters. James Isham recorded in 1743 that ice six or eight inches thick had collected on the *inside* walls of houses and was "every day cutt away with hatchetts." The rooms were dark with smoke from the wood stoves, and except for a few hours at mid-day the windows were covered with thick wooden shutters in an attempt to keep out the cold. Isham saw a two-gallon bottle of water freeze solid right beside the stove; other accounts tell of brandy solidifying to the consistency of treacle. Cleanliness was difficult to maintain, and Isham described the typical fur trader as having at this season "a face as black as any Chimbly Sweepers."

The North West Company differed from the original Hudson's Bay Company in that its officers were not employees, but were actual profit-sharing partners, the "wintering partners." The *bourgeois*, as the gentlemen of the North West Company were still frequently called, were no longer French, but mostly Scottish, while the Hudson's Bay officers were mostly English. But the same kind of hierarchy prevailed, with the clerks counting as gentlemen, and the servants and *engagés* rarely rising to become officers. The voyageurs and the labourers were *canadiens* from the St Lawrence or, in later years, sometimes Iroquois. In the Hudson's Bay posts, on the other hand, the craftsmen tended to be English, and the labourers were either English townsmen or Orkneymen, who regarded themselves as a different people from the Scots. In its drive into Athabasca from 1815 on the Company changed its pattern of employment and engaged *canadien* voyageurs.

SOME WOMEN ALSO LIVED at the posts, although their presence has often been ignored. The Nor'Westers, in the manner of their French predecessors, were open-minded about sexual relationships, and both gentlemen and servants took native women as wives, often temporary ones. Sometimes they purchased women who had become slaves in Indian wars. The Hudson's Bay Company, in the interests of good seventeenth-century puritan morality, at first tried to prevent such liaisons, but the attempt was only imperfectly successful, and by the time the two companies were united — with all the officers from chief traders upward becoming profit-sharing partners — marriage *à la façon du pays* was widespread.

At first the wives were Indian women, and the alliances thus formed were often very advantageous to the trade, since the women acted as interpreters and intermediaries with their tribes, and often prevented Indian bands to whose chiefs they were related from trading with the rival company. Later, as the people of mixed blood — whether paternally French, English or Scots — increased in numbers, it became customary to form relationships with Métisses, or half-breed women, whose beauty was often greatly admired. Not until the 1830s did the first European women arrive in the trading posts of the West; often they were shocked to hear about the past relationships of their husbands, and, as with the memsahibs who began to arrive in India at about the same time, their presence created social and racial tensions of a kind that had not existed before. For the first time, under their influence, colour became an important factor in determining a person's social acceptability.

But by this time the influences that would bring irrevocable change to the old nomadic society of the West were already beginning to emerge. After the union of the two companies, the Red River colony, the nucleus of settlement which Lord Selkirk had planted there with his Scottish crofters in 1812, grew steadily in importance, offering an alternate, stable way of life to the wandering existence that Indians and voyageurs and their Métis offspring valued so much.

CHAPTER
5

The Passion for Gold

THE FIRST THREAT TO THE HEGEMONY of the fur trade in the West came not from settlement, but from the early nomadic phase of yet another primary industry, mining. Even before the arrival of the Europeans, mining of a kind had been going on, since the Stone Age economy of the Indians and the Inuit required material for tools and weapons. Obsidian and flint were quarried by the Indians and soapstone by the Inuit far back in prehistoric times. These commodities, along with the native copper found around Lake Superior and on the Coppermine River, were traded widely throughout central and western Canada. In the West and the North and on the Pacific coast, such primitive mining and trading of mineral products continued long after the first contact had been made between Europeans and aborigines on the Atlantic coast. It was not until the nineteenth century that the tribal cultures of the prairie and the Pacific coast Indians and of the Inuit in many parts of the Arctic actually began to move out of the Neolithic Age. The acquisition of stone tools by trading or quarrying and chipping was part of the nomadic pattern of their lives.

Early Europeans came with the thought of gold in their minds. Martin Frobisher was even more ambitious in his pursuit of the precious metal than Jacques Cartier, and at Baffin Island in 1577 he loaded into his ships two hundred tons of rock which he thought contained gold. Like Cartier's "diamonds," it turned out to be worthless. Later it was less precious minerals that attracted the Europeans who reached eastern Canada. A Maître Simon, who appears to have had some expert knowledge of mining, reported finding silver and iron deposits in Acadia in 1604, and about the middle of the seventeenth century ships from New England were sailing up to Cape Breton to mine the outcroppings of coal there. The Norsemen appear to have used bog iron found in the marshes of Newfoundland in their smithy at L'Anse aux Meadows at the beginning of the eleventh century, and the first regular iron works in Canada, the Forges St Maurice at Trois-Rivières, started production in 1738, using iron ore from local deposits. About a century later, after settlement had moved into Upper Canada and steam navigation had been established on the Great Lakes, the copper deposits which the Indians had long used to the west of Lake Superior were dug by Cornish miners imported in the 1840s for their expertise in hard-rock mining.

Such types of mining were really the offshoots of early settlement. They provided coal and metals that could be used in small societies seeking to reproduce the European pattern. These early operations were the beginnings of long-term extractive processes that would play their part in the development of an industrial society. However, gold mining played a larger role in the Canadian Far West and Northwest from the 1850s to the end of the century. It was this industry that also initiated the disintegration of the Hudson's Bay Company's hegemony over the Northwest.

The discovery of gold in the Californian riverbeds in 1848 began one of the first mass movements of white men in North American history, fuelled by a strange mixture of greed and adventurousness. Like the fur trade, the first gold mining was nomadic. When an ancient deposit of virgin gold was discovered in the sand and gravel of stream beds, word would spread, miners would flock there, and rough-and-ready towns or villages would spring up to house and entertain the entrepreneurs. After a period of resolute placer mining based on rather primitive manual methods, gold would cease to show up in the miners' pans, and they would move on to other sites they had heard of, leaving their temporary settlements to become decaying ghost towns over which the bush would eventually re-establish its empire.

Though gold fever created a concerted movement of people from the eastern parts of the continent and from many countries abroad to the western mining areas, and of miners from one goldfield to the next, placer mining itself was a highly individualistic process. A solitary miner who set up his sluice box and wielded his pan at the right gravel bar could — as many of them did — make a fortune in a single season of work. In some of the goldfields, like the Cariboo and the Klondike, the best deposits lay underground, in submerged ancient streambeds, but even here it was a matter of digging shafts through the earth rather than hacking rock, and a partnership of three or four men could easily work such a deposit if they did not run into problems like underground water. At the end they could divide the take. It was only when the placer deposits were worked out and hard-rock ore had to be excavated that gold-mining capitalists came in to organize the process industrially and the miners became wage workers, rather than individual fortune seekers. Then gold mining ceased to be nomadic. A touch of that past clung even to the early stages of hard-rock mining, however, for the mineral deposits were generally discovered by wandering prospectors. In fact, nomadic gold mining has never entirely vanished; any increase in the price of gold will send adventurers out to pan for what is left in the famous old deposits of Gold Rush days, and will send prospectors wandering through the mountains in search of outcroppings of ore.

A gold rush immediately changed the social and economic pattern of whatever remote locality it descended upon, and this applied to the rudimentary communities that in western Canada had grown up in the shadow of the fur trade. When the gold miners arrived on Vancouver Island in 1858 Fort Victoria was the first fur trade post to be affected this way.

AT THAT TIME VANCOUVER ISLAND was in a somewhat different political position from the rest of the Hudson's Bay Company's empire and even from the colonial mainland of what was still called New Caledonia. After the Oregon boundary dispute came to an end in 1846 with the loss of the Columbia River territory, the British government realized that some kind of political claim must be made to the region north of the forty-ninth parallel if further American incursions into unorganized territory were to be prevented. Accordingly, Vancouver Island was created a Crown colony in 1849, thus becoming the first regular outpost of British government in North America west of Upper Canada. In fact, little was changed by this, since the Hudson's Bay Company was granted a licence of exclusive trade on the island, provided that it encouraged settlement.

But the Company carried out an obstructionist policy, discouraging individual settlers by the conditions it imposed, and virtually boycotting Richard Blanshard, the governor sent out by the Colonial Office. He resigned in disgust in 1851, and rather than send out a replacement, the imperial government offered the position to the incumbent chief factor of Fort Victoria, the leading fur trader in the west, James Douglas. Thus, political and economic power were united in one man, and the fur trade's interests were for the time being effectively protected. Sheltered in this way, the Company developed around Victoria a more varied pattern of commercial activities than anywhere else in Canada. It started the western mining industry by importing Scottish colliers to tap the coal deposits that were discovered in 1849 at Fort Rupert and shortly afterwards at Nanaimo. It started the timber industry in its modern form by building the first sawmill at Victoria in 1848. Lumber began to be exported to San Francisco from there the following year. The salting of salmon for export at Fort Langley on the Fraser launched the west coast commercial fishing industry, and the Company's subsidiary, the Puget Sound Agricultural Company, initiated the last of the basic industries in the region by establishing a number of farms in the open parkland of southern Vancouver Island.

By 1858 the non-Indian population of British North America west of the Rockies was considerably less than a thousand, scattered in the trading posts from Fort St James in the north to Fort Kamloops in the south, and in lesser centres on Vancouver Island like Fort Rupert, Nanaimo and Sooke. Most of the population was found in Victoria, which had between four and five hundred inhabitants and thus adopted the air of a Lilliputian capital. Most of its inhabitants were directly or indirectly linked with the Company; past and present employees formed the entire membership of the seven-man Legislative Assembly, whose Speaker, Dr John Sebastian Helmcken, was the Company's surgeon and the governor's son-in-law.

The intermittent presence of naval survey ships in Esquimalt Harbour helped to create a social life in this fur-trading village. There were annual horse races and balls and parties, to which the people picked their way down muddy lanes. A school was opened in 1851, and for the daughters of those who considered themselves gentry, there was even a Young Ladies' Academy. Everyone, young and old, joined in picnics on the

beaches and in riding parties over the open parklands; if
it had not been for the Indians who came down the
coast in their great carved canoes to trade and who
camped on the foreshore, Fort Victoria might have
seemed to offer an only slightly exotic version of the life
of a mid-nineteenth century small town on the English
south coast.

Gold changed it all. Scale gold — tiny flat nuggets
rather than dust — had been found on the North
Thompson River in 1857, and the Company had authorized the local traders to provide the Indians with metal
spoons to dig the scales out of the cracks in the bedrock.
Shortly afterwards dust was found in the sandbars of
the Fraser River above Hope. The nearest assay office
was in San Francisco, and there the Company sent it. It
arrived at a time when the easily panned gold was running out in the California fields, and the people of Victoria soon witnessed the first effects of the news. On
Sunday morning, April 23, 1858, just as the townsfolk
were leaving their recently built church, an American
side-wheeler, the *Commodore*, pulled into the harbour
just below the Fort and began disgorging its freight of
passengers. There were 450 of them, roughly the equivalent of Fort Victoria's population at the time, and most
of them were red-shirted, high-booted miners who had
arrived too late in California to make their fortunes and
wanted to try their luck in the new field. As the summer went on crowded steamers sailed in rapid succession up the coast, and the Victorians rejoiced in the
sudden increase in trading possibilities, not realizing
how much it would change their surroundings and their
leisurely way of life.

Most of the men who came were at least aspiring
miners, and, having stocked up at the Hudson's Bay
store and the rapidly increasing number of independent
shops, they hurried across the Strait of Georgia to the
mainland in whatever craft were available, making their
way upriver to the gold bars in the Fraser Canyon:

Boston Bar, China Bar, Kanaka Bar and a score of others. By the end of the first season twenty-five thousand men had passed through Victoria and up the Fraser, where they built their cabin settlements at the bars and rapidly exhausted the gold that could be obtained by the primitive placer methods.

Like any other flood this one left its remnants behind, and in Victoria they consisted of the merchants and other entrepreneurs who accompanied the miners in the hope of making a profit out of their activities. Among them were a number of middle-class blacks fleeing from the racial discrimination they had experienced even in San Francisco, and a Nova Scotian photographer originally christened William Smith, who had given himself in California the resounding name of Amor de Cosmos because of the plethora of Smiths demanding their mail at the post office. He had now transformed himself into a crusading editor, founding the *British Colonist* in Victoria to introduce a voice of opposition to the Company's power, and in the fullness of time, after he had helped to usher the western province into Confederation, he became premier of British Columbia.

A street plan of Victoria had already been created by a surveyor commissioned by the Colonial Office in 1851, and now its outlines began to fill out with hastily erected wooden buildings and a few brick ones. In one period of six weeks no less than 225 structures were built. Two hundred of them were stores and saloons, mostly owned and operated by San Franciscans who realized that surer fortunes would be made by staying away from the gravel bars than by toiling on them. The Hudson's Bay Company's trading monopoly had collapsed, and as a kind of symbolic recognition of the new order, Fort Victoria itself was demolished between 1860 and 1864, its site giving way to new streets, while the merchants began to build elegant houses on the wooded slopes overlooking the harbour. By 1866 there were six thousand people in Victoria, served by eighty-five saloons and hundreds of stores. The British population of early 1858 had been transformed into a cosmopolitan one, including native-born Americans (white and black), French, Germans and Italians, as well as the Chinese who had followed the gold miners from San Francisco and became an enduring element in the population of Canada's west coast.

Even on the mainland, as far as the Rockies, the gold rush had brought an end to the Hudson's Bay Company's dominance. Up to 1858 this had been a country with no real government other than that embodied in the Company's shadowy power. However, when the miners came in 1858 James Douglas feared the influx of Americans might be used by the United States to claim the region for itself. His fears were not ungrounded, as the influx of pioneers into the Oregon territory south of the border was used to that very end. So, illegally, he gave a semblance of government by issuing licences to miners. Lord Lytton the novelist, who happened to be colonial secretary at the time, was as alert as Douglas to the urgency of the situation, and in August 1858, the British government transformed New Caledonia into a Crown colony separate from Vancouver Island, with the title British Columbia — a designation chosen by Queen Victoria. Douglas was appointed governor of the new colony as well as of Vancouver Island, but at the same time he was forced to abandon his role as the Hudson's Bay Company's chief factor. The shadow government of the Company beyond the Rockies thus came to an end just as its commercial monopoly in the area was collapsing.

HAVING CAUSED THESE DRASTIC CHANGES, the miners were soon on the move again, following reports and rumours in a nearly unstoppable surge that in the end would probe as far as the Arctic Ocean. The Fraser Canyon bars were virtually exhausted by 1859, though the

Chinese stayed on to repan the tailings left by the original miners. They were content with smaller returns and a less flamboyant way of living than that of their white counterparts, who would often squander their gains in the saloons and dance halls of their transient communities and go on their way with the next wave of prospectors into the wilderness. By 1860 the miners were already on the verge of the Cariboo goldfield, and during the following winter "Dutch" William Dietz found the rich deep gravels of Williams Creek, which was named after him. Almost equally productive deposits were found in other nearby creeks, and by 1862 an even bigger stampede was on.

Before the Cariboo Road was completed in 1863 by the Royal Engineers, the gold seekers found their way by difficult trails up the Fraser Canyon and into the plateau country beyond it. By this time the fame of the western Canadian goldfields had spread, and tens of thousands of hopeful men — and not a few women — made their way to Williams Creek and its environs. On every creek of the Cariboo instant towns sprang up as soon as anyone made a rich find. Miners' cabins would be perched on the hillsides above the claims they had hurriedly made, and there would be a rough semblance of a main street lined with spartan hotels, gambling houses and stores, which sold goods at several times the prices in Victoria. In most cases the yield of gold dust soon diminished and the miners departed, leaving another ghost town behind them.

But one gold-mining community did continue to prosper for many years. This was Barkerville on Williams Creek, which for a while was the largest town in British Columbia, with ten thousand inhabitants, compared to the six thousand in Victoria and the two thousand or so who then inhabited the recently created capital of the mainland colony, New Westminster. Named after Billy Barker, a Cornish miner who struck it rich and died a pauper like so many of his kind, Barker-

ville was in fact for a number of years the largest town
west of the Rockies and north of San Francisco. Its narrow street with elevated sidewalks was lined with buildings of whipsawed lumber that housed hotels and
banks, laundries and barber shops, bakeries and smithies. There was a theatre that was visited by touring
companies from the United States, a library for the stu-
dious and a twice-weekly newspaper, the *Cariboo
Sentinel*. There was even a resident poet, James Ander-
son, who wrote verse in the manner of Robert Burns
and whose *Sawney's Letters*, written in Barkerville and
published there in 1868, makes him the pioneer British
Columbian poet. The terpsichorean art was somewhat
inelegantly served by the Hurdy Gurdies, German girls
dressed in vaguely Bavarian peasant garb, who acted as
dancing partners for the miners. As "Sawney" put it in
his serviceable doggerel:

Bonnie are the hurdies, O!
The German hurdy-gurdies, O!
The daftest hours that e'er I spent
Were dancing' wi' the hurdies O!

Barkerville survived, but it changed when the easily
gettable gold ran out. Syndicates appeared which used
newer mining methods requiring considerable capital,
such as hydraulic sluicing and dredges in the valley bottom, and the miners became employees of these companies. The independent ones moved off through the
mountainous interior of British Columbia, opening up
new goldfields like Omineca and Atlin in the northern
parts of the colony. Miniature replicas of Barkerville
sprang up, to vanish in their turn.

Then, in the 1880s, a rush of a different kind occurred in the Kootenay region in the south of the province. This time metals less precious than gold were the
centre of attention. Silver and lead were found near Nelson in 1882 and copper at Phoenix in 1883. For the next

two decades prospectors roamed the mountains and valleys north of the international boundary, and mine after
mine was discovered. These were hard-rock mines, most
of which lasted for a few years before the ore was
worked out, and this time the miners were usually employees of the speculators who financed the operations.
They were almost as independent and nomadic as the
placer miners had been, however, moving from one instant town to the next, living riotously and initiating,
through their militant and bitter disputes with their employees, the confrontational relationship between bosses
and workers that is still an active tradition in British Columbia.

Some of the mining towns in southern British Columbia, like Nelson and Grand Forks, survived to become centres of settlement. Others, like Phoenix, Elko
and Sandon, did not outlive the exhaustion of the
mines. Their inhabitants moved on, many of them to
take part in the greatest of all the gold rushes of history,
the rush to the Klondike in 1896–99.

THE KLONDIKE GOLD RUSH, which led tens of thousands of
people to the remote banks of the Yukon River, was one
of the most remarkable spontaneous mass movements in
modern times. It attracted more people than the California or Cariboo rushes or the diggings of Australia had,
and it attracted them at a time when the hunger for
news fostered by the burgeoning popular press of the
age was reaching its peak. No single event in Canada's
history up to that time drew so much attention abroad,
and no event at home made Canadians so aware of their
northern frontier.

Until 1898 the Yukon region, which lies just north of
the sixtieth parallel, was largely detached from developments in southern Canada. A few trading posts along
the river bought furs from the Indians of the territory,
and there were some small nomadic mining camps
which represented the last, forlorn remnant of the

migratory prospectors of the mid-century. There was no railway and no telegraph. During the summer a steamboat came up the Yukon River, but the annual freeze-up meant that for long periods each year the region was cut off except for dog teams that took weeks to reach any outpost of civilization. The contrast between that backward country and the world outside can be illustrated by comparing the slowness with which the news of the discovery of gold on Bonanza Creek reached the outside world and the rapidity with which it then spread.

Squaw-man Lying George Carmack made his strike in the latter part of August 1896. Word spread among the miners along the river, and as soon as they were finally convinced that Lying George was telling the truth for once, they staked their claims along the local creeks and worked over the winter as the weather allowed them. Not until the ice broke in the spring did the news get out, but then it assumed dramatic form. The first ships sailing from the mouth of the Yukon that spring reached American ports with eighty miners bearing fortunes in gold dust in their pokes. Some went on the *Excelsior*, which reached San Francisco on July 15, 1897, and others on the *Portland*, which docked at Seattle on the 17th. The news spread fast, and the effect was immediate.

Once again, as in the early days of California and Cariboo, it was placer gold that had been found, and the idea that a man on his own might strike it rich and make a great fortune was appealing to thousands of romantically minded people at the time. Within days the first cheechakos (aspiring miners) were on their way north. Enough reached the Klondike before winter for the instant city of Dawson to spring up in the late autumn of 1897, though the greater proportion of the people who set off from every corner of the western world fought their way over the passes from the Pacific coast in the winter of 1897–98 and waited at Lake Bennett. They built boats from whipsawn local wood and stayed there until the ice broke in the late northern spring. Then the vast fleet of their ramshackle craft sailed down through the canyons of the Yukon River to the gold-fields.

It has been estimated that no less than a hundred thousand people started out on the rush. Probably half of them reached Dawson City, which at its height was much larger than Barkerville, with an unstable population of thirty thousand. They included people of all races and all classes, for greed is a great leveller. Most of those infected by the gold fever were men, but women were by no means absent.

Not all of them were the dance-hall girls and prostitutes of Klondike legend. One woman making the great northern journey was a fashionable Chicago socialite, Martha Louise Purdy, who was stirred by the current excitement, and when her prosaic husband refused to accompany her, left for the Klondike with her three children. Martha Louise staked a claim and earned a modest profit from working it with hired labour. Later she managed a sawmill. After her stay-at-home husband died, she married a local civil servant, George Black, became an authority on the flora of the Yukon and eventually, as representative of the Yukon, became one of the first Canadian female MPs.

Few of the Klondike stampeders stayed on as long as Martha (Purdy) Black. In fact, one of the striking aspects of the Klondike rush was that of those who arrived at Dawson at least half never went out of the city to try their luck along the overcrowded creeks. Some of them — merchants, saloon keepers, gamblers, tarts — made their fortunes by mining in various ways the pokes of the actual miners. But there were many who, having made the trip, took one look at the wilderness and returned to their own ordinary world. The adventure of the journey had been sufficient to establish the self-image they needed; the destination was not important in the end.

Of course, other factors besides the mere sense of adventure motivated many to come. Profit may have been one of them, but poverty was not, for the cost of getting to the Yukon and buying the outfit needed to pass the Mounted Police at the White Pass on Chilkoot Pass was beyond the means of any destitute person. You had to have money to start off for the Klondike, even if you returned penniless.

But there was also a *fin de siècle, fin du monde* quality in this phenomenon that in so many other ways made the nineties seem like a last great fling. The world — at least the western world — was becoming urbanized, and large numbers of people, reacting against its creeping homogenization, found a kind of vicarious escape in this last of the great gold rushes. For them it embodied the supposedly free life followed by obsolescent frontier types like prospectors, cowboys and trappers. And in this sense the Klondike rush played a double role. It drew the curtain down on that period when the white intruders moved over the land as latter-day nomads, without establishing themselves as a stable society. But with it the romantic sanctification of that period also began. It is significant that no previous gold rush resulted in such a rich literature as the Klondike, because no other occurred when urban humanity was ready to regard the wilderness as something less than a threat.

Following on the fishermen and the fur traders, the placer miners were the last of those great nomadic waves of Europeans who sought to exploit the land economically without wanting to possess it by settlement or to dominate it politically. Yet, like their predecessors, they left the land changed, for they explored its intricacies, pioneered its highways and encouraged the establishment of farms to feed their transient towns. Just as a few of the fur traders' many temporary posts developed into permanent communities, so a handful of lasting cities were created from among the multitude of miners' ghost towns lost to the encroaching bush.

Their effect on the native population was less profound than that of the fur traders, since they set out to establish no symbiotic relationship like the one that existed between trader and trapper. Wherever they passed they tended to crowd the Indian temporarily off part of the land, and sometimes to encroach on his hunting grounds, though most miners were too obsessed with hunting gold to spend much time pursuing game.

Moreover, the areas where they operated were inhabited by relatively timid tribes who tended to keep out of the way of the miners, and the miners in their turn had no desire to provoke attacks. Violent incidents were therefore surprisingly few, and almost certainly fewer than would have taken place if the intruders had been operating among the fiercer peoples of the plains or the Pacific coast. The only really serious clash between Indians and whites that took place during the placer mining period in the interior of British Columbia was the 1864 massacre by the Chilcotins of workmen who were building a pack trail from Bute Inlet to Quesnel on the Fraser River. The motives for the massacre, which led to the brief expedition in search of the killers known somewhat grandiosely as the Chilcotin War, have never been clearly elucidated. Sir Matthew Baillie Begbie, then chief justice of British Columbia, was probably right, however, when he regarded it as an early manifestation of Indian concern about the threat of losing their lands. But the miners were not interested in land; they only wanted what lay in the streambeds.

Although they had no more desire for land than the fur traders or the fishermen, they prepared the way for the settlers, to whom land was all-important, and for the transitional class of colonial officers and soldiers who prepared the way for its possession.

PART
III

BRITISH POSSESSIONS
IN NORTH AMERICA.

Upper and Lower Canada, 1827

CHAPTER

6

The Monarch's Men

THE GOVERNMENTS OF BRITAIN AND FRANCE were slow to
impose direct government over their territories in what
later became Canada. They encouraged and even subsidized explorers like Cabot and Cartier on the Atlantic
shores, Frobisher in the Arctic and James Cook and
George Vancouver two centuries later on the Pacific,
and they considered that the successful arrival of these
voyagers gave them royal title to the new lands. But
they were in no hurry to establish governments. Instead, both the British and the French preferred to act
indirectly through the mercantile interests in their respective countries, encouraging chartered companies
and even favoured individuals to exploit the fish and fur
trades and, where possible, to establish settlements. Indeed, the earliest attempts at settlement on Nova Scotia
were conducted by individuals.

In 1599 the Marquis de la Roche made the first abortive French attempt at colonization when he landed fifty
unfortunates on desolate, weather-beaten Sable Island
off the coast of Nova Scotia. The sandy soil proved in-
tractable, the promised supply ships failed to arrive, and

most of the colonists had died from sickness or starvation when the few survivors were taken off the island in 1603. All this happened before a more lasting and better-known French settlement in Acadia was established at Port Royal. Both the English and the Scots disputed the French title to Acadia, and in 1621, after he had united the English and the Scottish crowns, King James I gave the peninsula its present name of Nova Scotia, making a grant of it to his Scottish friend, Sir William Alexander. He even allowed Alexander to attract capital by instituting an order of Baronets of Nova Scotia, who would receive titles in return for their investments. Alexander actually landed some settlers in 1629, but his venture came to an end when the next king, Charles I, decided to acknowledge the French claim to what became once again Acadia.

Thus, colonial government, with its attendant apparatus of short-term colonial administrators and garrison forces, was slow to establish itself in the eastern provinces of what eventually became Canada. Government came even more slowly to the West, where it did not appear until the second half of the nineteenth century.

No governor was appointed to Newfoundland until 1729. Even then he was usually the commander of the naval convoy, coming to the colony every season with the fishing fleet and leaving again when the season was over. Although a resident administration was created by dividing the island into districts and appointing a justice of the peace to each one, a resident governor was not appointed until 1817. It was not until 1825 that he was given a council of executive officers to advise him and a House of Assembly was elected as the first recognition that the island was a settled area and not merely a haunt of transient fishermen.

Government came somewhat earlier to Nova Scotia, which was returned to Britain under the Treaty of Utrecht in 1713. The French interpreted the cession as not including Île Royale, which is now Cape Breton Island. There, in 1717, they built the great fortress of Louisbourg to guard the approaches to the St Lawrence, and established a full-scale administration with a governor, civil officials and a garrison. There had been a small garrison at Port Royal before 1713, but no administration on the scale of the one now created. And it was in response to the threat of Louisbourg that the British transformed their vague suzerainty over Nova Scotia into effective sovereignty: in 1749 they sent Edward Cornwallis to found Halifax and establish a garrison and a provincial administration.

THE FRENCH IN QUEBEC HAD CREATED a colonial administration more than ninety years before the English established theirs at Halifax. By 1663 it was evident that indirect government through Richelieu's chartered companies could no longer, with its limited resources, protect the fur trade or the missionaries against the perpetual attacks of the Iroquois. Even less could such corporations sustain the pattern of alliances with and dependencies on friendly tribes which the court at Versailles considered necessary if France were to appear as a rival of Spain in the Americas and if the English were to be prevented from spreading eastward over the Alleghenies from the seaboard colonies. The French at that time did not seem to have perceived to the south of them the varied collection of provinces of different origin that would in the end be united only by their shared resentment of the British government. They saw another Britain growing up there, whose successful enlargement would immensely strengthen France's traditional enemy.

In 1663, shortly after he assumed absolute power with the departure of Cardinal Mazarin, Louis XIV cancelled the company charters and transformed New France into a colony royally administered through the Ministry of Marine. Under this new rule, power was shared between three authoritative figures, which represented the triple aspect of French power overseas. The governor was the titular head and commander-in-chief, responsible directly for military affairs, which in the case of active governors meant a busy life fighting the Iroquois and the English and building forts as the frontiers of New France steadily moved into the forests of what later became Ontario and the American Midwest.

In general charge of civil affairs was an official called the intendant of justice, public order and finances. The office had been created by French kings during the Middle Ages when they found it necessary to appoint officials to check the power of the baronial magnates. In effect, the old intendants had consolidated and unified the French monarchy. Such an office in the hands of a conscientious and imaginative official was admirably suited to a colonial society in the early and difficult stages when it was being transformed from a primitive trading enterprise into the settled community the king wished to establish. The third great figure of New France, with almost as much power as the governor and the intendant, was the bishop of Quebec.

Right to the last days of New France all these officials were metropolitan French, and all, except the bishops, were transients, returning to France when their terms of office came to an end. They administered the colonies primarily in the interests of the king and the mother country. In doing so they were laying the foundations of what would later become integrated and eventually autonomous communities, and in the end an independent nation. But if they could have been made aware of this, it would have seemed to them a secondary matter.

The most important of these offices in terms of French imperial interests was probably that of the governor, who organized defence and sometimes offence, conducted external relations with Indian tribes and with imperial rivals like the English and who gave support to energetic officers like Alexandre Prouville de Tracy. This military man arrived with the Carignan-Salières regiment in 1665 and built a series of forts to protect the approaches of Quebec from the mouth of the Richelieu River to Lake Champlain and then, with a small mixed army of regulars, *canadien* militia and Indian allies, took the initiative by marching into Mohawk territory and ravaging the Iroquois villages. In this way the governors and their officers established the defences behind which the intendants were able to carry on their work of developing the growing community of French- and native-born people who became, in name and fact, the first Canadians.

The welfare of New France as a community was undoubtedly most dependent on the office of the intendant, for the most successful military campaigns were pointless if the colony was not well administered. Certainly one of the main reasons why New France failed effectively to resist British invasion during the 1759–60 war was the fact that in its whole history the colony had only one "Great Intendant." This title was given justly to Jean Talon, whose tenure of office extended from 1665 to 1672, and who established industries and promoted agriculture so that New France would have to rely less on the fur trade. He also imported eleven hundred women — the famous *filles du roi* — to adjust the population balance and induce a steady natural increase, and he encouraged immigration and exploration. During the eighteenth century, a series of incompetent or corrupt intendants undermined the economy of the colony. The last and most disastrous of them was François Bigot, who created an intricate system of peculating government funds. He also gained vast profits by establishing a Society of Canada — later called the Great Company — which exacted a toll from all trade passing in and out of the colony. By the time the fall of Quebec forced Bigot to return to Paris, the colony was on the edge of economic ruin.

As later experience in British times would show, this kind of callous disregard for the interests of an administered territory or of its people is an ever-present danger when the administrators come from the metropolis and have no intention of becoming permanent residents of the colony. The temptation to make one's pile and leave is always great. Even Jean Talon was more dedicated to his career than to New France, though he was the kind of man who did conscientiously and ably what he had undertaken to do. In 1670 he petitioned to be released from service in such a primitive setting, and he was recalled and appointed to the powerful position of secretary to the king. Had he decided his loyalties were with New France and stayed the remaining twenty years of his life, the continuity that was so necessary in the early stages of the colony might have been sustained. But after he left, New France went three years without an intendant, and the industries, agriculture and West Indian trade he had developed were allowed to languish.

The bishop was not an officer of state in quite the same way as the governor and the intendant, yet he was much more powerful than his ecclesiastical position might suggest. This was largely because of the form of local administration assumed in New France. Having neutralized the power of the aristocrats in the mother country, the French kings had no intention of resurrecting it in the colony. Consequently it was not the seigneury that became the basic unit of rural government, but the parish. The parish corresponded to the local militia district, public meetings were held in the church, and the priest rather than the landowner became the most influential member of the community.

The power that derived from this arrangement was used not so much in the interests of France as to the greater glory of the Church. For, by a strange twist of circumstances, the church in New France was not Gallican — dedicated to supporting the state — as it was in France. It had an ultramontanist outlook, dedicated to upholding the papal ascendancy. The first missionaries, the Récollet friars, were expelled in 1629, and would not return until 1670. In their absence the Sulpicians, who represented the Gallican church and were strong in Montreal, struggled for ascendancy with the Jesuits of Quebec. The Jesuits won, and the first bishop of New France, François de Laval de Montigny, was a dedicated ultramontanist who set the pattern of French Canadian Catholicism for two centuries, partly by establishing a seminary in which generations of priests were trained according to the doctrines of Bishop Laval. The establishment of obligatory tithes confirmed the Church's role as part of the state apparatus in spite of its enduring loyalty to Rome. Tithing also gave it financial security and strengthened its power over the *habitants*. Later, as education developed, the Church remained in complete control of it, and thus reinforced its own strength.

The varying interests of military and civil authority and of a Church that owed its first allegiance to Rome and not to Versailles, resulted in perpetual conflicts between the three great officers. These were reflected in the Sovereign Council, or Superior Council, as it was called after 1702. The Council fulfilled in part the role of the *Parlement* in France; it was a supreme court that established legal precedents and reinterpreted the ancient code known as the Custom of Paris to fit the new colonial conditions. It was also an advisory body whose appointed members, drawn from the various districts, provided information and discussed proposed ordinances, although they did not enact them. Beyond this advisory role, which was restricted to representatives of the seigneurs, the merchants and the professional classes, the *canadiens* had little say in how they were governed; the *habitants* and other people of humble occupations and antecedents had none at all. The disunity that already existed within the administration was projected in the local strife between landowner and priest, and it was emphasized even more by the resentments that were felt by born Canadians towards the civil

officials and military commanders sent out from France
to occupy the most important positions in the country.
Undoubtedly one of the principal reasons why the
Church retained its prestige in New France while that of
the colonial administration steadily declined was the fact
that as time went on most of the priests were locally
trained *canadiens*, rather than emigrants from France.

In the end, because it retained this influence among
the people, and because it was not Gallican, the Church
was the one wing of French administration that not only
survived the Conquest, but continued to gather
influence to itself. Owing allegiance to the Pope and not
to the French king, the bishops were able to preach acceptance of British rule, and they succeeded in lobbying
for religious tolerance, embodied in the Quebec Act of
1774, which eliminated in Canada the onerous tests that
prevented Catholics in Britain from holding public
office. The Church retained a power over education
which gained importance as the French Canadian population became more literate. It also sustained a potent
influence in the country districts, where the *curés*
remained arbiters of morals and political advisers. In return, the Church guaranteed loyalty or at least neutrality
at times when British power was threatened in North
America — notably during the American revolutionary
period of the 1770s, during the war of 1812–14 and during the Lower Canadian rebellions of 1837–38.

THE BRITISH COLONIAL ADMINISTRATIONS AFTER 1760 were so
ready to accommodate the French church partly because
they were in no haste to establish a British system of
government in the newly acquired province of Quebec,
as New France had become. Indeed, for thirty years
they followed an authoritarian pattern not unlike the
one they had superseded, imposed by British career officers and officials who had little personal interest in the
country except to do their duty in administering and defending it. From 1760 to 1763 the military ruled. Then,

from 1763 to 1792, a civil governor ruled with the advice of an appointed council, which consisted principally of British officials like himself. But even in this period and for a considerable time afterwards the so-called civil governor was in fact a military man. It was not until long after Upper and Lower Canada were created under the Constitutional Act of 1791 that the colony was governed by a civilian. That civilian was the Duke of Richmond, who arrived in 1818.

As well as dividing Quebec into two provinces, the Constitutional Act at least modestly diluted the authoritarian character of colonial administration by giving each of the new provinces a political structure, in which a lieutenant-governor ruled with appointed executive and legislative councils and an elected assembly. In fact, the assembly had little direct power, except to approve or disapprove the government's budget, and the imported colonial officials, who dominated both of the councils, were in no way responsible to the assembly. In effect, the government remained in the hands of the governor or lieutenant-governor and the career officials who were his closest advisers until responsible government was instituted in the Canadas and the Atlantic provinces late in the 1840s.

In the far western province of British Columbia responsible government was not established until the colony entered Confederation in 1871. Up to that time the local judiciary and civil service remained mainly in the hands of Colonial Office appointees. In the prairies Manitoba acquired responsible government under the compromise that ended the Red River rebellion in 1870, but in the western plains it was not gained until Saskatchewan and Alberta were carved out of the Northwest Territories in 1905.

After the achievement of responsible government, after Confederation and even after Canada's virtual independence was recognized under the Statute of Westminster in 1931, vestiges of the transient class of imported colonial officials remained. Although the last British troops departed in 1870, apart from those staying at small seaport garrisons at Halifax and Esquimalt, the generals commanding the Canadian Armed Forces were imported British officers until 1904.

TO THIS DAY THE HEAD OF STATE is a British monarch residing in England and making periodic visits to her or his Canadian domain, and until the middle of the present century the monarch's resident deputy, the governor general, was always a distinguished Briton and usually a member of the peerage.

It is true that for more than a century the duties of governors general have been mainly formal, but there were occasions when they were called on to play an important and active part in Canadian affairs. During the crucial years of the 1860s, when Confederation was being discussed by both British and colonial politicians, the incumbent governor general, Lord Monck, played a key part. In his role as Queen's representative Monck felt that he was at least partly responsible for furthering the policies of the imperial government, and he actively did so by smoothing over the differences between the various provinces and ensuring that the hesitations of the Atlantic colonies, Nova Scotia and New Brunswick, were effectively overcome.

Once Canada was a self-governing dominion, responsible for its own defence, the governor general's role of defending and interpreting British interests in North America diminished. His role as surrogate head of state in a constitutional monarchy remained, and this meant that his influence, wherever it was exerted, operated indirectly: advice replaced direction. In 1952 the last vestige of the succession of transient colonial officials came to an end with the departure of the last British governor general, Viscount Alexander. Vincent Massey, a native-born Canadian, was appointed in his place.

CHAPTER

7

Colonial Bureaucrats and the Failure of Feudalism

THE RELATIONSHIP BETWEEN THE POLITICAL structure of a country and its life as a society is rather like the relationship between a house and a home. The Chinese philosopher Lao Tzu once said:

> You build a house with walls
> but you live in the space
> between the walls, which is empty.
> You use a bowl because of
> the part that is empty,
> but the emptiness
> depends on the bowl.

The house in fact becomes a home because of the way people live in its emptiness, and so long as the same family inhabits a house, it is what happens in the inner space that is the constant. The structure of the house can be changed, enlarged, even rebuilt, and still

161

the life that goes on within it belongs to the inhabitants and not to the house.

It is the same with a country; the political structure may contain the society that develops within it and it may protect the culture, but the society and the culture are the enduring if not unchanging realities. The shape society assumes is derived from the collective impulses of its people or peoples, and the culture that emerges is an expression of those impulses. A political structure can be constructive and beneficial only insofar as it is a consensual structure based on an arrangement of those collective impulses and the desires they reflect. Only in this way can it guarantee fairness to all sections of society. Where politics does not fulfill these requirements, as in the case of a dictatorship or an oligarchy of interest or doctrine, it is antisocial, and the house begins to take on the look of a prison.

Canada's evolution from a colonial society under authoritarian rule to a mature pluralist society with democratic self-government cannot be considered entirely without reference to those who presided, often unwillingly, over that transition.

The clash of interest between transitory colonial administrators interpreting changing imperial interests and a colonial population that over the years became increasingly native-born was present in Canada from the beginning. As we have seen, it was not many decades after Champlain's establishment of Quebec in 1608 that a class of traders and trappers, the *coureurs de bois*, began to defy the laws imposed by the governors of New France in order to enjoy the free and profitable life of wanderers in the *pays d'en haut*, the Indian country. But for the most part, in the seventeenth century, the *coureurs de bois* were not a group separate from the rest of *canadien* society. They were usually young *habitants* from the farms that were beginning to appear along the St Lawrence, stretching in narrow strips between the river and the forest, so that their inhabitants learned early to be fishermen and hunters, as well as tillers of the land. In this sense the *coureurs* simply reflected a widespread feeling among the French men and women who migrated to Canada and even more among their children, that they had liberated themselves from the restricted, over-regulated and class-ridden society of Old France.

And, indeed, the attempt to establish a replica of French society through the creation of *seigneuries*, whose tenants — like tenants in France — were obliged to carry out certain *corvées*, or work tasks, in return for their land, was never completely successful. Society was too mobile; the *seigneuries* often fell into the hands of merchants or men who had risen from the peasantry; the rank of seigneur failed to inspire the respect or fear (or for that matter the hatred) it had inspired in Old France. This mobility gave *canadien* society a resilience that enabled it to withstand the shock of the Conquest and accept a new set of colonial rulers. But also, paradoxically, it decreased the possibility of violent internal change, so that the *canadiens* were responsive neither to the Revolution in Old France in 1789, nor, by and large, to the approaches of the geographically closer republicans from the insurgent states south of the border.

IN UPPER CANADA THERE WAS A SIMILAR ATTEMPT on the part of early colonial administrators to recreate on North American soil the replica of a traditional European society. The first lieutenant-governor of Upper Canada, John Graves Simcoe, who held office in the colony's formative years, from 1791 to 1796, was a man of considerable intelligence and culture who had gone through Eton and Oxford. He had intended to embark on a career as a lawyer before he took up a commission in the British army. During the American Revolution he had been the resourceful commander of a famous Loyalist regiment, the Queen's Rangers, and so he may have seemed the ideal first administrator of a colony inhabited largely by Loyalists.

The task that Simcoe faced — that of creating a working community in a virtually trackless wilderness — was enormous, and there is no doubt that in some respects his achievements in promoting road building and in encouraging immigrants were considerable. But his guiding vision was to reproduce in North America the existing English hierarchy of king, gentry and commoners, with the Church also incorporated into the establishment. The plan was not very clearly related to the realities of life in Upper Canada or of its heterogeneously developing population.

Simcoe's plan was also based on his classical education. He hoped to establish in Upper Canada something resembling the old Roman system of military colonies, which allowed for defence and settlement at the same time. His old regiment, the Queen's Rangers, would be recreated, and its twelve companies would become the nuclei of twelve settlements. The original settlers would be disbanded members of the regiment, and the active soldiers — while serving as a potential defence force — would be occupied in laying out townsites, clearing forest and building roads, the whole network centring on Simcoe's new capital of York. But the scheme failed for lack of support from both the Colonial Office and the military authorities. Simcoe was allotted two companies instead of twelve and used them mostly for road building.

At the same time, Simcoe sought to shape the actual order of Upper Canada by giving large grants of land — sometimes whole townships — to individuals, who were then expected to attract settlers, among whom they would become a kind of local squire. In this way an untitled aristocracy would appear in the colony and act as a barrier to the spread of excessively democratic ideas from south of the border. Most of these grants were made to British half-pay officers and to officials in the colonial government, including Simcoe himself, who claimed five thousand acres as a military grant, which his family was able to sell at a considerable profit in the 1830s.

Simcoe's policy of land grants was continued under later governors, and the beneficiary who came closest to Simcoe's ideal of the transplanted landed magnate was Thomas Talbot, who had been Simcoe's private secretary during his early years in office. Travelling with Simcoe, Talbot had been impressed with the possibilities of western Upper Canada, and when the Peace of Amiens came in 1801 he resigned his commission and was granted several townships to develop in the area of present-day London, Ontario. Subsequently he received a vast area of more than sixty thousand acres on the north shore of Lake Erie. Talbot acted the benevolent despot, living in patriarchal state among his settlers, insisting that houses be built and land improved as a condition of granting his land, and creating one of the best road systems in the province.

Talbot, however, was an exception among landowners in the interest he displayed in effective settlement, and Simcoe's ideal of the dedicated squire tended to be replaced in the next generation by the more openly commercial operations of syndicates like the Canada Company. In 1825 this enterprise was allowed to purchase two and a half million acres at a price of about twelve cents an acre with the connivance of the colonial officials and against the opposition of the elected assembly. Again it was a question of British bureaucrats encouraging British beneficiaries, for the Scots novelist John Galt was the leading figure in the Canada Company, and another British writer, the former military surgeon William Dunlop, was one of his principal managers.

Under the Constitutional Act of 1791, a seventh of the land in the two Canadas had been set aside as "Clergy Reserves," to be sold for the benefit of the Church of England; later the Church of Scotland was

regarded as an equally acceptable beneficiary. Simcoe
had hoped to use funds raised from the sale of these
lands to endow an Anglican state church in Upper
Canada. But with plenty of free land to be got from
grants or mere squatting, nobody in the still thinly populated territory of Upper Canada was inclined to spend
money on uncleared land, and the Clergy Reserves remained a subject of bitter controversy for the next two
generations. Meanwhile, the imperial government refused to give Simcoe any other funds to endow a state
church.

SIMCOE'S HOPES OF CREATING A GRADED SOCIETY were equally
vain, mainly because he had wrongly assessed the loyalties of the Loyalists. The Loyalists differed from the
American rebels in maintaining their loyalty to the king
and to the British connection. But they and their families
had been living, often for generations, in the more open
society of the colonies, and they had no desire to retreat
to a class-ridden society on the English model, with its
squires and yeomen and labourers. Moreover, the Loyalist body of settlers in Upper Canada was being permeated by Americans who were crossing the border not
out of any consideration for the Hanoverian kings, by
now represented by the weak-minded George III, but
because there was good land to be had for the taking.
Such men leavened the legislative bodies with which
Simcoe had to deal, and it was only with difficulty that
he fended off a proposal by the assembly to institute
town meetings on the New England model to deal with
local affairs. Instead, he had justices of the peace appointed in the English style. This was one of his few tri-
umphs in imposing a traditional system on the emergent
Canadian society.

Simcoe was somewhat distressed to find that the
elected representatives in the assembly were men of little education compared to British members of Parliament, but he had even greater difficulties with the

appointed legislative council. It included merchants and men who were land speculators rather than landowners, and who were much more concerned with defending their own interests and those of their fellows than with establishing an old-fashioned Tory social order. With only a few exceptions like Thomas Talbot, the few English officers who settled in Upper Canada prior to the War of 1812 offered no real counterbalance to the general Loyalist desire to create a society that may have been monarchist in sentiment but was in practice more open and less traditionally divided on class lines than that of England.

Yet there were times when the officials, who represented the imperial fatherland rather than the actual colonists, could have a cohesive influence on this barely formed society, because they were in some sense above local problems and situations. Isaac Brock was one such official, who epitomized Toryism at its early Canadian best. He was neither a native Canadian nor a Loyalist, but a British career officer who certainly did not expect that he would die, as he shortly did, on Canadian soil. He was commander of the armed forces in Upper Canada, and when the Americans started the war in 1812 he happened also by chance to be the administrator of the colony in the absence of the lieutenant-governor. It was a decade since Simcoe's failure to recreate an idealized English rural society in the dark woods of Ontario, and Brock found himself in charge of a province that by 1812 had been settled largely by Americans of dubious allegiance to the Crown. He faced an initially obstructive assembly and was partly dependent on a demoralized and unreliable militia, recruited under the outdated laws of New France, to support his small force of British regulars.

"Most of the people have lost all confidence," Brock remarked as the war began. "I however speak loud and look big." Brock not only looked big; he acted decisively. He entered into alliance with Tecumseh and his

Indians, who wished to save the old West from complete absorption by American frontiersmen and settlers and had their own quarrel with the American Longknives, and he chose to deploy the most reliable Loyalist units among the Canadian militia. Combining these disparate elements with his regular regiments, he created a small but effective army that, with a combination of boldness and ruse, drove out the Americans who at the beginning of the war had crossed into Upper Canada and occupied Amherstburg. He followed them over the border and captured Detroit, a symbolic action that immediately changed the look of the war and rallied the waverers.

Brock's stance was clearly revealed in his speech to the assembly of Upper Canada on July 27, 1812, a few weeks before the capture of Detroit.

> We are engaged in an awful and eventful contest. By unanimity and despatch in our council and vigour in our operations we will teach the enemy this lesson, that a country defended by free men, enthusiastically supported by their King and Constitution, can never be conquered.[12]

Brock was defending the British system of government against the American, which to him was obviously repugnant, but he was also making the English Tory argument that men are most free in a hierarchical situation where roles are understood. "King and constitution," in Brock's terms, meant the graded pattern of king, lords and commons, a system that was uneasily accepted by his supporters. But he gathered them together more by force of personality and by the exhibition of complete honesty and courage than by force of policy. Apart from the British regulars, who were there under imperial orders, and Tecumseh's Indians, who vanished like migrant birds as soon as their great chief was slain at Moraviantown, Brock's reliable supporters were a small group of young Loyalists and a few British office holders and officers. They had come to Canada before 1812, encouraged by the offer of land grants, and it was they who carried on the struggle beside the regulars after his death at the battle of Queenston Heights in 1813. The whole alliance, however, was one reached in time of crisis and it did not last.

ACCORDING TO CONVENTIONAL READINGS of Canadian history, there was a return to the *status quo ante bellum* after the War of 1812. The Tory ideal was sustained by the loose and ill-defined alliances of establishment figures known in Upper Canada as the Family Compact and in Lower Canada as the Château Clique. And there is indeed no doubt that during the three decades or more between the end of the war in 1814 and the institution of responsible government in the late 1840s, tacit but shifting understandings did exist among those who shared power in the colonies and who were unwilling to surrender it quietly to a more democratic system.

In both colonies the governors and the imported career officials — colonial secretaries, treasurers, solicitors general and surveyors general, judges, customs officials and postmasters — constituted the cores of the imposed administrations. From among these the executive councils, which were the nearest equivalents to cabinets, would be selected. Such officials dominated whatever scanty civil service existed. The local support for their administrations consisted of those whose interests were maintained by the defence of existing power and property relations. These were the merchants and fur traders, the speculators in land and officials in land companies, the canal builders and the earliest railway speculators. Multiple entrepreneurs like the famous Molson family, who from the late eighteenth century pioneered not only in brewing and other manufactures but also in steamships and in Canada's first banks, also had interests to protect. Some of these influential citizens were British immigrants, some were Loyalists and a growing number were Canadian born.

The title Family Compact, invented by the radical journalists of the time and much used by democratic polemicists like William Lyon Mackenzie in their campaigns against the reigning establishment, gives the impression that there were close personal links within the ruling groups of the Canadas between 1814 and about 1850. It is true that there were social relations and intermarriages between the leading mercantile and professional families in both Montreal and York (which became Toronto in 1834). These were probably no more prevalent, however, than in any town dominated by mercantile patricians — such as Bristol in its heyday or the Hansa towns of Germany whose interconnections Thomas Mann presented so compellingly in *The Buddenbrooks*. There was also a kind of Old Boy network which began in the school for young gentlemen that Dr John Strachan ran at Cornwall in the early 1800s and was continued in Upper Canada College, founded by Sir John Colborne in York in 1829. People linked in this way and united by common interests tended to work together as Old Boy networks still do in Canada. However, there was a gradual transformation of the Canadian upper classes, particularly after the War of 1812, which diminished not only the social influence but even the political power of the career officials who came from Britain.

Loyalists, and the Canadian-born sons of Loyalists, who had shown their loyalty once again by their service during the war, began to find a place beside the British-born officials in the administration of the North American provinces. John Beverley Robinson, born in Lower Canada in 1791, was one such official. The son of a Loyalist officer in the Queen's Rangers, he was one of Strachan's pupils at Cornwall, and after studying law he served as a militia officer under General Brock at the capture of Detroit. After John Macdonell, the Scottish-born attorney general of Upper Canada, was killed fighting at Queenston Heights in October 1812, Robinson was named acting attorney general in his place, and eventually in 1829 he was appointed Chief Justice of Upper Canada.

In many ways Robinson personified the differences between the traditions of the North American Loyalists and those of the transient British officials. At first sight it is easy to dismiss him as a conservative like Simcoe, dedicated to a British Tory view of society. This impression might seem to be reinforced upon observing that, as chief justice, he presided with implacability over the trials that followed the defeat of William Lyon Mackenzie's 1837 Upper Canadian insurrection. It was he who sentenced the rebel leaders Samuel Lount and Peter Matthews to death after Mackenzie, the prime mover of the pathetic little uprising of a few hundred badly armed farmers, had fled safely over the border into the United States. Yet, like the other Loyalists who gathered to support the absurd governor, Sir Francis Bond Head, against the rebels, Robinson was concerned mainly to prevent Canada from falling under what to him seemed an alien type of democratic republicanism. However, he was as loath as the rebels were to see Upper Canada and the other British North American colonies condemned to the perpetual tutelage of the mother country. He saw, rather, a North American community eventually developing on its own and taking responsibility for its own affairs. It was he who invented the term, "the Kingdom of Canada," conceiving a coordinate realm to that of Britain, which would follow its own course according to good Tory principles. This Canadian conservative was in fact one of the earliest advocates of the union of all the British North American colonies into a single Canadian nation capable of developing its own institutions and defending them.

The rebellions of 1837–38 in fact heralded the end of the influence and even the presence of the British career officials, even though in Lower Canada especially they were suppressed by British regular soldiers with some brutality. Order was re-established with strictness, but it was obvious that in neither Upper nor Lower Canada could there be a lasting return to the old condition of colonial subordination. And just over a decade after the rebellions, the granting of responsible government in the Atlantic provinces and the Canadas brought an end to the old system of appointed executive officers; elected politicians took their places. Not all these ministers among the people would be native Canadians. The first two prime ministers of the Dominion of Canada were immigrants. But they were non-returning immigrants, who had elected to make their lives in Canada, unlike the transient career officials who had preceded them.

Two governors general, who were among the last of the active administrators sent out from Britain to the North American colonies, illustrate admirably the evolution of attitudes that led the British official class to accept and indeed to facilitate its own replacement. The first of the two was the Earl of Durham, who was sent out in 1838 as governor-in-chief and lord high commissioner to make recommendations for a form of government that would prevent the repetition of the rebellions. The second was Lord Elgin, Durham's son-in-law, who was sent out in 1846 by a reform-minded imperial government to preside over the effective dismantling of the old colonial system of administration.

DURHAM WAS A CAPABLE, SENSITIVE MAN attached to the reform wing of the Whig party in Britain, and so open in his views that in England he was popularly known as "Radical Jack." But his investigations in Canada and the famous *Report on the Affairs of British North America* show how difficult it had become for an outsider to understand the complexities that had developed in Canadian society during the eighty years since the Conquest.

In Upper Canada Durham got in touch with the moderate reformers who had not joined Mackenzie in his rebellion, but who were deeply critical of the oligarchical way in which Canada was governed. Here he understood the situation very clearly, recommending the granting of responsible government so as to liberate the people from the rule of what, with good partisan ire, he described as "a petty, corrupt, insolent Tory clique."

But when he came to consider Lower Canada, Durham fell into the error he had avoided in the other province. He seems to have had little contact with the French-speaking radicals and reformers, perhaps because most of them had either fled or were lying low for fear of prosecution. Instead, he took his views from the English-speaking merchants of Montreal and the other St Lawrence towns, who represented the very kind of "insolent Tory clique" he had condemned in Upper Canada. He let himself be persuaded to see the Lower Canadian situation in racial and cultural rather than in political and social terms; he perceived "two nations warring in the bosom of a single state" and showed his contempt for the traditions of the *canadiens*, which seemed meagre and rustic to a man of European culture.

> There can hardly be conceived a nationality more destitute of all that can invigorate and elevate a people than that which is exhibited by the descendants of the French in Lower Canada, owing to their retaining their peculiar language and manners. They are a people with no history and no literature.[13]

Resentment against such strictures was in later years to become one of the major factors in the revival of a French Canadian culture in Quebec. But immediate attention centred around Durham's conclusion that the conflict which had resulted in the Lower Canadian rebellions would recur unless the French were assimilated into the English population of British North America.

Therefore, while on the one hand he recommended the granting of responsible government that would increase the general autonomy of the North American colonies, on the other hand he declared that the subordination of the French Canadians was essential for the peace of the region. With this end in view he recommended the union of the two Canadas so that the French-speaking voters would be dominated by an English-speaking minority.

The British government, at that time Tory in inclination, accepted Durham's recommendation of the union of the two provinces, but rejected the proposal of responsible government. The Act of Union brought Upper and Lower Canada together in a single province in 1840, and the Legislative Assembly now contained, as had been expected, a majority of English-speaking members. Merchant-dominated constituencies in Montreal and Trois-Rivières and Loyalist settlements in the Eastern Townships of Quebec had returned anglophone representatives, and a minority of French-speakers.

What ensued defied both Durham's expectations and the calculations of the British government of the time. The Assembly of the united province did not erupt in racial strife, nor was there a peaceful re-enactment of the Conquest, with the French-speaking members relegated to a perpetual minority. The moderate reformers in the two language groups formed an alliance which became a politically inspired liberal majority rather than a linguistically inspired English-speaking one. Thus the situation was an ideal one for the appointment in 1846 of Lord Elgin, who had instructions from the new reform-minded colonial secretary, Lord Grey, to institute responsible government at the opportune moment. Early in 1848 an election for the Assembly was won by a reform alliance led by the Upper Canadian Robert Baldwin and the Lower Canadian Louis-Hippolyte LaFontaine, and LaFontaine, who a decade before had been briefly imprisoned under suspicion of engaging in rebel activities, was called upon to form the first truly responsible government in Canada. He did this by creating a cabinet in which the Upper and Lower Canadian reformers, English-speakers and French-speakers, were fairly evenly balanced. In that way the model of the multicultural and pluralist Canada we know today was created as the two most numerous Canadian peoples set about learning to work together harmoniously.

The new responsible government was not without its touch of melodrama. The first sparks flew in more ways than one when the Rebellion Losses bill came before the Assembly. This bill aimed to compensate Lower Canadians whose property had been damaged during the rebellions of 1837–38. LaFontaine saw the proposed legislation as an assertion of French Canadian equality within the united province and also as a means of countering the radical influence of Louis-Joseph Papineau, the leader of the rebellion. Like William Lyon Mackenzie in Upper Canada, he had discreetly fled when he saw defeat ahead, but had recently returned under an amnesty. Some of the claimants under the bill were suspected of sympathy for the rebel cause, or even of participation in the rebellion, and for this reason the legislation was strongly denounced by the Tory opposition and the remaining British officials. With a reform alliance majority, however, the bill was passed.

Elgin himself was personally unsympathetic to the legislation, but in accordance with the policy of responsible government he signed the bill as the Queen's representative on April 25, 1849. That night an English-speaking mob attacked Elgin and burned down the Parliament building, which at that time was in Montreal. But Elgin refused to prevent passage of the bill, the Colonial Office supported him and in its first real test responsible government was confirmed.

Once that had happened, the need for British career officials in Canada, except as ceremonial representatives of the monarchy, came to an end. But as a class they

had played their part in maintaining the political structure of the North American colonies until a genuine Canadian society could develop and demand its own
political expression.

CHAPTER
8

Soldiers of the King and Queen

THE BRITISH CAREER OFFICIALS who came and went in Canada undoubtedly had a peripheral influence on upper-class life there, but the English lifestyle could not be imported without modification. Immigrant gentry like Susanna Moodie who tried to settle in the bush quickly found that the upper-class veneer was thin in the Canadas. Even among Loyalists of the landowning class there was a North American openness and frankness of behaviour that could only have been disconcerting to anyone brought up on the combination of upper-class politeness and lower-class deference that was the norm in England. Attempts might be made to perpetuate British upper-class behaviour, through such institutions as English-style private schools and social clubs, which survive to this day, but at no point, even during the height of Queen Victoria's reign, was a true replica of English aristocratic society ever established in Canada. One has only to read the accounts of English gentlewomen, like Anna Jameson's narrative of her seasons in Canada during the 1830s, or Frances Monck's diary of her experiences as the governor general's daughter-in-law in the 1860s, to realize how gauche and rustic the "polite society" of Toronto, Montreal and later Ottawa must have appeared to them.

It is true that in far-off British Columbia, where the career officials lingered until the province entered Confederation in 1871, an anglophile society of émigré gentry did develop, so that parts of Victoria came to resemble a cross between an English country town and a south coast resort. But Victoria was a mere enclave in a province inhabited by miners and loggers, fishermen and farmers, with the largest proportion of Indians and Chinese in the country.

Much the same might be said of the social influence of the British soldiers who shared with civil officials the care of the British North American colonies in the early days. As soon as direct colonial government began in 1663 in New France, the matter of defending the colonies came to the fore, and from the beginning a two-level system was put in place. It consisted of local forces that carried out mainly home guard duties and regular troops sent from France and later from Britain whenever major threats had to be countered.

In the case of New France, regular regiments were sent usually in times of crisis. The Carignan-Salières regiment, for instance, was dispatched in the 1660s to deal with the Iroquois menace and a considerable body of regular regiments were sent to Quebec under the Marquis de Montcalm during the Seven Years' War (1756–63). But more often New France was defended by the Troupes de la Marine, a corps established in 1696 for guarding naval dockyards and for colonial services. It was under the direct control of the Ministry of Marine. The Troupes de la Marine were more flexibly organized than the units of the French army; they consisted not of regiments but of companies of about one hundred men, which could be moved about more easily and were more suitable for the forest warfare that occurred on the borders of New France. There were usually about thirty companies of Troupes de la Marine in New France and another twenty were stationed in the fortress of Louisbourg once it was built.

Unlike the regular regiments, which consisted entirely of soldiers from France and whose officers were usually French aristocrats whose arrogance offended the *canadiens*, the Troupes de la Marine soon began to recruit young men from among the *habitant* population. Their companies were often officered by *canadiens*, as well, who had a close knowledge of the country and were familiar with the methods of warfare of the Iroquois, their principal enemies. The Troupes de la Marine mingled easily with the local population, and the French who served in them often elected to remain beside the St Lawrence after they were demobilized.

The other line of defence for New France consisted of the militia, which was really a reactivated form of the obsolescent *milices* of France itself, that by the late seventeenth century had little more than a ceremonial function. Even before colonial government was established in 1663, hunters and *habitants* were being armed and loosely organized for self-defence against the Iroquois, who were constantly indulging in surprise attacks on French settlements and on fur convoys from the *pays d'en haut*.

After the establishment of colonial government, and particularly under the governorship of Count Frontenac, a regular militia was organized, with a unit in each parish, headed by an honorary *capitaine de milices*. All males from sixteen to sixty were required to train in their parish unit for at least one month a year and to turn out in case of war, as they did in a *levée en masse* when the British invaded New France during the Seven Years' War. When there was no war, the militia were often used during their training period for road construction. Since many of the militia were men who had visited the

pays d'en haut as *coureurs* or voyageurs, they were familiar with the Indian forms of guerilla warfare, which they
used not only against their Iroquois enemies, but also,
when the occasion demanded it, in surprise attacks and
ambushes directed against the British in New England
and on the Hudson River. Combination forces of
Troupes de la Marine, militia and friendly Indians
proved effective in the border fighting that took place
during the wars with Britain, and on the whole they
were more efficient than the French regulars. A similar
militia was formed by the French in Acadia during the
eighteenth century and was much feared by the inhabitants of Maine when it served in combination with the
Micmac Indians, sometimes led by local missionary
priests.

After the Conquest, the British continued to use the
French structure of defence. The captains of militia units
were designated agents of local government, since they
knew their districts well and enjoyed the confidence of
their parishioners. The *canadien* militia remained a functioning entity for some time, and was called out as a defence corps during the Indian rebellion led by Pontiac in
1763 and again during the American Revolution.

The earliest militia in English-speaking Canada was
formed in Halifax in 1749, and Governor Simcoe attempted to set up a compulsory system in Upper
Canada shortly after the colony was established. Not
until shortly before the War of 1812, however, were facilities made available to train the militia. It was part of
this militia that Isaac Brock used in combination with his
regulars and Tecumseh's men during the war. Those
who served under compulsion were relied on only for
non-combatant transport and labour duties, but a number of highly motivated volunteer companies, composed
mostly of Loyalists and British immigrants, fought beside the regulars and on occasion served with a great
deal of courage and skill. However, the credit that has
often been given them by over-patriotic historians for

the victory over the Americans, if such it was, is more a matter of myth than of fact.

The real brunt of withstanding the American attacks, of saving Canada from absorption by its greater neighbour and of carrying the war into enemy territory was borne by the British regulars and by a number of provincial regiments, or fencibles, recruited in the colonies to serve only on North American soil. One of the provincial regiments that served with special distinction at that time was the Voltigeurs Canadiens under Colonel de Salaberry, which defeated at Châteauguay an American army that was blundering its way towards Montreal.

BETWEEN THE WAR OF 1812 AND CONFEDERATION IN 1867, a double defensive structure existed in Canada. The various Militia Acts retained the option of compulsion, and theoretically every man between sixteen and sixty remained liable for service when called upon. But there never were any *levées en masse* until conscription came in a different form during the Great War, and the Sedentary Militia, as it was euphemistically called, remained for the most part an entirely untrained and unarmed reserve force. When the call went out to the militia during the 1837 rebellion in Upper Canada, the men responded in larger numbers than they did to William Lyon Mackenzie's insurrectionary proclamations, but probably less than half of them came with firearms of any kind or even knew how to use them properly.

In practice the volunteer principle prevailed, and the volunteer principle was linked to social standing. Smart young gentlemen trained in camp together for a week or two every year, but more important to many of them was the life of parades and balls and parties that went on around the armouries in the cities and towns. Far from stressing universality of training, many militia units were highly selective in their choice of recruits, and the mere cost of the elaborate uniforms often cho-

sen was usually enough to discourage the artisan or the
labourer who might have patriotic thoughts.

These militia regiments, troops and batteries, many
of which still survive in the names at least of volunteer
or even regular units, set out to imitate the regular
troops. Some of the models were highly prestigious regiments like the Guards, who served on garrison duty in
Halifax from 1749 until as late as 1905. Most British regiments gave up their duties in Canada shortly after Confederation, at which time the imperial government
intimated that henceforth the newly constituted dominion would be responsible for its own defence.

After Pontiac's rising the Indian threat had largely re-
ceded, as the Americans on their ever-advancing frontier
began to take on the more westerly tribes. But throughout the Napoleonic Wars the threat of French invasion
remained, and the danger of attack from the United
States was a closer and even more real one, as the
American attack on Canada in 1812 demonstrated. The
principal garrison points were Halifax, which also
served as a naval depot for the North Atlantic, and Quebec, which guarded the western approaches to the heart
of the continent up the St Lawrence River. Other points,
like Kingston and Niagara, were of lesser defensive importance, but troops were stationed there, as well as in
provincial centres and centres of commerce like Toronto,
Montreal and Fredericton. It was in this last city that
William Cobbett, probably the most distinguished "other
rank" in the British army in Canada, served from 1784
to 1791, rising eventually to the rank of sergeant-major
and causing a major scandal on his return to England by
accusing the officers there of corruption.

Far to the west, on Vancouver Island, Esquimalt Harbour became a permanent naval base, and there, as in
Halifax, a small garrison remained until the dockyards
were handed over to the newly formed Royal Canadian
Navy in 1905. Elsewhere other units appeared for short
periods and special purposes. A unit of Royal Engineers

served in British Columbia at the time of the Fraser Valley Gold Rush, suppressed that absurd little miners' rebellion known as Ned McGowan's War and built a great part of the highroad into the Cariboo mining country. In 1870 a battalion of the 1st Royal Rifles accompanied a group of Canadian militia units in the last British action in Canada when General Garnet Wolseley's expeditionary force went to Fort Garry at the end of the Red River rebellion in 1870.

The number of British soldiers in Canada changed constantly during the nineteenth century as crisis alternated with calm. After the wars in America and Europe came to an end in 1814 and 1815, respectively, the British North American territories were rapidly demilitarized, partly because of imperial economies, but partly because the Iron Duke believed that a few key fortifications (which in the event were never completed) would be enough to hold Canada against the Americans now they had no French allies to rely on. The local regiments of fencibles were dismissed in 1816, and by 1819 the British garrison had been reduced to seven regiments. Many of the militia formations mustered in the recent war maintained a paper existence, but for political rather than military reasons, since they produced a multitude of military titles for worthy citizens who might gather once a year for a disorderly parade like that which Anna Jameson witnessed in 1837, which ended "in a drunken bout and a riot, in which, as I was afterwards informed, the colonel had been knocked down."

The Upper Canadian rebellion, following closely after the parade which Anna described, led to a doubling of British forces in the Canadas. Fluctuations in the strength of the military establishment continued into the 1860s, reaching a crescendo in 1861 during the Civil War when a Union vessel stopped the British steamer *Trent* and precipitated an international crisis by seizing two Confederate agents who were on board. Fourteen thousand troops, including artillery and engineers and regiments of the Guards, were rushed to Canada in case of war. It was the largest contingent of British troops to cross the Atlantic since 1814, and it was also the last. Within a decade, as a result of Confederation, the British military presence in North America would be almost at an end. At the same time, however, the British naval presence was building up on the Pacific coast, first as a reaction to the American threat during the Oregon boundary dispute of 1846, and later to the Russian threat during the Crimean War. A good harbour at Esquimalt near Victoria and coal deposits on Vancouver Island led to the creation of a naval depot that still exists as a Canadian navy base today.

THE CONTINUED PRESENCE UNTIL THE 1860S of the garrisons in Halifax and Quebec and of British detachments in other urban centres was socially important in a number of ways. Since there were comparatively few married officers, and just as few married men in other ranks, they naturally sought links with the civilian life that went on outside the garrison walls. Of the life of the men, as they were curiously called in distinction from the officers, we have little knowledge beyond the round of barracks and tavern. More is known about the officers, who influenced the life of the towns in which they lived and the culture of Canada in general in a number of ways.

Many of them were aristocrats or at least members of the English country gentry, and their presence encouraged the survival of a kind of social protocol that no longer existed south of the border, or for that matter in the Upper Canadian bush or the villages along the St Lawrence. Their social life was ordered and led to a considerable flowering of snobbery. Quebec was protected to some extent by the duality of its own culture, but Halifax was another matter. It was entirely British and the garrison — not counting any naval ships that might be stationed there — accounted for an eighth of the

population. A traveller describing the city in 1859 remarked that

> as it is a garrison town, as well as a naval station, you
> meet in the streets red-coats and blue-jackets without
> number; yonder, with a brilliant staff, is the Gover-
> nor, Sir John Gaspard le Marchant, and here, in a car-
> riage, is Admiral Fanshawe, C.B., of the *Boscawen*
> flag-ship. Everything is suggestive of impending hos-
> tilities; war, in burnished trappings, encounters you at
> the street corners, and the air vibrates from time to
> time with bugles, fifes and drums.[14]

Though familiar, the military as a class were still somewhat exotic in the eyes of the mercantile Haligonians
and, as another traveller noted: "A young officer . . .
finds himself raised at once to a level above that ac-
corded to the scarlet cloth at home — his society generally sought, frequently courted, and himself esteemed."
Whatever the effect of this situation on the young officer, there were many including the radical journalist
and politician Joseph Howe, who regarded its general
influence on Nova Scotian society as highly question-
able.

> We by no means wish to undervalue the benefits
> which Halifax derives from the expenditures of the
> British and local governments . . . but the whole ten-
> dency of military society in a town like this is towards
> habits of idleness, dissipation and expense. We have
> colonels, majors, captains, and subalterns — all hav-
> ing fixed incomes provided by the crown — many of
> them gentlemen of fortune, and polished manners. If
> our population would be content to borrow only what
> is estimable, to copy only what was worthy of imita-
> tion, we might derive from it a great deal of good and
> but very little harm. But unfortunately we are all
> prone to copy each other's vices and virtues, and too
> many of our young men, without acquiring the grace
> and polish of their Garrison associates, have learnt

their disregard of time, their habits of expense and
their contempt for the low pursuits of business.[15]

But more people probably welcomed the young officers than deplored them, and they gave a touch of liveli-
ness and sophistication to the very provincial existences
of towns like Toronto and Kingston. In such a remote
and miniature capital as Victoria, hovering in the late
1850s between the fur age and the gold age, the naval
officers provided much of the social entertainment. In
1859, for example, the officers of two men of war, the
Satellite and the *Plumper*, gave "a grand ball to the ladies
of Vancouver Island," which Lieutenant Charles Wilson
described with a touch of condescension, hinting at the
gap between social pretensions and realities in colonial
Victoria.

> Every body came to the great ball from the governor
> downwards nearly 200 in all & we kept dancing up
> with great spirit until ½ past three in the morning.
> Every body was quite delighted & it goes by the name
> of "the Party par excellence"; nobody says ball in this
> part of the world, it is always party. The ladies looked
> very nicely dressed, & some of them danced very
> well, though they would look better if they would
> only learn to wear their crinolines properly, it is most
> lamentable to see the objects they make of them-
> selves, some of the hoops being quite oval, while oth-
> ers had only one hoop rather high up, the remainder
> of the dress hanging down perpendicularly.[16]

One way in which the garrison society contributed
notably to the emergent culture of Canada was in its
fostering of the arts. The first novel set in Canada, *The
History of Emily Montague* (1769), was written by Frances
Brooke, friend of Dr Johnson and wife of the garrison
chaplain at Quebec. It concerned the lives and loves of
officers and ladies during the occupation period after the
Conquest. One of the first important novels written by a

Canadian was a Gothic tale about garrison life, John Richardson's *Wacousta* — which was set in the British fortress of Detroit during Pontiac's rebellion in 1763. John Richardson was the son of a medical officer in a British regiment and himself served as a gentleman volunteer in the War of 1812, later being commissioned in the regular British forces.

The British garrisons were also responsible for developing the theatre in Canada, if not actually introducing it there. A masque of a kind, *Le Théâtre de Neptune dans la Nouvelle France*, by Marc Lescarbot, had been produced at Port Royal as early as 1606, but though occasional amateur performances of Corneille and Racine were put on by French officials and officers stationed in Quebec, the Church kept a watchful eye and an inhibiting hand on dramatic performances. An attempt to stage Molière's *Tartuffe* was halted in 1694 by the intervention of the bishop. The ban on Molière continued until, ironically, he was first performed in Canada in English, by officers and men of the British garrison in Montreal.

In Quebec and Halifax as well, the initiative in theatre was taken by the garrisons. At first they played, as in Shakespeare's time, with all-male casts in taverns and public rooms. Not content with such makeshift accommodations, the Halifax garrison built the New Grand Theatre in 1789. Even in more remote places, like York, Kingston and London, the theatrical impetus came from groups of soldiers, and here an unusually democratic spirit prevailed, with members of other ranks who had acting talent playing alongside the officers. Gradually, as civilian amateurs began to mingle with the soldiers and women were persuaded to act, the theatre tended to be supported by the community in general, with a certain puritanical opposition on the part of the Methodists.

But perhaps the most important contribution that the British officers made to Canadian cultural life was in the visual arts. Unlike the muscularly Christian Victorian era, when amateur painting, like the writing of poetry, was seen as a pastime for women and effeminates, a degree of accomplishment in the arts was regarded in the eighteenth century and the subsequent Regency period as a desirable attribute for a gentleman. (Skill in music had had similar status in the Elizabethan age.) Among the officers who sailed with Wolfe to the invasion of Canada there were several who were adept with pen and watercolour, notably the Marquess of Townshend and Richard Short.

More important, artillery and engineer officers who went through the military academy at Woolwich were instructed in topographical drawing, which was essential in the days before photography to provide information about the terrain on which troops would campaign and attack. The courses at Woolwich were given by professional artists, and they included instruction in the theory and history of art as well as in drawing and in watercolour sketching.

Many of the officers who received this training put it to use to fill their considerable leisure time. This resulted in not only some of the earliest Canadian landscape painting, but also studies of early Canadian towns and their street life which are now invaluable resources for historians. The succession of officer painters continued from 1757 when Thomas Davies, ranking as "Lieutenant of Fireworks," reached Halifax to the 1840s when Captain Henry Warre was sent on a mission to the disputed Columbia River territory and returned with some of the earliest landscape paintings of the Rockies. Thomas Davies has since been recognized as a painter of genuine originality and stature, and a number of the garrison painters, like James Peachey, James Cockburn and Richard Levinge, have their secure places in the history of Canadian painting. The tradition of officer painters, like the garrisons to which they belonged, vanished in the mid-nineteenth century, but by this time a notable contribution had been made to Canada's social and artistic life.

CHAPTER
9

The Other Kingdom

Of the three great branches of imperial power that
the French introduced into Canada during the seventeenth century, the civil and the military establishments
came to an end, as we have seen, after two centuries or
less. At this time there was a Canadian-born community
that both desired and was able to establish its own government and defence. But the third great body, the
Church, adapted itself to the changing society and, in its
many forms, tenaciously remained.

For the seventeenth-century French, and in a different way for the eighteenth-century English who succeeded them, the existence of a temporal power without
a coordinate spiritual power was almost unthinkable,
and both governments attempted to create a religious
establishment. The French did so to the extent of actually excluding Huguenots from New France and making
it impossible for non-French Protestants to settle there.
While the British found dissenting sects even more numerous and active in the Atlantic provinces and in Upper Canada than they were at home in Britain, they did
their best to create an Anglican establishment, and failed

only because the opposition to a state church became linked to the struggle for democratic rights and responsible government. In the long run the domination of Protestant Canada by the Church of England was never a political possibility in the same way that domination by the Church of Rome was possible in Catholic French Canada.

Thus, in the beginning, the two official churches were as much institutions imported from outside for the purpose of ruling as were the colonial civil establishments and the military garrisons. Their strength and their power of survival lay in their ability to adapt to changing social and demographic conditions, to detach themselves from obsolescent colonial political establishments and to fit with as much ease into a population of native-born Canadians as they had originally fitted into the populations of their countries of origin.

Some religious communities in Canada have never sought to proselytize, like the Jewish community and certain ethnically oriented Christian sects (the Doukhobors, the Mennonites, the Russian Orthodox Church, the Ukrainian Uniates, for instance). However, most of the main religions were established on Canadian soil with a double aim. To begin with, they were garrison churches, catering to the needs of their members and making sure that in a new country they kept the old faith. For this purpose they created ecclesiastical structures that were offshoots of the parent churches, and offered familiar settings by building churches that looked like the ones in the Old Country, even if they were of wood rather than of stone. They also sustained the familiar liturgies. On the other hand they were also mission churches, intent on the work of converting the heathen, which many of the seventeenth-century French and nineteenth-century English regarded as the great task under heaven.

Unlike the claim of the old adage, trade in Canada did not follow the flag; rather, it preceded civil government. Religion often appeared between trade and government after the first impact of European intrusion. Like exploration and settlement, Christianity moved across the country in a kind of space-time continuum, showing up first in the St Lawrence valley, then on the Atlantic seaboard and later in Upper Canada. Not until the nineteenth century did it reach the prairies and the Pacific coast, and it was late in that century or early in the twentieth that it arrived in the North.

MOST MISSIONARY ENDEAVOURS BEGAN on the assumption that in the end it would be possible to achieve a complete triumph of Christianity, and that in the process it would be possible to convert pagan and largely nomadic Indians into pious and settled replicas of Frenchmen or Englishmen. Even secular rulers saw this as a way of solving the problems involved in taking a continent away from its original inhabitants and owners. Colbert demonstrated this in 1671 when he urged Jean Talon, the intendant, to support the missionaries.

> Always endeavour by every possible means to encourage the clergy to bring up in their communities as many Indian children as possible, so that being educated in the maxims of our religion and in our customs, they, along with the settlers, may evolve into a single nation and so strengthen the colony.[17]

Without such political motives, the Protestant missionaries shared the same aim of total conversion, preferably to the tenets of their own sects, and as late as the 1970s I heard in mission stations in the Arctic Bishop Heber's grand old hymn of proselytization, "From Greenland's Icy Mountains" sung by Inuit under the direction of their English-born pastor.

Salvation! O, salvation!
The joyful sound proclaim,
Till each remotest nation
Has learn'd Messiah's name.

In fact, even by the time Colbert wrote to Talon,
there had been a change in the attitudes of missionaries
and in the scope of their activities. Cartier had claimed
the land for Christ as well as for France when he raised
his great cross beside the St Lawrence in 1534, and it is
possible that priests accompanied him on his second
voyage but did not stay. The first missionaries to begin
actual work among the Indians were the Récollets, who
came in 1615 at the invitation of Samuel de Champlain.
In 1625 they were joined by the Jesuits, who had hardly
begun their mission work when Quebec was captured
by the British in 1629 and all the priests returned home.
By the time the colony was returned to France in 1632,
the Jesuits had lobbied in court so successfully that they
were the only missionaries allowed to return. The Récollets were kept out of Canada until 1670. There followed
the high period of Jesuit activity, during which the
members of the order founded their ambitious mission,
Ste Marie-among-the-Hurons, and attempted to convert
that powerful tribe in its entirety. However, by 1650 the
Iroquois attacks not only destroyed the Huron nation,
but also put an end to such grand attempts at proselytization.

From that point on the Jesuits and other missionaries
contented themselves with maintaining scattered missions among the Indians, and devoted more of their attention to the growing population of immigrants and
Canadian-born French. By 1680, these had reached
about twelve thousand in number, including the
Troupes de la Marine. The change in emphasis and direction by the Church was accompanied by a change in
policy on the part of the colonial authorities, who no
longer felt that French people and converted Indians

could easily form a single, homogeneous community. They abandoned thoughts of acculturation on any wide scale, preferring now to accept the Indians as they were. They had decided to regard them as potential allies and providers of furs with whom treaty relations were to be established on the basis of nominal equality. This did not prevent missionary priests from attempting their conversion and the priests still had the official support of the authorities. This support, however, was tempered at times by annoyance at the priests' inclination to interfere periodically with the fur trade. The men of the cloth often claimed that the *coureurs de bois* and the merchants were corrupting the native population, which they doubtless were, since they took with them not only alcohol but a wide assortment of white men's diseases, all the way from smallpox and syphilis to measles and influenza.

In 1657 the Sulpician fathers arrived and established themselves in Montreal, which had already been founded as the mission settlement Ville-Marie in 1642. They devoted themselves to work among the French-speaking population, but soon Canadian-born priests, trained in the seminary that Bishop Laval founded at Quebec in 1660, were added to their numbers. By the time of the Conquest four-fifths of the eighty-four parishes were served by Canadian-born *curés* who stayed on, thus providing the continuity which the Church sustained under British rule in Quebec. Just as important as the creation of a secular clergy drawn from the people to whom they ministered was the domination of welfare and educational activities in New France by members of religious orders. Among these were not only the Jesuits, Sulpicians and Récollets, but also the members of seven communities of nuns.

This involvement of the Church with the social concerns of the community had begun almost immediately after the return of the French to Canada in 1632. In 1639 a community of Augustinian nuns founded the Hôtel-

Dieu at Quebec, the first hospital in Canada. In the same year the Ursulines arrived under Marie de L'Incarnation and opened a church for French and Indian girls as a counterpart to the schools the Jesuits were already providing for boys. From the beginning, the king supported the work of these orders by endowing them with lands and giving them financial subsidies. In practice, then, they acted as agents of the state in dealing with the temporal needs of the *habitants* and the people of the small towns — Quebec, Trois-Rivières, Montreal — that were slowly growing up in the valley of the St Lawrence. The religious also used the opportunity to gain and keep spiritual domination over the *canadiens*.

In these ways, and also in providing the parish structure that laid the foundations of administration in the St Lawrence valley, the Church presided more closely than the state over the transition of New France from a fur-trading frontier to a complete society. The Church shepherded French Canada through its transition from being a nomadic society dominated by fur traders, career officials and soldiers, to being a rooted settlement dominated by farmers and artisans, and professionals and priests bred from the people. The role of the Church did not change greatly in Quebec after the Conquest. The Church ceased in law to be supported by the state and became instead a tolerated communion, but its good will was so vital to the British that they were content to allow Catholicism to reign in Quebec as a kind of coordinate power. Indeed, it retained its control in fields like welfare and education far into the present century.

NO PROTESTANT CHURCH ACQUIRED SIMILAR power or influence either in the country as a whole or in a limited region. This was mainly because the Protestants were divided from the beginning. Not only was there a division dating from the sixteenth century between the Anglican Church of England and the Presbyterian Church of Scotland, but both of these bodies had suffered schisms that had produced a variety of dissident sects. These included the Baptists and the Congregationalists, as well as a clutch of Scottish "free churches," but most important were the strongly evangelical Methodists. The Methodist movement had been born within the Church of England and did not withdraw as a separate communion until 1791, but by the time of the American Revolution it was already a powerful organization. The first Methodist congregations in North America appeared in the 1760s, and among the Loyalists and the other immigrant Americans who reached Upper Canada during the last decades of the eighteenth century the followers of this rapidly growing movement were numerous. At the same time a parallel movement was developing in the Maritimes under the influence of John Wesley's disciples in England.

Although the Church of England was the unestablished "official" church in Canada, it never enjoyed the standing or the widespread membership of the parent Church of England, mostly because of the activities of the other Protestant denominations. For a long time, indeed, it was almost literally a garrison church, its clergy being sent out to minister where large numbers of troops were stationed. The fur traders were generally hostile to clergy of any kind, whose influence on the Indians they regarded as harmful to trade. The Hudson's Bay Company required that the heads of its posts conduct simple services, but ministers of religion appeared in the West only with the beginning of settlement. For example, the first Anglican priest on the Red River was John West, sent out rather reluctantly by the Hudson's Bay Company in 1820, eight years after Lord Selkirk founded the settlement there, and the first Anglican priest on the Pacific coast, Robert John Staines, reached Fort Victoria in 1849 at roughly the same time as the earliest settler on Vancouver Island, Captain Walter Colquhoun Grant.

It was a generation after the arrival of the first British garrisons that the Church of England began to create an ecclesiastical structure by appointing the Loyalist Charles Inglis as Bishop of Nova Scotia, and five years later, in 1791, creating a diocese in Quebec, where Jacob Mountain sustained a rather isolated dignity in a land of Roman Catholics. The Methodists, with their more flexible organization of circuit riders, or wandering lay preachers, were usually ahead of the Anglicans in the rural districts of the Atlantic provinces and in the rapidly filling backwoods of Upper Canada. So in these regions Anglicanism tended to become a middle-class urban sect, while Methodism reigned in the countryside and the small communities.

In the West and the Far West the situation was somewhat different because of the activities of the evangelical wing of the Church of England, which was represented in Canada by three missionary organizations, the Society for the Propagation of the Gospel, the Church Missionary Society and the Colonial and Continental Church Society. The last group concentrated on providing churches for settlers and training clergy to minister to them, while the first two were more interested in converting the native population. In parts of the West and North, however, their activities laid the foundations of Anglican communities as settlers and ranchers followed them in.

Since most of the Protestant sects believed in the separation of education from sectarian religion, they did not usually set out to create school systems like the one the Catholics had established in Quebec. The Anglicans did make an unsuccessful attempt to control education in Upper Canada, but eventually an entirely secular and non-denominational system was established there by the Methodist, Egerton Ryerson. Nor were the Protestants in this early period greatly involved in welfare activities; they saw their task as the saving of souls rather than of bodies and looked mostly with suspicion on any approach that seemed to favour "works" as opposed to "faith." Not until the end of the nineteenth century would their perspective radically change as the "social gospel" movement (to which we shall refer again) directed itself to the problems of poverty and other kinds of misery that rapid immigration was creating at the time.

WHEN IT CAME TO THE INDIANS, the attitude of the churches was different, for here they seem widely to have believed that conversion was impossible without acculturation. Outside Quebec the country became for a while a free battleground of the sects. The French-speaking Métis were generally left to the Catholic Oblate fathers, many of whom came from France and Belgium, but as far as both Indians and Inuit in the West and North were concerned, all the major sects joined in the scramble for proselytes, with Catholics, Anglicans, Methodists, Presbyterians and Baptists competing, and even the Salvation Army joining in later in the day. The Army worked effectively among the Gitskan Indians of the Skeena Valley, who became especially devoted to the music of brass bands. Once the patchwork was established, a kind of lassitude seemed to replace the initial missionary zeal. A status quo was established, with surprisingly little subsequent raiding, so that now a journey down a single western river will take one past little wooden mission churches representing a wide variety of denominations.

Most of these mid-nineteenth century missionaries, and especially the Protestants, were convinced that real conversions could take place only if the native people could be induced to abandon entirely their pagan way of life and all the customs connected with it; otherwise, there would always be the danger of backsliding. This led not only to a frontal attack on institutions and ceremonials that were intimately linked with the Indians' sense of identity as peoples possessing their own cultures; it also resulted in some extraordinary acts of vandalism in the name of religion.

The missionaries induced the federal government to introduce legislation forbidding the rain dance of the prairie Indians and also the potlatch, the great giving feast of the Pacific coast peoples, as well as other localized ceremonials like the spirit dance of the Salish tribes in southwestern British Columbia. At the same time the clergy on the Nass River, where the Nishga were remarkable wood carvers, persuaded the converted bands to burn their totem poles and ceremonial regalia such as masks and rattles, almost wiping out what the few surviving relics tell us must have been one of the most vital of the artistic traditions on the Pacific coast.

The results of these attacks on the native culture were disastrous. In the case of the Pacific Coast Indians, the arrival of white traders had led to a brief upsurge of the arts as metal tools made wood carving easier and an inflow of cash made feasts and winter ceremonials more lavish and extravagant. The ban on the potlatch and missionary antagonism to native forms of art completed the demoralization and decline of these peoples that had begun with their decimation through imported sicknesses. For many years they seemed to be doomed, if Christianized, peoples as their numbers declined and their creative energies vanished. The trend was not reversed until the 1950s when the greatness of their artistic traditions began to be recognized and their culture began to revive in new ways. Much of the blame for their long period of decline undoubtedly lies with missionaries who were blinkered by Victorian prejudices.

Yet there was a certain realism in the attempts of the missionaries to persuade the native peoples to abandon their nomadic lives and settle down to the agrarian patterns that were alien to their traditions. The Catholic priests who inspired and largely directed the establishment of Métis settlements like St Laurent on the South Saskatchewan and St Albert near Fort Edmonton in the early 1870s, and the Protestant missionaries who made similar endeavours among the prairie Indians, were partly motivated by the anticipation of two events that would inevitably destroy the old nomadic lifestyle. The first was the disastrous decline in the bison herds; the second, the surge of settlers into the prairies that would consume the tribal hunting grounds.

William Duncan on the Pacific coast was not only appalled by some of the more sensational aspects of Tsimshian ceremonials — notably the ritual cannibalism of the Hamatsa secret society initiates — but he was also alarmed by the way in which the Indians were being preyed upon and demoralized by unscrupulous white men. To protect them he established in 1862 a missionary community at Metlakatla near the present city of Prince Rupert. It was probably the most complete and in some ways the most successful attempt at acculturation. Family dwellings with little gardens and neat picket fences were built instead of the old clan community houses, a large school was constructed, and over the village towered an immense wooden church, with Gothic spires, that held 1,100 people. The Indians were put into European clothes and trained as craftsmen, so that the community became largely self-sufficient. The community had its own sawmill that provided wood for houses and for furniture made by the local carpenters and joiners, it had its own rope-making and net-making shops, a cooperative store and trading schooner, and was able to feed itself for the most part with seafood and garden produce.

It can be argued that the Indians of Metlakatla and of similar though less ambitious mission settlements in the prairies, were better prepared than other less assimilated groups for the time when the tribes were forced to sign their ancestral lands over to the Canadian government. After the treaty signings the Indians were segregated on reserves, where they were intended to begin farming. Those who had not previously lived in mission settlements would have much more difficulty adapting to the restrictions of this life. Whatever the rights and wrongs of this situation, there is no doubt that the churches in their missionary phases, whether around the Great Lakes in the seventeenth century or in the West during the nineteenth century, acted as the harbingers of the settlers who would destroy the great forests of Upper Canada, annex the prairies and make the old nomadic ways impossible.

PART
IV

CHAPTER
10

The Habitants

IN MOST PARTS OF CANADA THE FARMER has been the agent of settlement. It was the farmer who populated the shores of the St Lawrence, who — with the help of the loggers — felled the great deciduous forests of Ontario, who ploughed the thick ancient turf of the bison pastures in the prairies. Where the fur trader had wanted to preserve the wilderness as the habitat of the animals on which he preyed, the farmer set out to destroy it. Immigration went hand in hand with settlement; until the early twentieth century there were never enough native-born Canadians to occupy the lands that were available for farming. Urbanization followed soon afterwards, for if trade established a few communities like Halifax on the seaboard, it was the settling of the backwoods that built up the towns of Upper Canada. In the same way the breaking of the prairies turned trade posts into cities like Calgary, Regina and Saskatoon that rose up on the bare plains where nothing had existed before but the temporary camps of wandering Indians.

Only one province was an exception to this pattern and that was Newfoundland, the great bare rock in the

Atlantic. To this day agriculture plays only a minor role in Newfoundland's economy, and it has been estimated, perhaps pessimistically, that only one-tenth of one percent of the island's area is suitable for cultivation. Yet non-agrarian settlement took place, in spite of the opposition of the European merchants who controlled the early fishing industry. Eventually fishing changed from a seasonal activity of visiting fleets to the main occupation — directly or undirectly — of most of the island's population. And by the end of the eighteenth century Newfoundland had twenty thousand inhabitants who all depended on this industry. Fishing and trade to Europe, the West Indies and New England turned St John's into a thriving seaport with five thousand inhabitants, making it a major centre by British North American standards of the time.

But most of the Newfoundlanders, then and well into the twentieth century, lived in the hundreds of small coastal settlements known as outports, where they mostly survived by means of a complex subsistence economy. It was not unlike that of the western isles of Ireland, the country from which many of them had come. They had fish and seal-meat in season, netted migrating waterfowl and sometimes hunted for caribou in the bleak interior. They gathered wild herbs and berries and grew potatoes in soil laboriously scraped out of crevices in the rock, they baked bread and made homebrew and supplemented it all with cheap rum smuggled from St Pierre and Miquelon, the French islands in the Gulf of St Lawrence.

Everything that could be made by hand was produced in the village, from the locally built fishing boats to the knitted guernseys and homespun trousers the men wore. The clothing was made from the wool of sheep that grazed in the meagre pastures around the bare wooden houses, many of which were painted red with a malodorous mixture of ochre and fish oil. Money rarely changed hands, and goods needed from outside, including salt to cure the fish, were obtained mostly through a truck system by which the merchants bartered them for the fish caught and dried in the outports, often trading in such a way that the fisherman remained perpetually in debt. As one of the songs of the outport people had it:

> Now I am intending to sing you a song
> About the poor people, how they get along;
> They start in the spring and they work to the fall
> And when it's all over they have nothing at all,
> And it's hard, hard times.

The outport people did not have many links with the more prosperous outside world. Few of these small coastal communities could be reached by road. The only links were by water, and for long periods they would be isolated by bad weather. But the Newfoundlanders created a unique poor man's culture of their own, still speaking in the ways of seventeenth-century Irishmen or Devon men, using old-fashioned locutions and proverbs, still singing folk songs and ballads that had been forgotten in Britain but preserved in the amber of Newfoundland isolation. They composed their own folksongs, too, about recent events, and they were as full of wayward wit and whimsy as the names they gave to the places around the rugged coastscape: names like God Almighty Cove and Harbour Grace, Famish Gut and Lushes Bight, Happy Adventure and Seldom Come By.

In the rest of Canada, apart from British Columbia, the other special case, the arrival of the farmers meant the beginning of real settlement. Here we can actually point to a pioneer among pioneers, in the person of Louis Hébert, an apothecary at the court of King Henry IV of France who accompanied the Sieur de Monts to Acadia in 1604.

HÉBERT WAS ESPECIALLY INTERESTED IN MEDICINAL herbs, and this led him to start gardening and farming in a small way. He first broke soil at Port Royal in 1606, a year before the earliest settlers arrived at Jamestown in Virginia. Shortly afterwards, when the Sieur de Monts lost interest in Acadia and turned his energies and interest to the St Lawrence valley, Hébert returned to France. In 1617, however, he went to Quebec at the invitation of Samuel de Champlain, and there also became the first agricultural settler, working with his wife Marie Rollet on a patch of about nine acres that was granted to him in the Upper Town of Quebec. The fur traders discouraged him, as they automatically discouraged all farmers, but Champlain supported the venture, and in 1623 Hébert was granted land "en fief noble," thus becoming the first seigneur in New France. He grew grain and vegetables, pastured cattle and even had apple trees brought from Normandy to start an orchard. By the time of his death from a fall in 1627 he was growing enough to feed his family and had established the pattern of subsistence farming that dominated early agriculture in most parts of Canada.

Louis Hébert farmed the hard way, by turning the land with a spade, and it was not until 1628, the year after his death, that the first ox team drew the first plough through the earth of New France. Even so, by the late 1620s there were no more than a score of settlers beside the St Lawrence. Cardinal Richelieu had made it a condition of the charter of the Compagnie des Cents-Associés that they should bring four thousand settlers to Canada in the fifteen years after 1627, but their programme suffered a major setback when the convoy of four ships carrying the first four hundred colonists was captured by the British force that seized Quebec in 1629.

After the recovery of New France, agricultural settlement proceeded far more slowly than Richelieu had expected. In 1666, when the first census was taken three

years after the establishment of direct colonial government, there were only 3,215 French people in the colony. These included not only the inhabitants of Quebec
but also people living in the two more recent settlements of Trois-Rivières, founded at the mouth of the St
Maurice River in 1634, and Montreal, founded on the
site of the old Iroquois settlement of Hochelaga in 1642.

Those who settled in New France did so under the
seigneurial system which was elaborated under the charter of 1627, but did not really begin to operate until
1634. It was in this year that the Company began to
make seigneurial grants in the neighbourhood of Quebec. By the time the Crown took over the administration
of the colony in 1663 about sixty grants of seigneuries
had been made, some to noblemen and some to religious orders, but others to merchants and others who
would not normally be accepted as seigneurs in Old
France. From the beginning it was evident that, despite
appearances, the European feudal system was not being
reproduced in Canada.

By the end of the seventeenth century about two
hundred seigneuries had been granted. They covered
most of the arable land on either side of the St Lawrence, from the Gaspé to west of Montreal, as well as
the farmable land in the valleys of the Chaudière and
Richelieu rivers, and the lower Ottawa.

On average, a seigneury would cover about thirty
square miles, but some were expanded by further
grants, or *augmentations*. The seigneur granted *concessions*
or *habitations* to his tenants, who were called *habitants*.
Most seigneurs retained a considerable parcel of land for
themselves, like the home farm on a traditional English
estate, and they would manage it themselves or through
some kind of share-cropping arrangement.

The relationship between the *habitant* and the seigneur was one of mutual obligation. So long as he paid
the seigneurial dues and met the obligations under the
title deed, the *habitant*'s right of possession was secure;

his children could inherit the land, and he could deed or even sell it. These were some of the title deed obligations: rent of a few bushels of grain a year, plus charges for milling flour, which was a seigneurial monopoly, and a tax on land sales, which amounted to about 8 percent. Once a church had been built in the parish, the *habitants* had to pay a yearly tithe of about 4 percent. In addition, they had to perform road work and serve in the militia when they were called upon. The seigneurial system continued under the British until it was finally abolished in 1854, almost a hundred years after the Conquest, by a law that allowed tenants to claim ownership rights to their land. At that time no less than 75 percent of the people of Quebec (or Canada East as it was then called) were still living on seigneurial land.

The farms occupied by the *habitants* were narrow strips stretching back from the river and about ten times as long as the river frontage, which was usually between one hundred and two hundred yards. Often more than a mile in depth, the strip farm would contain between fifty and a hundred acres. Roads were slow to be built, largely for lack of manpower in the early days, and the principal means of transportation and communication was by water. On the other hand, the narrowness of the river frontages, where the houses were usually built, meant that the *habitants* were never lacking in neighbours, and voyagers on the St Lawrence in the early eighteenth century remarked that it was like sailing beside a continuous village, as travellers to this day still feel. When the roads were eventually built along the back of the river lots, a second line of strip farms was often laid out on their further sides.

There were several advantages to the strip farm, apart from the closeness of neighbours and the access to the river for transport and fishing. It often gave the farmer access to a variety of soils on which he could grow different crops, and a long, rectangular field was easier to plough than an irregularly shaped one.

Most of the farms were originally heavily wooded, and with the primitive equipment and tools at the disposal of the *habitants* it was difficult to clear more than an acre or two of land for cultivation each year. Two or three years would usually pass before the farm began to produce enough grain and vegetables to feed a family, and several years more before an orchard could begin to bear fruit and enough pasture had been cleared to graze cattle. That resourceful animal, the pig, was usually present from the beginning, however.

In the early days, before the *habitants* had cleared a great deal of land, the French settlers led a life that was no more comfortable than that of agrarian Indians like the Huron and the Iroquois. The original *habitants* ploughed shallowly, knew little about crop rotation and rarely fertilized. They grew enough for a rather monotonous subsistence diet, often supplemented by game and fish. In many ways, in fact, they continued to live on the edge of a hunting society, and there were times when food was critically short in New France, particularly during the seventeenth century. Still, most of the *habitants* had more to eat and all of them had more freedom than they would have enjoyed if they had stayed in France.

Gradually, as more land was cleared, the *habitants* paid greater attention to their farms and less to fur trading and hunting, though the *pays d'en haut* always remained a temptation for their sons. A simple kind of two-year rotation became customary, with crops of grain or legumes alternating with fallow years. As more animals were kept — oxen for draught, cows for meat and milk, sheep for wool — the farmers began to manure their fields. Chickens were reared, and the wood lot that remained at the far end of even the best-cultivated farm provided fuel and timber for construction, as well as maple syrup to be tapped each winter and boiled into sugar. A farm with twenty acres of cleared land would enable a family to subsist comfortably, and on anything larger than that it was possible to earn enough, by selling surplus produce to wandering merchants from the towns, to pay for whatever tools and utensils were needed, and to have something left over for the priest and the doctor, for buying new stock, for dowries and for loans to sons starting their own farms.

It was quite a long time before the ribbon-like pattern of the strip farms began to knot itself into villages. Wandering pedlars took the place of shopkeepers, and some of the *habitants* had artisan skills — as blacksmiths or harness makers or wheelwrights — which they combined with farming and would put at the disposal of their neighbours, often on a barter basis. At each seigneury there would be a flour mill operated by wind or more often water, usually near the manor house, and often a sawmill as well, serving a few dozen farms. Soon the churches began to appear, also near the riverbank and towering over the small *habitants'* houses, which in those days were built of squared logs and whitewashed, their steep roofs thatched with reeds or straw. Local craftsmen made the furniture and often carved and painted it in traditional French ways.

The neighbourliness of riverfront life meant that the *habitants* had little reason to form villages, and though the government of New France did try to create village nuclei to act as market or service centres, there was so little demand for them that until the British period after the Conquest, the three towns of Quebec, Montreal and Trois-Rivières remained the only real centres of population. But towards the end of the eighteenth century, though the *habitants* clung to their decentralized patterns of living, villages did begin to spring up around the churches, each of them usually containing new shops, a doctor, a smithy or two and a handful of other craftsmen.

THE POPULATION OF NEW FRANCE grew slowly. By 1698 it had reached fifteen thousand, and this was largely due to a special effort on Intendant Talon's part to attract immigrants, including not only men to start farms but also women — among them the famous eleven hundred *filles du roi*. After the end of the seventeenth century, immigration slowed down, and it has been estimated that during the whole period when the colony was in French hands no more than 9,500 immigrants actually settled there, though many other people did arrive, as officials, as soldiers, as indentured servants, and returned to France at the end of their terms of duty. The rest of the population of New France — which amounted to about 65,000 at the time of the Conquest and to about 200,000 by the end of the eighteenth century — came from natural increase.

Urbanization went hand in hand with settlement in New France, and by the middle of the eighteenth century both Quebec and Montreal had grown into real towns. Their populations were still small — Quebec's was about five thousand and Montreal's about three thousand — but Quebec in particular was already winning the admiration of visitors because of its architecture. The large number of handsome baroque buildings in the Upper Town had been built almost entirely by the state and by religious orders, and all its streets had stone-fronted, steep-roofed houses — wooden houses had already been forbidden as fire hazards.

Both of these major centres of New France stood somewhat apart from the life of the riverside farms, aside from buying much of their food from the countryside farmers. Montreal, a fortified city with a large garrison, was essentially the trans-shipment centre for the fur trade and the Indian country. From here the fur brigades were outfitted, the furs were sent downriver to Quebec and goods were transported upriver into the *pays d'en haut* and the surrounding countryside. By the eighteenth century, when the farms were beginning to grow surpluses of grain for sale, Montreal started what may well have been the first exports of Canadian wheat, from the farms on the flatlands around its own boundaries. Montreal was a provincial administrative centre and also the local headquarters of the Sulpicians, who owned the seigneury of the Island of Montreal.

But in the seventeenth and most of the eighteenth century, it was Quebec that enjoyed the importance of an inland seaport. In the later age of steamships, that position would be usurped by Montreal. It not only exported to France the furs that came down by small boat from Montreal, it also sent locally grown foodstuffs to Louisbourg and the West Indies, while all the imports from France into the colony found their way through its port. A royal shipyard was established for constructing and repairing naval vessels and there were several private shipyards for making smaller boats.

In the crowded streets of the Lower Town the crafts flourished. A man of fashion could have a wig or a coat or a pair of shoes skilfully made. His wife could buy a well-crafted *armoire* or a pair of locally made silver candlesticks. The needs of the Church encouraged architects and masons, carvers in stone and wood, and the first in a long tradition of Quebec church painters, who occasionally ventured into portraiture and who represent the real beginnings of the fine arts in Canada.

Yet despite their commercial and industrial enterprise and their flickerings of artistic activity, both Montreal and Quebec under the French kingdom were intellectually and morally repressed communities. A strain of puritanism in the priesthood that has often been mistaken for Jansenism led to constraints on life that partly explain the attraction that the free life of the Indian country held for so many young people. There were no newspapers or journals of any kind and no books were published locally, for the simple reason that there was not a single printing press in the towns of the St Lawrence until after the Conquest; the priests discouraged any such venture. They also kept a sharp eye on the importation of books that projected the philosophies of the

Enlightenment. Anyone who possessed a volume of Voltaire or Diderot concealed it from all but his most trusted friends. Attempts to put on plays in either Quebec or Montreal were usually obstructed as well.

Nor was New France an educated society either in the towns or in the countryside, though a number of establishments were dedicated to teaching. The Seminary founded by Bishop Laval provided a kind of classical higher education for those who were likely to become priests and for other sons of prosperous or genteel families, and there were other schools mainly intended for privileged children, though occasionally a brilliant *habitant*'s son would find his way into one or another of them. Nevertheless, by 1784 only one *canadien* in five could write. Largely as a result of this widespread illiteracy, the *habitants* of New France were a people of simple beliefs and simple life, tenacious of tradition, doggedly Catholic, and in spite of the good opinion they had of themselves, inclined to defer to the prestige of the priests. That prestige actually grew after the British Conquest, as the authority of the seigneurs began to decline and the rapport between the church and the conquerors grew closer. This was only one of many ways in which the arrival of the British affected the life of New France.

BRITISH MERCHANTS QUICKLY GAINED CONTROL of the fur trade out of Montreal and of the export trade out of Quebec, redirecting it from France to England, and very soon the towns along the St Lawrence became overshadowed by the new Anglo-Celtic military and commercial elite. And that commercial domination of Quebec by English Canadian and British interests was to continue far into the twentieth century.

In the countryside, the Conquest changed the patterns of local society. Some of the seigneurs remained, as most of the priests did, but many of them decided to return to France rather than live under British rule. Often they sold their estates cheaply to the newcomers, while some British officers acquired properties as dowries when they married the daughters of local landowners.

But the greatest influx of people of non-French stock resulted from the American Revolution, when nearly twenty thousand Loyalists found their way into Quebec by travelling up the Richelieu River. Some of them bought already cleared farms from the *habitants* along that river, and some chose to live in the cities, but the largest group of them settled in the region to the southeast of Montreal that became known as the Eastern Townships.

The new British seigneurs and the Loyalist settlers brought with them more modern farming techniques than those used by the *canadiens*, but they had comparatively little influence on the methods of the *habitants*. Well into the present century, Quebec agriculture, unlike that of Ontario and the West, consisted mostly of subsistence farming, with comparatively little cash coming in from the sale of produce to the towns and comparatively little going out for industrial products.

The influx of British farmers contributed to radical changes in the rural society of Quebec mostly by aggravating the land shortage that became evident in the early decades of the nineteenth century. But even here forces within French Canadian society were largely responsible for the crisis, and none more so than the famous *revanche du berceau*, the "revenge of the cradle." Early French Canadian nationalists and their priestly allies encouraged the raising of large families because they believed that by natural increase they could counter the flood of British immigrants that began with the arrival of the Loyalists in the 1780s. The *revanche* was so dramatically successful that the 140,000 *canadiens* of 1791 had increased to at least 1,000,000 by 1871, a figure that did not include considerable numbers who had to emigrate because of the increasing strain on the land available to the many sons of philoprogenitive *habitants*. By the third

decade of the nineteenth century all the arable land in
Lower Canada south of the Laurentians and north of the
American border had been taken up. Country people
were beginning to find their way into the cities, and
particularly into rapidly growing Montreal, where they
competed for labouring jobs with the floods of Irish immigrants who appeared at the same time.

IN THE 1840s YOUNG FRENCH CANADIANS who had no hope of
either land or work began to emigrate to New England,
where they found jobs in the textile mills. By the time of
the Great Depression of the 1930s, less than a century
later, about nine hundred thousand French Canadians
had made their way to the northeastern United States,
and become part of the Franco-American community
that had sprung up there as a result of earlier emigration from Acadia on the east coast. The Canadian nationalists and their clerical associates began to realize
that the *revanche du berceau* had proved a pyrrhic victory.
It had indeed kept the francophones at a steady level of
30 percent of the population of Canada, in spite of the
myriads of immigrants entering the country from Britain
and continental Europe throughout the nineteenth century and well into the twentieth. But it had also led to a
kind of racial hæmorrhage, since the inhabitants of that
ever-renewed cradle found it impossible to survive in
their own country and as a consequence were lost to it
forever.

The result was the last phase of the original wave of
settlement in Canada, which had begun with Champlain's first *habitation* on the St Lawrence. Patriotic French
Canadians began to devise schemes of colonization that
would keep *canadiens* in Canada by going beyond the
old seigneurial lands in the only direction possible —
that is, to the north, where the growing season was
much shorter than beside the St Lawrence but land was
still available. The Saguenay, the great northern tribu-
tary of the St Lawrence, had once seemed a forbidding

river, but by the 1830s colonization societies were beginning to open the lands along its banks, and by the next decade settlers were pouring onto the alluvial soils around remote Lac St Jean, which in earlier generations had been merely a stopping place on the routes of the fur traders.

Finally, by the later decades of the nineteenth century, the pioneer urges that had begun beside the St Lawrence with Louis Hébert almost three centuries before reached their final stage. The sons of the *habitants* began to filter westward and set up farms in the marginal lands of northern Ontario on the edge of the Canadian Shield. There they became the nucleus of the half a million Canadians who now call themselves Franco-Ontarians.

Beyond Ontario, in the prairies, the Catholic missionaries encouraged immigration from Quebec, and also directly from France and Belgium, to strengthen the Catholic minority there. That community at first consisted mainly of French-speaking Métis, the descendants of the original voyageurs from Quebec. The French Canadian nationalists, already alarmed by the exodus to New England, did their best to discourage this last manifestation of *canadien* settlement, and only a few small groups found their way west. Some of those who did go went far, and a group of sawmill workers from Quebec actually founded a French-speaking community, Maillardville, in the vicinity of Vancouver. The French-speaking communities of the West were tiny, but they produced a surprising number of notable Canadians, including the novelist Gabrielle Roy, the man-of-letters Georges Bugnet, and the sixth Canadian governor general of Canada, Jeanne Sauvé. Even in its farthest western trickle, the stream of French settlement, three centuries on the way, did not lose itself entirely in the dry lands of the wilderness, but produced its own blossoms.

CHAPTER
11

Atlantic Origins

THERE WERE MANY WAYS IN WHICH THE SETTLEMENT of the Atlantic provinces paralleled that of New France. The first attempts were made by the French and were in fact initiated by the men later responsible for founding Quebec: the Sieur de Monts and Samuel de Champlain. As in Quebec, the French were temporarily displaced from the Atlantic region by the English during the reign of Charles I, but Acadia — as the area now known as Nova Scotia and New Brunswick was then called — was also handed back to France in 1632. This was part of the settlement made when Charles married Henrietta Maria, the daughter of the French King Henry IV. Nova Scotia eventually fell to the British as the spoils of war, like Quebec, but it was in an earlier conflict, the War of the Spanish Succession, ended by the Treaty of Utrecht in 1713. And the 1758 fall of Louisbourg, the fortress that France retained on Cape Breton Island, was the prelude to the later capture of Quebec. Only in one important detail — and that a tragic one — would the history of the settlement of the Atlantic provinces differ profoundly from that of settlement in Quebec. The *canadiens* in Quebec were allowed to stay on their land after the Conquest and to increase and multiply there. The Acadians in Nova Scotia were expelled from their long-occupied farms, and many of them never returned, so that the final settlement of the Atlantic region was carried out mainly by other peoples under the aegis of British rule.

Long before anyone attempted to create a permanent colony based on farming anywhere in Atlantic Canada, the fishermen and fur traders had been working off its shores. The Basque and Breton fishermen who operated in the Gulf of St Lawrence also fished around Île Royale (Cape Breton), and farther south along the Nova Scotian peninsula, around Canso and Chedabucto, during the sixteenth century. Early in the seventeenth century New England fishermen in small ships pushed up the Atlantic shore of the peninsula, though the French maintained their presence on Île Royale. That presence was to become even stronger when Louisbourg was built and the fish merchants of Plaisance moved there after British domination of Newfoundland was recognized under the Treaty of Utrecht.

Agricultural settlement was hardly fitted for the rocky and storm-lashed Atlantic coast, where the fishermen would often winter in sheltered coves and harbours, fishing in-shore when they could and quickly curing their catch. It was one of these harbours, the sheltered Bay of Fundy, that attracted the Sieur de Monts and his companions. In 1604 they made their first attempt at a settlement, on the western side of the Bay at the mouth of the St Croix River, which now forms the boundary between New Brunswick and Maine. The following year they moved over to the estuary of the Rivière du Dauphin (now the Annapolis River) and established Port Royal. There was good arable land in the region, but the Sieur de Monts was more concerned with fur trading than with agriculture. Since Port Royal was not a particularly good fur-trading centre, he and

Champlain eventually turned their attention to the valley of the St Lawrence, and the future character of the settlement at Port Royal was determined when Biencourt de Poutrincourt arrived in 1606 with a group of French peasants intent on farming.

The name of "Acadie" seems to have been applied to the region even in those early days, but its origin is obscure. It seems likely, though, that it was a corruption of "Arcadia," the name of a Greek region that became a byword for rustic peace. Giovanni da Verrazzano, who sailed off these shores in the 1520s, even before Cartier, had applied that name to the whole region, and the men of culture who were part of Poutrincourt's entourage could hardly have been unaware of this fact.

One such man was the young lawyer Marc Lescarbot, the first poet to write in Canada, who had composed the masque, *Le Théâtre de Neptune dans la Nouvelle France*. He also wrote what must surely be the first of all Canadian immigrant's laments, in a poem he addressed in August 1606 to a party of friends who were returning to France.

> 'Tis you who go to see congenial friends
> In language, habits, customs and religion,
> And all the lovely scenes of your own nation,
> While we among the savages are lost
> And dwell bewildered on this clammy coast
> Deprived of due content and pleasures bright
> Which you at once enjoy when France you sight.
> (Translated by F. R. Scott)[18]

FROM THE BEGINNING THE NEW COLONY, geographically separated from New France, was harassed by the English. In 1613 Samuel Argall led a force from Virginia which destroyed the French installations at Port Royal, and in 1629 Sir William Alexander, as part of his short-lived attempt to create a Scottish realm on the peninsula, landed a few settlers. They departed after Acadia was returned to the French in 1632.

The early French settlers soon realized the possibilities of the tidal marshes along the Rivière du Dauphin and at the head of the Bay of Fundy. Once they were dyked and allowed to freshen for a few seasons, they proved extremely fertile, and soon, when the available marshland around Port Royal had been taken up, the children of the original settlers moved to the more extensive marshes at the upper end of the Bay, around Grand Pré and Beaubassin. The dykes were considerable works, built up of marshgrass sods and reinforced by logs and branches, to a height of seven or eight feet and a thickness of twelve to fifteen feet. Many of them were wide enough for a road to run along the top, and they were fitted with simple but effective sluices that had wooden valves, allowing drainage water to escape at low tide and preventing salt water from entering at high tide.

Immigration to Acadia was even slower than to New France, and the increase in the population was mostly a natural one in a closely knit community of families that quickly became interrelated. There were about 350 people in 1670 and about 2,000 at the time of the Treaty of Utrecht when Acadia was handed back to the British. Almost all of them were the descendants of the forty original families who had arrived in the mid-seventeenth century. They lived an almost forgotten and autonomous existence, building their simple houses of clay-plastered wood and thatch, cultivating large gardens and subsisting well on their farms and their herds. Few could read and they were served by an excessive number of priests.

Although the Church had a strong hold on the community, the seigneurial system was never effectively established in Acadia, and the farmers enjoyed most of the privileges of freeholders. They traded whatever surplus produce they had with the New Englanders, but had little connection with New France, and to this day the descendants of the original Acadians still consider themselves a different people, with separate traditions, from the Québécois. The royal government in France sustained an intermittent interest in Acadia, and at intervals a governor would appear, and then depart shortly afterwards. The colony was not always even considered worth the cost of defending, and it was only in the early eighteenth century that a regular garrison of 150 men was established there. It was sufficient, with the help of the local militia, to fight off a British attack in 1707; the invaders had to content themselves with breaching the dykes near Port Royal and burning the church. But in 1710 they came back in force, overwhelmed the defenders and established a rule over Acadia which was confirmed when the peninsula was ceded to the British under the Treaty of Utrecht. The region became Nova Scotia once again. Port Royal became Annapolis Royal, renamed in honour of Queen Anne, then reigning in England, and for a while, until the foundation of Halifax, it was the capital of the province.

Halifax owed its existence to an ambiguity in the terms of cession that in the end was to work out to the detriment of the Acadians. For their own purposes the French interpreted Acadia to mean, under the treaty, merely the peninsula of Nova Scotia, and not Île Royale, which they continued to occupy and on which they built Louisbourg. For the British, Louisbourg was a perpetual threat, and its presence made them suspicious of the Acadians, who for their part tried to maintain an impossible neutrality. They did not resist the conquerors, but they would not swear allegiance to the English monarch. Consequently, they were suspected of harbouring rebellious intents and of being in contact with the French at Louisbourg, as some of them doubtless were. The threat of Louisbourg was taken seriously enough for Halifax to be founded in 1749 as a garrison town and naval depot on the eastern shore of Nova Scotia nearer to Île Royale. Increasingly, the Acadians were seen as a potential fifth column in the event of warfare, particularly as the French maintained a post at Fort Beauséjour on the border between New France and Nova Scotia and were inciting the local Micmac and Malecite tribes to harry non-French settlers.

In 1754, two years before the Seven Years' War actually became a full-scale conflict, fighting had already started in the Ohio territory. And the next year, under pressure from the New Englanders and from Admiral Boscawen, who commanded the navy in Halifax, the incumbent governor, Colonel Thomas Lawrence, decided, without authority from the imperial government, to expel the Acadians as a threat to this strategically sensitive area. By now they had increased rapidly, and there were about fifteen thousand of them. More than ten thousand of them were expelled, though there is no record of how the process of selection worked. Colonel John Winslow was in charge of the actual operation of shipping the Acadians away, and the very confusion of the entry he made in his journal for October 8, 1755, gives one some idea of the reluctance with which he supervised the uprooting of these harmless peasants, whose only desire was to live untroubled by men of power.

> October 8th. Began to Embarke the Inhabitants who went of Very Soletarily and unwillingly, the women in Great Distress Carrying off their children in their arms. Others carrying their Decript Parents in their Carts and all their Goods Moving in great Confusion & appeard a Scene of Woe & Diestress.[19]

Winslow had received orders not to parley with the Acadians and to allow no delays, and, though he "Did not Love to use Harsh Means," he had at one point to order his troops "to fix their Bayonets & advance towards the French." It was, he concluded, a "Troublesome Jobb."

Some of the exiled Acadians were allowed to join the
French in Louisiana and together they became the Cajun
population of that area. Others went to New England
where they pioneered the considerable Franco-American
presence there. A few of them went to the scantily populated Île St Jean. (In 1799 that island would be renamed
Prince Edward Island in honour of the Duke of Kent,
the eventual father of Queen Victoria, who was then
stationed at Halifax.) Many of those who went to New
England found it impossible to adapt to a new language
and a different culture, and eventually, after the Seven
Years' War was over, they found their way back to
Nova Scotia. Discovering that their farms around the
Bay of Fundy had been appropriated by later settlers,
they moved north to join those who in 1755 had fled
into the Miramichi region of what is now New Brunswick. From 1764 they were once again allowed to take
up land there. These were the people about whom
Henry Wadsworth Longfellow wrote at the end of his
poem, "Evangeline":

Only along the shore of the mournful and misty Atlantic
Linger a few Acadian peasants, whose fathers from exile
Wandered back to their native land to die in its bosom.
In the fisherman's cot the wheel and the loom are still busy;
Maidens still wear their Norman caps and their kirtles of home-
spun,
And by the evening fire repeat Evangeline's story,
While from its rocky caverns the deep-voiced neighbour-
ing ocean
Speaks and in accents disconsolate answers the wail of the
forest.

Actually Longfellow underestimated the number of
Acadians who returned. By 1800 there were 8,000 of
them once again, and they proceeded to carry out their
own *revanche du berceau*, so that by the end of the nineteenth century their numbers had increased to 140,000,

and now there are more than 300,000. Forming three-eighths of the population of New Brunswick and a fifth of the population of the Atlantic provinces in general, they have maintained a culture of their own quite different from that of Quebec.

AFTER THE CESSION OF NOVA SCOTIA in 1713, there followed a period of what at the time was contemptuously called "counterfeit suzerainty," when no real attempt was made to Anglicize the colony. A garrison was maintained at Annapolis Royal and a few merchants settled there, but the best land was occupied by the Acadians until the 1750s, and settlers were discouraged from settling elsewhere by the intermittent warfare which mixed guerilla bands of Canadians and Indians carried over the border from New France. The first serious attempt at settlement took place in 1749, when Edward Cornwallis arrived with 2,500 potential English settlers to found Halifax. Shortly afterwards about 2,500 Germans from King George's Hanoverian domains arrived, and for a brief period Halifax was a crowded community with about 5,000 inhabitants outside the garrison. In 1753 the Germans moved south down the coast to Lunenburg, where they established a long-standing and very conservative community, in which old German peasant beliefs long dominated farming practices. Until comparatively recently the Lunenburgers sowed their seed according to the phases of the moon. It was they who initiated the industry of shipbuilding in the Atlantic provinces.

It was only after the expulsion of the Acadians in 1755 and the destruction of French power between 1758 and 1760 that agrarian immigration began in the rest of Nova Scotia, though there was a small community of New England fishermen at Canso to the north of Halifax. In 1759 the colonial government began to employ surveyors to lay out the land in townships and offered generous allotments: one hundred acres for the head of a family and another fifty acres for each additional member. The already land-hungry New Englanders were attracted by the offers, now that the colony had become more peaceful. By 1765, while the population of Halifax had shrunk to about two thousand, some seven thousand farmers and fishermen had come north to occupy the old Acadian lands around the Bay of Fundy, and to build their fish-curing flakes along the southern shore of the peninsula.

During this period the first British immigrants to the mainland of what later became Canada began to appear. About five hundred Ulstermen came in the 1760s to settle near Halifax, and in 1772 a thousand Yorkshire tenant farmers arrived in the Chignecto area because of the high and uneconomic rents that the English landowners were imposing. At least some of them soon regretted the move, like Luke Harrison, who wrote home in 1774:

> We do not like the country, nor never shall. The mosquitoes are a terrible plague in this country. You may think that mosquitos cannot hurt, but if you do you are mistaken, for they will swell your legs and hands so that some persons are both blind and lame for some days. They grow worse every year and they bite the English the worst.[20]

Shortly afterwards a couple of hundred Highland Scots settled at Pictou and gave some justification to the province's name, while other Scots joined the Acadians who had settled on the Île St Jean.

By 1775, on the eve of the American Revolution, the population of Nova Scotia had increased to a thinly scattered seventeen thousand. Half of them — which meant the majority of the country dwellers outside Halifax — were New Englanders, and their sympathies inclined towards the Americans who wanted to separate from Britain, but the stand they took during the revolutionary war resembled that of the Acadians. Again, a watchful neutrality prevailed. The Nova Scotia Yankees would not rebel in support of the insurrectionary colonists, and they were prepared to fight to keep their lands if that were needed, but they preferred not to commit themselves prematurely to the British Crown. It was a tense situation, but this time the British did not make the mistake of attempting an expulsion of the doubtfully loyal. The war ended with no uprising on the part of the Nova Scotia Yankees, although — as happened later on during the War of 1812 — they maintained a busy trading connection with their fellow New Englanders.

The aftermath of the American Revolution greatly accelerated settlement in the Atlantic region. Of the Loyalists who moved northward at the war's end, about thirty thousand came up the coast to Atlantic Canada and stayed there. About nineteen thousand of them, including some three thousand blacks who had fought on the British side, settled on the peninsula of Nova Scotia, where they established a large mushroom settlement at Shelburne on the southeast coast. For a brief period the settlement had a population of about five thousand, but it declined into a mere village as the refugees moved into the countryside and into Halifax. That town's population grew rapidly to eight thousand, so that it rivalled Quebec as the largest community in British North America at the time. Small numbers of Loyalists went to Prince Edward Island and Cape Breton, and about eleven thousand settled to the west of the Bay of Fundy, where a few squatters had begun to farm along the St John River. There they founded the city of Saint John, which, unlike Shelburne, grew slowly and steadily and soon vied with Halifax as the leading community in the region. It became evident that it was impractical to administer the large area of original Acadia and its growing population from Halifax on the eastern seaboard. In 1784 the colony was divided and New Brunswick and Cape Breton became separate provinces, each with its governor, its small garrison and its miniature colonial service.

THE COMING OF THE LOYALISTS RADICALLY CHANGED the society of the Atlantic provinces and of Nova Scotia especially, where the population doubled as a result of the influx. Although the Loyalists had come from all classes in the colonies that became the United States, many of them were educated and cultured people. Because of their presence and that of Scottish immigrants Nova Scotia became a pioneer among the English-speaking parts of Canada in higher education. As early as 1789 Loyalists founded the Anglican King's College at Windsor, and twenty years later the Scots founded a rival Presbyterian academy at Pictou. It was presided over by Thomas McCulloch, the author of that early work of Canadian fiction, *The Letters of Mephibosheth Stepsure*. Not long after, inspired largely by these examples, Dalhousie University would be established in 1818 in Halifax. It was a non-denominational institution and the first actual university in Canada.

After the Loyalists arrived Nova Scotia became a province of divisions and contrasts. The newcomers, many of whom had held important offices in the rebel states and expected to be rewarded with similar posts in their new home, did not get along well with the original Yankee settlers, whose loyalty they regarded as suspect. A great difference quickly developed between the prosperous and active life of Halifax, with its commerce and its garrison, and the slowly changing and still primitive existence of the countryside, where most of the farmers, even after the departure of the Acadians, aimed for little better than subsistence. With its wealthy merchants and officers of the army and the navy, Halifax became not only a busy but also a relatively cultured town. The first printing press in Canada was set up there shortly after the city's founding, and by 1752 the first newspaper was being published, *The Halifax Gazette*. As we have already seen, the first theatre in Canada was built in the 1780s by the Halifax garrison, and the country's first literary magazine was also a Halifax production, the *Nova Scotia*

Magazine, which began to appear in 1789. In these early years the spirit of Toryism was strong in Halifax, but loyalism was never politically homogeneous. It had its liberal as well as its conservative sides. Eventually the establishment of another Halifax newspaper, the *Nova Scotian,* published and edited by Joseph Howe, the son of a Loyalist exile, would lead the struggle for responsible government and take Howe to the heights of provincial political eminence.

The contrast between Halifax, commercially active and intellectually alive, and the stagnant countryside, was one of the early motivating factors in the native literature that began to emerge in Nova Scotia early in the nineteenth century, with McCulloch's *Stepsure Letters* and Thomas Chandler Haliburton's *The Clockmaker.* These works, the earliest Canadian fiction of any consequence, consisted of satirical sketches aimed at exposing the backwardness and lack of enterprise of Nova Scotian country people.

Satire often contains exaggeration that verges on caricature, and in fact Nova Scotian bucolic life in the early nineteenth century was not quite so sluggish as one might assume from reading McCulloch and Haliburton. The influx of the Loyalists did provide better local markets for the farmers, and it also brought in a considerable number of artisans, including the men who helped to develop the local shipbuilding industry.

Since the ships were built of local timber and the making of wooden vessels required no great installations, it was an industry that lent itself to decentralization. It was carried on in dozens of small towns and villages on the shores of New Brunswick and Prince Edward Island as well as Nova Scotia. Eventually it reached such proportions that in the single year of 1865 no fewer than 650 wooden ships were launched from the slipways of the three provinces, and some of them — the famous clippers — were among the most handsome and efficient sailing craft ever built.

SHIPBUILDING RECEIVED A GREAT IMPETUS during the Napoleonic Wars, and so did the timber industry. After the
closing of the Baltic, demand for ships and timber increased even more, as Swedish wood was no longer
available to the British. The Navy turned to the North
American colonies and their splendid pine forests for its
supplies of spars and masts. This prosperity continued
through the War of 1812, from which Maritimers profited when privateers sailed out of the ports on the Bay of
Fundy to attack American shipping (carefully avoiding
that of the covertly friendly New England states). Small
towns grew rich on the spoils.

With shipbuilding came ship owning. In the 1860s
Nova Scotians alone owned some 350,000 tons of shipping, at a time when vessels of 1,500 tons were considered large craft. But ship owning in the end killed
shipbuilding in the Atlantic provinces, for the most successful owners, like Samuel Cunard, turned quickly to
steamships and then to iron ships, and with these enterprises the builders of wooden ships were unable to compete. By the end of the nineteenth century the Atlantic
shipbuilding industry was almost dead, though one of
its last products, the famous schooner *Bluenose*, constructed at Lunenburg in 1921, has been regarded as one
of the finest sailing ships ever built.

After the end of the Napoleonic Wars more waves of
immigration hit the Atlantic provinces, even larger than
that of the Loyalists. From 1814 the Scots began to arrive, perhaps attracted by the name of the colony and its
flag, which featured the St Andrew's cross. They included Highlanders who had been expelled from their
crofts to make way for sheep farming, and Lowlanders
who were seeking a better way of life. The Highlanders
settled particularly on Cape Breton Island, where they
soon formed the majority of the population. Whole villages and clans of them came and settled close together,
retaining their stern Calvinist religion, and even keeping
their language so obstinately that Gaelic is spoken in

Cape Breton to this day. But it was impossible for all of them to reconstruct on Canadian soil their old Scottish patterns of simple farming and fishing, and they became the principal pool of labour as the coal deposits on Cape Breton began to be worked extensively. The Lowland Scots tended to come individually and to be absorbed into the population.

Between them, the Scots and the Irish fleeing from the potato famines constituted the majority of the roughly one hundred thousand immigrants who flooded into the Atlantic colonies between the end of the Napoleonic Wars and the middle of the nineteenth century. They submerged the former Loyalist majority, taking up the vacant lands and working in the logging industry that by the end of the century had almost exhausted the great forests of pine and spruce.

The rise of shipbuilding and of logging as major industries had a considerable influence on the occupational patterns of people in the Atlantic provinces and resulted in a certain versatility among the population. Farmers and their sons would often do spells as loggers or seamen, and people who lived near the seacoast would combine fishing and logging, while the men who built the wooden ships were usually familiar with all these occupations.

This meant that Atlantic society was never so completely agrarian as that of the rural districts of Upper Canada in the same period, or of the prairies later on. There were always other ways of making a living, and during the mid-nineteenth century these resulted in what Maritimers ever since have looked back on as their Golden Age. The little shipyards were turning out their hundreds of craft, ships from Nova Scotia and New Brunswick sailed over the whole world and even little ports like Yarmouth and Liverpool were great centres of trade. Timber was so abundant and in such demand that 85 percent of New Brunswick men earned their living from the forests, the seas were still full of fish and even the simple farmers who had once been content with a bare subsistence were profiting from the general prosperity.

It was the kind of boom that could not survive when the forests were exhausted and the demand for wooden ships declined, and when the industrial and urban age came to Canada the Maritime provinces would be impoverished in comparison to the others. Yet the kind of versatility they had gained in good times stood the people of the Atlantic provinces in good stead when they fell upon bad times. Joseph Howe once remarked that "Nova Scotia is an excellent poor man's country, because almost every man, in any walk of industry, by perseverance and economy can secure the comforts of life." The Maritimers had a certain hardiness of temperament, a combination of individualism and of the cooperativeness that comes in small and rather intimate communities and the taste for intellectual pursuits that has bred so many scholars and writers among them. All these qualities were to stand the peoples of the eastern colonies in good stead when the phase of settlement in Canada moved into the phase of urbanization and industry and they seemed to be left behind in the race.

CHAPTER

12

Pioneers on the Great Lakes

THE FIRST AGRICULTURAL CLEARINGS IN THE FOREST hinterland of the *pays d'en haut* were made by the French. Already in the late seventeenth century they had established Fort Cataraqui (which later became Fort Frontenac) at the point where Lake Ontario flows away into the St Lawrence, and in 1701 Antoine de la Mothe Cadillac founded the settlement of Detroit. Detroit combined a military fort with a fur-trading post, and there was a nearby Jesuit mission, all fairly common elements of initial penetration into the wilderness. What made it different from any other place in this region was the fact that outside the fort, along the Detroit River, a number of *habitants* had set up their strip farms. By the time of the Conquest the rural population outside the confines of the fort had already reached five hundred.

Detroit, of course, eventually became American territory, and so did the settlements in the Illinois country along the Mississippi, which represented the other French attempt at farming in the *pays d'en haut*. What makes the Detroit settlement of interest in Canada's history is that in the middle of the eighteenth century the farmers began to spill over to the eastern side of the St Clair River, opposite Detroit. The first land grants were made in 1749 where the Canadian city of Windsor now stands, and by the time the province of Quebec was divided and Upper Canada came into existence in 1791, there were about two thousand people of French descent living there, the first settlers in what eventually became Ontario.

By 1791 a variety of other settlers had moved into the region, introducing a predominantly English-speaking population, which was one of the reasons why the new province was created. The largest influx was that of the Loyalists who, as in Nova Scotia and Quebec, began to arrive during the American Revolution. Their numbers rapidly increased as the war drew to an end, so that by 1783 nearly ten thousand had arrived. They were of a different type from the Loyalists who reached the Atlantic provinces. The latter had been mostly townspeople, but most of those who crossed the frontier into the region north of the Great Lakes were soldiers from locally raised Loyalist regiments that had been disbanded at the end of the war. Many of them, whether they were veterans or not, came from the frontier regions south of the Canadian border, and the clearing of wild land did not present such problems to them as it would do shortly afterwards to the immigrants who came from an England of long-established farms. Common soldiers were given a hundred acres of land per family, and the difficulties of settling in were cushioned by the provision of tools and of seed, food and clothing for the first three years. Officers were even better treated, receiving up to a thousand acres of land each.

Not all the new immigrants were British. Mingled with the majority, who were of English and Scots descent, came hundreds of Germans, some of them civilians and the rest members of disbanded regiments from King George's German principality of Brunswick, who had served on the British side during the recent war.

Indians, too, were among the Loyalist immigrants, for Chief Joseph Brant led a contingent of Iroquois, members of the Six Nations who had been Britain's allies to the end, and who were given land on the Grand River, near the later site of the town of Brantford.

The Loyalists not only began to farm the wilderness. They also founded the first small towns, including Kingston, near the site of Fort Frontenac, and Newark (which later became Niagara-on-the-Lake) near the site of another old French post, Fort Niagara. Newark was the first capital of Upper Canada, but later Governor Simcoe decided it was too near the American border for comfort. So he set up his village capital of York on the north shore of Lake Ontario near the site of a small French fur-trading post called Fort Rouillé. The shift of terrain did not prevent York and its spartan government buildings from being attacked and burned down by the Americans during the War of 1812, however.

After the creation of Upper Canada, officially encouraged immigration continued. It included more Americans, the so-called "late Loyalists," who were really much more concerned with cheap land than with political allegiances. Even if they did not get grants of free acreage like the soldiers, they could buy Crown land for sixpence an acre plus survey costs if they were willing to take an oath of allegiance to King George. Most of these former republicans seem to have treated the procedure as a mere formality.

Variety was added to the population pattern by the arrival, towards the end of the eighteenth century, of some three thousand Gaelic-speaking Highlanders, who settled in Glengarry County near the Lower Canadian border. They farmed, worked as loggers when the forest industry began to spread in the Ottawa valley, and retained the martial traditions of their clans. The Glengarry Fencibles were one of the most reliable of the provincial regiments raised during the War of 1812, and they later played an enthusiastic part in suppressing the Lower Canadian rebellions of 1837–38.

A contrast to these eager warriors was offered by a new wave of German immigrants, who were encouraged by Simcoe's relatively liberal immigration policies. These were the so-called "Pennsylvania Dutch," who were descended from German farmers, mostly of the Mennonite faith, who had suffered persecution in Europe for their pacifist beliefs. They had first been offered refuge by William Penn, himself a pacifist Quaker. During the Revolution, however, the Mennonites refused to take up arms for either side and thus excited the hostility of the rebels. Once the United States was independent, they found it an inhospitable land. Upper Canada was willing to accept them on their own terms, and a clause giving exemption from service to Mennonites and other pacifist sects found its due place in the Canadian militia acts. The Mennonites and other Germans settled mostly in Waterloo County, where their principal town was called Berlin. Later, during the Great War, patriotic prejudice caused its name to be changed to Kitchener.

THE ENDING OF THE WAR WITH THE AMERICANS in 1814 and of the Napoleonic Wars in 1815 greatly changed the pattern of immigration into Upper Canada. Americans were now regarded with suspicion as recent enemies and possible agents of republican subversion. British immigrants were therefore given a warm welcome. Many of them were officers who had been discharged after the Napoleonic Wars, and could not afford to live in Britain on their half-pay. Others were ordinary soldiers and sailors. The officers were often granted generous parcels of land and sometimes given posts in the colonial administration.

But there was another kind of unprivileged immigrant from Britain who soon outnumbered the military land seekers. This group so submerged the original Loyalist population that present-day claims to pure Loyalist blood in Ontario are really impossible to substantiate. Some of them were people who had enough money to pay their passages and buy some cheap land from the government or through one of the land companies. Often they were experienced farmers or farm workers who thought they could do better for themselves in the Canadas than in Britain, and often their expectations proved correct. But others came because there was simply nothing left for them in Britain. Between the 1820s and the 1840s there were crop failures and acute unemployment in England, the crofters had been dispossessed in Scotland, and poverty was general and persistent — aggravated by potato famines — in Ireland. This whole series of crises led to many dubious assisted-immigration schemes.

One of the most bitter critics of such schemes was William Cobbett, the radical author of *Rural Rides*, who knew both Canada and the English countryside from direct experience. He believed that if agriculture had been properly organized in England there would have been no need to send people to the New World. And of that place he had no great opinion after his period of military service in New Brunswick. Cobbett's indignation was justified to a great extent, since many people were sent from England by the Poor Law authorities merely to reduce expenses for their parishes. (The parishes were responsible for maintaining the poor at that time.) The "assisted immigrants" were often landed in Canada with no money and none of the abilities that might be useful to them in a pioneer society. Even for those who came with the advantages of health, skills and a modicum of cash, the process of transfer must have been a traumatic one.

To begin with, there was the journey across the Atlantic, which in the early days of the nineteenth century was usually by sail and could take weeks or even months, depending on the weather. Those who were better off sailed on reasonably well-appointed passenger ships, and by the late 1830s some of them even travelled on the new Cunard steam packets. The poor, however, were often packed into roughly converted timber ships which were making the return voyage to Quebec. There were many shipwrecks with all passengers lost, but an even greater threat was death by sickness at sea.

Epidemic sicknesses bred quickly in the crowded holds of the timber ships, and cholera and typhus spread to Canada with the emigrants from Britain. The first of the bad years was 1832; Asian cholera had devastated Europe in the preceding year, and fearing that it would reach Canada, the authorities there established a quarantine station at Grosse Île in the estuary of the St Lawrence where all ships were stopped for inspection. In spite of these precautions, the sickness reached Quebec and Montreal. More than five thousand people died in these two cities alone and six thousand altogether in the two Canadas. Even passengers who came on the better ships were afflicted. Catharine Parr Traill, whose writings about life in early Upper Canada later became famous, was one of those who barely survived an attack of the cholera. The great typhus epidemic of 1847 was even more devastating. It coincided with an especially large migration of Irish people fleeing the famines. More than nine thousand immigrants died on shipboard during this time, plus a further ten thousand at Grosse Île and in the hospitals of Quebec, Montreal and even Toronto. Smaller epidemics continued into the 1850s.

Yet in spite of these difficulties and all the deaths on the way, and in spite of the fact that tens of thousands of immigrants used Canada only as a passageway to the United States, enough remained to increase the population of Upper Canada tenfold in thirty-seven years. The 1814 population of 95,000 had grown to 952,000 by 1851, by which time the mainly English-speaking population of Upper Canada had decisively leapt ahead of the largely French-speaking population of Lower Canada.

Only half of these people were Canadian-born; the rest consisted of people born elsewhere.

In the mid-nineteenth century immigration continued to be predominantly British. In the 1851 census 93,000 of the people enumerated were English or Welsh by birth, and 90,000 were Scots, but the Irish greatly outnumbered either group; there were 227,000 of them, divided sharply between the Protestants from Ulster and the Catholics from the rest of Ireland. Over the years the combination led to great violence, Irishman fighting against Irishman, and deeply affected Canadian political life. By now the American element in the population had declined in importance, and in 1851 only 56,000 of the inhabitants of Upper Canada had been born south of the border.

Within another ten years the population of Upper Canada increased even more sensationally, by more than 40 percent, reaching 1,396,000 in 1861. This placed Upper Canada almost 300,000 ahead of Lower Canada and fuelled a campaign by local politicians for "Rep by Pop" (representation by population). Up to that point the Assembly of the province of Canada, which had been formed from Upper and Lower Canada in 1840, consisted of equal numbers of representatives from Canada East and Canada West (the new names for Lower and Upper Canada). It was French fears of being submerged if the anglophone Rep-by-Poppers had their will that led to the compromise plan of a federal dominion consisting of largely autonomous provinces. The plan became reality at Confederation in 1867.

The rapidly growing population flooded into the countryside and took up most of the available land, so that by the mid-1860s there was already a shortage, and the people of Canada West — soon to become Ontarians after the province's name changed in 1867 — began to look westward to the empty prairies for living space. The towns and cities were still comparatively small. It is true that since 1831, when York's population was only

four thousand, that tiny capital had increased elevenfold
in size. Now called Toronto, its population was still only
forty-five thousand, however. Its nearest rival, Hamilton
at the western end of Lake Ontario, had nineteen thousand inhabitants, and Ottawa, which had been the Canadian capital for four years after Queen Victoria
prodded her pin at the map in 1857, had a population of
less than fifteen thousand. More of these were connected with the logging industry than with the tasks of
government. London at this time was just under the
twelve thousand mark, and no other cities in Canada
West even reached ten thousand. Most people still lived
in small communities or on their farms.

The situation in Canada East was not much different.
Its two real cities — Montreal with more than ninety
thousand and Quebec with fifty-one thousand people —
were larger than any in the upper province, but their
nearest competitor, Trois-Rivières, had barely six thousand. The rest of the communities in Canada East were
little more than villages. Canadians everywhere were
mostly country dwellers, though it is true that some of
the immigrants who came during these years never proceeded beyond Montreal, where many found work as
skilled craftsmen, and others sank into the pool of casual labour, inhabiting the slums that began to appear in
Canada as the towns became more populated.

Those who continued from Montreal to Upper
Canada in the 1820s and the 1830s faced a hard journey,
for there were few roads and as yet no railways. The
trek between the two provinces had to be made by water, and this meant first negotiating the rapid-strewn
stretch of the St Lawrence extending from Montreal to
Prescott in Upper Canada. For this part of the journey
Durham boats and *bâteaux* were used. The difference between them was mainly in size, for both were flat-
bottomed craft that were worked up the river by oar and
pole, and sometimes by sail, but even more often by
towing. The *bâteau* was a short, sturdy boat usually

about forty feet long, but the Durham boat, which was built according to an American design, was often a hundred feet long or more. At some parts of the journey there would be horses to do the towing, but often the passengers had to man the ropes, and at the worst rapids there would be long delays while the freight was portaged and reshipped to the next stretch of relatively quiet water. The hundred and twenty miles of bad water between Montreal and Prescott often took twelve days to traverse before steamboats came into operation, and frequently the immigrants — adults and children — sat unprotected by any shelter from the rain and the sun. At Prescott the passengers had to transfer to sailing ships for the rest of the journey up Lake Ontario to the landing nearest their final destination. Here again there was the risk of shipwreck, for the wind and weather of the Great Lakes were as uncertain as those of the ocean.

Even within Upper Canada, water was usually the most convenient means of transport, and the fortunate settlers were those who had land on a lakeshore or a river. Soon, however, the waterfront lots were taken, and there was no alternative but to seek land away from the shore.

UNLIKE THE SEIGNEURIES ALONG THE ST LAWRENCE, the land in Upper Canada was divided according to the township system derived from American experience. Most townships were great squares of land, ten miles each way, divided into a checkerboard pattern of lots or concessions. Provision was made in the survey for a pattern of concession roads running through the township, onto one of which each lot would face; few of these roads actually existed, however. The lots varied in size according to the districts, but on average they consisted of two hundred acres. In the early days a seventh of the lots in each township was reserved for the benefit of the Protestant clergy and another seventh for the Crown. This created a ragged pattern of settlement, with the occupied lots of individual farmers alternating with un-occupied Crown or clergy lots. By 1825 the Crown lands had been sold at a cut rate to the speculative Canada Company, which meant that they gradually became oc-cupied. The last of the clergy reserve plots were not sur-rendered until 1854. In the end the townships were not merely surveyors' abstractions; they became the basic units of local government in Upper Canada, and groups of townships surrounding local villages or towns were formed into counties.

In the early days the stretches of real road uniting the townships were very few and very short. Even the streets of early Toronto were notorious for their mud, and what often passed for roads beyond the towns were mere tracks where trees had been felled. Wagons had to jolt over the ground that had been cleared, sometimes none too efficiently, since they often encountered stumps in the middle of the road and the cart wheels had to be carefully manœuvred between them. Gravel roads were unknown, and for a long period the only kind of surfacing in use consisted of logs laid crosswise across the track in muddy stretches. They became known as "corduroy" roads after the material they vaguely resembled. At best, corduroy caused an almost unbearable jolting in the often springless carts, and with or without it many of the roads were almost impassable bogs for long periods of the year. They were probably at their best during winter when a firm snow surface would build up, over which sleighs could pass without great difficulty.

The settlers' problems did not end when they reached their land, which was likely to be a forest that had to be felled before any crop could be sown even be-tween the stumps. (The lumber did provide material for houses, barns and fencing, however, as well as ash for making lye soap.) Frequently, the settlers' land was marshy into the bargain. Settlements were few and scat-tered, often consisting of little more than a store, a grist mill, a sawmill, a smithy, a tavern, and perhaps a Methodist meeting house. Little cash was in circulation and barter flourished.

Early farms in Upper Canada were of necessity mainly subsistence operations. Almost all the food used by the settler family was grown on the holding, the first house was built of the trees that had grown where it stood, much of the furniture was hand-carpentered and most clothes were made from homespun woven by the farmwife from the wool of the farmer's own sheep. Even items like soap and candles were made from the lye and animal fat that were produced on the holding. Though some of the journals of early gentlemen farmers tell of planting potatoes during the day and dancing the same evening at balls in York, many early settlers were lost in the great brooding woods and suffered acutely from loneliness.

Yet, as the country began to fill, a great communal spirit arose among the farmers. Although life was always rough and the people often rough-mannered, a kind of mutual aid was widely practised. Neighbours would gather at "bees" to cooperate in harvesting or in building each other's houses or barns. Such occasions were often festive, since locally distilled whiskey, which according to William Dunlop cost "one shilling sterling a gallon," would be dispensed by the bucket at these affairs. But even such neighbourliness could not compensate for the unrelenting toil and the difficulty of communications. Susanna Moodie spoke with the bitterness of the experience when she warned other prospective immigrants:

> In most instances, emigration is a matter of necessity, not of choice. Few educated persons accustomed to the refinement and luxuries of European society ever willingly relinquish these advantages. Emigration may generally be regarded as a severe duty performed at the expense of personal enjoyment.[21]

THE SITUATION BEGAN TO CHANGE RAPIDLY as the mechanical age reached Canada in the first decades of the nineteenth century. At the end of the War of 1812 the only signs of the forthcoming changes were the little steamboats which the multiple entrepreneur John Molson began to operate on the St Lawrence in 1809. The maiden voyage that his *Accommodation* made from Montreal to Quebec took thirty-six hours, but thereafter he improved the design of his ships. During the war he profited greatly by ferrying soldiers from Quebec, where they left their troopships, to the Lachine rapids where they began their journey into the hinterland.

By the 1830s visitors were commenting on the relative luxury of the accommodation enjoyed by passengers on the larger steamships operating on the St Lawrence. Even at this date, however, there were many immigrants who could not afford the fares on the paddleboats and who still had to be content to travel in *bâteaux*, now towed by steamboats. The steamboats made them more speedy, but they were no less uncomfortable than they had been in the past. For those who could afford it, travel was speeded up along the upper reaches of the St Lawrence by steamships operating on the stretches of calm water in combination with connecting stagecoaches on the portage roads between steamboat landings. The *Frontenac* made its first trip on Lake Ontario in 1817 and thus became the first steamship to appear on the Great Lakes in Canada. It was quickly followed by others as settlement spread along the lakeshores. Not everyone was impressed by them, however. Anna Jameson remarked in the 1830s that the little vessels operating between landings on Lake Erie looked like "tea kettles" in comparison with the large boats that already plied the American side of the waters. Even on the lesser lakes like Simcoe, small steamships appeared, and with competition the fares fell so far that relatively rapid water transport was soon available to almost every immigrant.

Travel by boat long remained the most convenient way of getting from place to place in Upper Canada, and it was facilitated from the 1820s onward by the building of a series of canals, which gave employment to many new immigrants before they established themselves on the land. The earliest, the Lachine Canal, was started by a group of Montreal merchants to provide a way around the formidable rapids at this point. It was built between 1821 and 1825, and public funds were needed to complete it. This established a precedent in Canada, a country of long distances and scattered population, where private and public initiative have of necessity gone hand in hand from the beginning. The Welland Canal was built between 1824 and 1829 to link Lake Erie with Lake Ontario, bypassing Niagara Falls. But the most ambitious of these early undertakings was the Rideau Canal, built between 1826 and 1832 under military supervision to provide a strategic link between Ottawa and Kingston that would be well removed from the American border. The Rideau Canal was rarely used for military purposes and never in warfare, but it did play a great part in opening up the backlands of eastern Ontario. Later, canal works were planned for the express purpose of opening up the country. The Trent system, for instance, begun in 1834, ran for more than two hundred miles between Lakes Ontario and Huron, linking up small lakes and rivers on the way and facilitating not only settlement, but also later activities like logging and grain handling.

The railways were relative latecomers to Upper Canada. In Lower Canada a small portage railway sixteen miles long had been completed between the St Lawrence and Richelieu rivers in 1836, and in Cape Breton a mining railway had been built in 1839. But in the upper province serious railway building did not begin until the 1850s, when the Great Western was built through southern Ontario. It went from Niagara Falls by way of Hamilton and London to Windsor on the St Clair

River, and a few years later the Grand Trunk was built from Montreal to Toronto and thence to Sarnia at the southern end of Lake Huron. The railways played an important role in opening up communication, since they released the lockgrip of the Canadian winter on transport. Once winter came even the steamships were frozen in their harbours and the roads became difficult. Only the railways kept going in all but the worst of weathers, and in this way they brought an end to the winter isolation that plagued so many early Canadian communities.

But the Great Western and the Grand Trunk also had their economic importance, for they opened up the fertile lands of southern Ontario to freight at a time when the productivity — and the character — of rural life were changing with the completion of settlement. By the 1860s most of the arable land in Canada West had been cleared, the great forests had been felled except in the northern part of the province along the Ottawa River, and the farms were no longer directed towards subsistence. They still tended to be mixed farms, however, with an emphasis on growing wheat. The wheat became an export crop that was sent out by railway.

During this period Canadian agricultural practices were radically changed by the technological revolution in farming. Sickle and scythe were replaced by implements like horse-drawn mowers, reapers and eventually reapers-and-binders. Daniel Massey and Alanson Harris were two of the first farm implement manufacturers in Canada West. Massey's foundry was established in Newcastle in 1847 and Harris's was set up in Brantford in 1857. They made implements according to their own designs or according to patents acquired from the United States. Not only did they help to change the whole nature of Canadian farming, but they also created one of the earliest important Canadian industries.

The country way of life also changed with growing prosperity. By the time the railways appeared to complete the communication links with the outer world, good roads had been made within and between the townships; corduroy belonged to an already romantic past. The log huts and shanties of the original pioneers had given way to frame houses or even, in some areas, to structures of brick or stone. Store-bought clothes and furniture took the place of homespun and the roughly carpentered chairs and tables of early days. Egerton Ryerson's School Acts of 1846 and 1850 had initiated the spread of educational facilities through the farming areas of the province, and, even if attendance was not compulsory, most children went at least part of the year to the schoolhouses directed by boards of local trustees. Churches and school buildings often served as the nuclei of an expanded social life. As crossroads hamlets grew into villages and villages grew into towns, the isolation of the pioneers was dissipated like the shadows of the vanishing forests.

By the 1860s Canada West, which was shortly to become Ontario, had developed into a prosperous and populous rural society. Its main dilemma was the growing pressure on the available land, a problem that would eventually find its solution as the next wave of settlement overleapt the barren expanses of the Canadian Shield to arrive in the rich and empty prairies.

PART
V

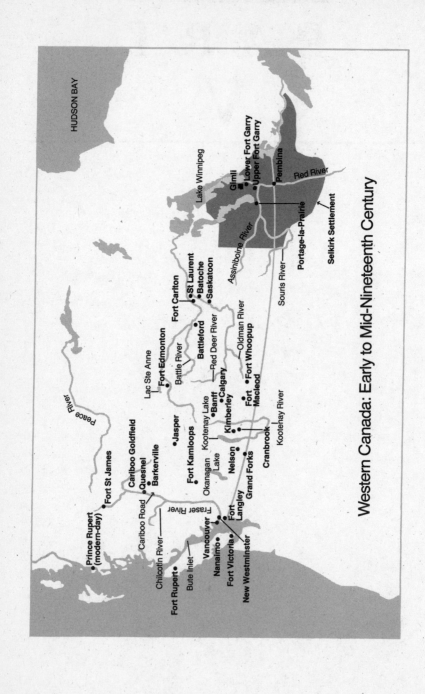

Western Canada: Early to Mid-Nineteenth Century

CHAPTER
13

The Death of the Great Wild Herds

THE ARRIVAL OF THE SETTLERS in the Canadian Prairie marked the end of at least a century of radical transition in the native cultures that led to their virtual breakdown. The penetration of alien influences was less direct here than in other parts of the vast domain of Rupert's Land, but it was no less profound. No real attempt was made to impose governmental authority over the region until the 1870s, and before that time even the fur traders, once they went beyond the Red River valley, tended to avoid the territory of fierce and independent peoples like the Blackfoot and the Sioux. Instead they veered off through the parklands to the northwest towards the Athabasca country.

Yet, as we have seen, the presence of the white men, even when they had little direct contact with the plains tribes, had a profound cumulative influence on the destinies of those peoples. Horses, originally imported by Spaniards of whom the Sioux and the Blackfoot had never even heard, were passed northward from tribe to tribe. By the time they had reached the Sarcee and the Cree on the edge of the northern woodlands, they had changed Indian ways of hunting and warfare more radically than any innovation since the tribes invented the buffalo pound millennia before. The acquisition of firearms by trade or capture affected the balance of power and the distribution of peoples in the plains, without any direct intervention of the white men. The new weapons enabled the Ojibwa to push the Assiniboine and the Sioux out of the more westerly woodlands into the prairie. They also allowed the Cree to establish themselves in the parklands bordering the plains and to compete with the Blackfoot for hunting grounds.

Old World diseases also preceded the white men, passing rapidly from tribe to tribe. Following on La Vérendrye's first tentative penetration of the plains, smallpox spread in 1736 among the Assiniboine and the Sioux, and in 1783 a worse epidemic of the same disease had reached the western tribes and killed many a Blackfoot who had never seen an Englishman or a Frenchman.

But there were still direct ways in which, even by their internecine rivalries, the fur traders profoundly changed life on the plains. The North West Company did it by encouraging the emergence of the Métis as a new and separate force on the prairies, and the Hudson's Bay Company, by allowing the creation of the first prairie settlement on the Red River in 1812.

These two initiatives were fatally intertwined and equally fatally linked with the philanthropic urges of Thomas Douglas, 5th Earl of Selkirk, the first man who seriously thought of the prairies as a potential destination for immigrants. Selkirk, a conscience-stricken Scottish nobleman, had taken up as his life's cause the plight of the displaced Highland crofters. In 1803 he settled eight hundred of them on Prince Edward Island, and in the following year he established another settlement at Baldoon in Upper Canada, which failed partly because the land was too marshy for sheep rearing and partly because it was looted and burned by the Americans in 1812. But Selkirk did not abandon his ambitions, and even before Baldoon was destroyed he and his relatives had bought into the Hudson's Bay Company and secured a controlling interest which he used to obtain a grant of 116,000 square miles of land. It included the Red River valley from the present boundary between North and South Dakota downriver to Lake Winnipeg, together with the valleys of the Assiniboine and Souris rivers.

Even many of the Hudson's Bay officials were opposed to the creation of a settlement in their territory, which they regarded as harmful to the fur trade, and the partners of the North West Company were more alarmed by the scheme. A concentration of farmers along the Red River would lie right across their routes of access to the Northwest. Furthermore, it would offer a competing market for the pemmican and buffalo meat on which they depended for the victualling of their brigades and of their forts in the Athabasca country.

Selkirk ignored this opposition and in July 1811 the first party of immigrants set off from Scotland for Hudson Bay. They wintered at York Factory and finally, after many privations, reached the junction of the Red and Assiniboine rivers in August 1812, followed by a second party in October of that year. During the first winter, the settlers had difficulty feeding themselves and were kept alive only by the help of local Indians and of the fur traders, who temporarily allowed compassion to stifle their misgivings. The situation changed quickly, owing to the impetuous arrogance of Miles Macdonell, Selkirk's governor. In his anxiety to ensure that his settlers would have adequate supplies, he rashly issued a proclamation in January 1814, in which he forbade the export of pemmican from the Red River to other parts of the Northwest. The Nor'Westers retaliated by arresting him under dubious authority and persuading many of the settlers to depart for Upper Canada. The rest, discouraged, withdrew in the direction of Hudson Bay, but were brought back by Colin Robertson, who re-established the settlement and then departed to combat the Nor'Westers in the Athabasca country, leaving Robert Semple as governor.

By now the Nor'Westers had made up their minds to destroy the colony. With this in mind they flattered the Métis, many of whom were now employed at their forts and in their brigades, persuading them that they were a "nation" which had aboriginal rights to the prairie lands that the settlers were violating. In June 1816 a clash took place at Seven Oaks between a party of Métis led by Cuthbert Grant and a party of settlers led by Governor Semple; Semple and twenty settlers were killed — and one Métis. It went down in the records of the Hudson's Bay Company as a "massacre" and in Métis oral history as a great victory, but it did not mean the end of the colony. When he first heard of the incident Selkirk was on his way across the Great Lakes with a party of discharged Swiss mercenaries from the De Meuron regiment whom he had persuaded to accompany him to the Red River. He immediately seized the Nor'Westers' depot at Fort William, arresting the partners of the company whom he found there, and proceeded to the Red River, where in the summer of 1817 he re-established the colony.

FROM THIS TIME ONWARD THE COLONY survived, though it went through many vicissitudes owing to floods, droughts and plagues of grasshoppers. In 1837 the Selkirk grant, by now named Assiniboia, was handed back to the Hudson's Bay Company. In order to administer the region's affairs the HBC created the first semblance of a government in the West, which consisted of a governor and an appointed council picked from among the local residents.

Over the years the population of the Red River changed considerably. The mercenaries whom Selkirk had brought with him and other Swiss settlers who followed them soon departed to warmer places in the United States. But the descendants of the original Scottish settlers for the most part remained. As the settlement grew, retired Hudson's Bay officials chose to settle there rather than return home and live as strangers in the haunts of their youth. People of mixed Scottish and Indian ancestry imitated the original Scots by taking to the land and establishing farms. And finally, largely under the influence of the Catholic Oblate fathers, many Métis took up a semi-settled existence, establishing strip farms beside the Red and Assiniboine rivers like those of their *habitant* ancestors on the St Lawrence. Other Métis in the Saskatchewan country still pursued a nomadic existence as free hunters, mingling with the Indians and in many ways living like them. Those who settled along the Red River would usually winter on their farms, cultivate a little land and sow a crop in the spring, and then set off for months with their families on their great summer hunts, returning to reap whatever crops had survived drought, pests and weeds.

The Red River settlement was really a series of ribbon villages merging into each other, with Fort Garry doubling as the seat of the government of Assiniboia and as the centre of the fur trade for the region. The Hudson's Bay Company tried to maintain a monopoly of that trade, but by the end of the 1840s a near rebellion of the Métis hunters led to the establishment of virtual free trade. Independent merchants gained control of so much of the commerce that during the 1850s they would send caravans of as many as five hundred Red River carts at a time, loaded with furs, buffalo robes and other Red River products, on a slow month-long journey down to the railhead at St Paul in American territory. Freighting of this kind was one of the principal occupations of the Red River Métis until 1859. In that year the

paddle steamer *Anson Northup* sailed downriver across
the international boundary to Fort Garry and brought
the mechanical age into the prairie. It was on the steamboats that the first prairie wheat was exported, the
scanty surplus harvests of the Red River farms. Commerce brought to the Red River the first semblance of a
town: the trader's village of Winnipeg, which was variously described by visitors as "unsightly" and "a sorry
scene." It consisted of about fifty log houses along a
mud street and "a few small stores with poor goods and
high prices." Colonel Wolseley, who led the military expedition there in 1870, remarked that "grog shops are
the principal feature of the place."

But grog shops were not all that the Red River settlement had to offer its inhabitants. The Oblate fathers
Provencher and Dumoulin had arrived in 1818 to establish a mission at St Boniface, and the Anglican priest
John West came two years later, though the Methodists
and Presbyterians did not arrive for another twenty
years. For all sects the Red River served as a springboard for further ventures into the West. Both Anglicans
and Catholics emphasized education, and between them
they created a loose network of schools that offered academic, religious and vocational training in the valley
and to some degree affected all but the most nomadic of
its inhabitants.

By 1870, when the Red River settlement finally entered Canada — with considerable reluctance — as the
province of Manitoba, its population had grown to almost twelve thousand. More than ten thousand of them
were Métis or Scottish half-breeds or Ojibwa Indians, by
now a dwindling group. About 1,500 were entirely European in ancestry, and these included not only descendants of the original Scottish settlers, but almost three
hundred Ontarians, the vanguard of the great immigration that in the next generation would flood the prairies.

By 1869, when they asserted themselves under Louis
Riel's leadership in the Red River rebellion, the Métis

had assumed in the prairies a role as important as that of any of the Indian confederations. They challenged the Indians for control of the one great natural resource of the great plains that was then being exploited. It was the resource on which aboriginal life in the region had been dependent from time immemorial, the bison herds — or buffalo herds, as they were generally called on both the Canadian and the American plains.

UNLIKE THEIR FRENCH FATHERS, WHO WERE content with the life of the voyageur, the Métis resembled their Indian ancestors in their passion for hunting. Circumstances encouraged them to follow this inclination. Since the fusion of the two fur-trading companies and the replacement of canoes by York boats diminished the need for voyageurs, the increasing number of Métis began to serve the fur traders as "freemen," or independent hunters, who provided the forts with meat and pemmican, and usually did a certain amount of trading on their own account at the same time. Like the Indians, they also depended mainly on the buffalo herds for their own subsistence. The only domestic animals they generally reared were horses, and apart from potatoes they grew very little in the way of crops. Trading furs and the products of the buffalo gave them enough cash or barter value to buy the bright clothes they liked, the tobacco, spirits and tea they consumed in considerable quantities and the powder and ammunition they needed to carry on their hunts.

Their economy was basically very little different from that of the native peoples of the plains, and they retained the nomadic inclinations of the Cree, to whom most of them were related. At the same time, however, they kept a great deal of the French culture of their fathers, including their own form of the French language (though most of them were at least bilingual, speaking a minimum of one Indian language as well). They retained a superstitious form of Catholicism and had a great love of dancing the whole night through to the tune of the fiddle. They shared with the Indians their love of gambling and an almost anarchic form of democracy, in which their leaders were recognized as chiefs only for limited purposes and at specific times, usually during the great communal hunts.

It was on these great hunts that the Métis challenged powerful Indian groups like the Blackfoot Confederacy, so they had to travel in almost military formation. In 1840 Alexander Ross, fur trader and author, observed one great Métis hunt. It left from the Red River to arrive on the plains bordering the Missouri, travelling over the international border, which neither Indians nor Métis recognized any more than the buffalo herds did. In all some sixteen hundred people from the Red River gathered at the rendez-vous at Pembina, including almost four hundred children. There were twelve hundred Red River carts in the procession, some drawn by horses and some by oxen, and the creaking of their ungreased wheels could be heard for miles. In addition to the draught animals, there were four hundred horses that had been chosen to be used by that many hunters as buffalo runners.

As soon as they assembled at Pembina the hunters elected ten captains, who in turn elected the head of the hunt. On this occasion, and many subsequent ones, the elected head was Jean-Baptiste Wilkie, who became the father-in-law of an even more famous hunter, Gabriel Dumont. Ten guides were also appointed, men with knowledge of the country where the hunt would take place, who would take turns leading the cavalcade as it moved across the plains and who would send out a screen of scouts to look out for Indian bands or buffalo herds. As soon as a halt was called for the night, the captains would take over to establish the camp, each with ten soldiers under him acting as a kind of police, and to ensure the carts were arranged in a kind of laager so that the camp could defend itself against any surprise attack.

Elaborate rules, similar to those of the Blackfoot, were drawn up to prevent the herds being frightened prematurely and to keep individuals from gaining an advantage over the hunters in general. The method the hunters used was to ride simultaneously into the herd, shooting the animals at point-blank range, a method which required the most exact coordination in starting off the hunt. Ross described one such occasion:

> No less than 400 huntsmen, all mounted, and anxiously waiting for the word "Start!" took up their position in a line at one end of the camp, while Captain Wilkie, with his spy-glass at his eye, surveyed the buffalo, examined the ground, and issued his orders. At 8 o'clock the whole cavalcade broke ground, and made for the buffalo; first at a slow trot, then at a gallop, and lastly at full speed. . . . When the horsemen started, the cattle might have been a mile and a half ahead; but they had approached to within four or five hundred yards before the bulls curved their tails or pawed the ground. In a moment more the herd took flight, and horse and rider are presently seen bursting in among them; shots are heard, and all is smoke, dust and hurry.[22]

But neither in the rules of the hunt nor in the general practice of Indian or Métis hunters was there any thought of conservation. Ross remarked that at least as much useable meat as had been eaten or dried was left on the prairie, to be devoured by the herds of wolves that followed each hunting camp or to rot among the white bones that already strewed the land like strange-shaped fungi. To make matters worse, those who hunted on horseback were selective, and usually shot the heifers and the young cows, who were potential or actual mothers. Both had flesh more delicate than that of the bulls.

APART FROM ALL THIS WASTE, THE DEMAND for buffalo meat had increased rapidly in the early nineteenth century; fur traders, settlers on the Red River and growing numbers of Métis competed with the Indians for this basic food of the wild plains. After the beginning of the nineteenth century, the numbers of buffalo and the range of their wandering began to diminish steadily and strikingly. It has been estimated that between 50 and 60 million bison roamed the plains in 1800, and they were still to be found in considerable numbers in the Red River valley at that time. By about 1830 they were diminished by almost half, to about 30 million, and they had deserted the Red River region. Now the hunters from there had to go south of the border into the Missouri country, while the Métis of the Far West developed a separate hunt in the area of the two Saskatchewan rivers. This meant clashes with the Indians, since the hunt from Red River was encroaching on Sioux hunting grounds and the Saskatchewan hunt on those of the Blackfoot Confederacy. The Métis were often involved in pitched battles with these tribes, who felt the plains belonged to them.

During the fifty years between 1830 and 1880 the herds declined even more rapidly, and this was partly because there was no way of keeping the buffalo within Canada. They roamed freely back and forth over the great plains that lay on each side of the border. In the United States they were subject to even greater perils than in Canada, since the frontier was moving forward more quickly there, and the hunt was rapidly becoming commercialized. Professional hunters began to appear, who killed the buffalo either for their pelts, which were turned into winter coats in the cities, or for their hides, which were often used to make industrial drive belts.

1880 was the last year in which Gabriel Dumont led the Saskatchewan Métis out on their hunt, and returned with very little meat. The Red River hunt had vanished years ago. And after 1880 the buffalo were virtually extinct on the great plains, though bison of another breed survived in the northern woodlands. In the mid-1870s, after Canada had taken over Rupert's Land, the newly created Council of the Northwestern Territory passed an ordinance forbidding wasteful ways of killing the buffalo, but it was already too late, and in any case the Indian and Métis hunters who would have benefited most by it regarded it as an intolerable infringement of their aboriginal rights.

Some people, especially the missionaries, foresaw the imminent end of the buffalo hunt, and it was because of their urging that the Métis began early in the 1870s to stake out strip farms along the Saskatchewan River at places like St Laurent and Batoche. Some resorted to places like Lac Ste Anne and Lac La Biche, where the diminishing returns from hunting could be complemented by fishing as well as a certain amount of cultivation. The Métis, proving more flexible than the Indians, also turned to occupations like freighting, and far into the 1880s the trains of Red River carts lumbered and screeched over the Carlton Trail from Fort Garry to Fort Carlton on the North Saskatchewan.

The Indian peoples of the prairies were more catastrophically affected by the disappearance of the great herds. As long as their memories or their traditions probed into the past they had lived off the bounty of the buffalo hunt. It had provided in abundance everything they needed for their highly specialized way of life. It not only sustained them physically; it also encompassed their myths and ceremonials, their entire patterns of work and play, and inspired what art they had. It sustained a whole culture, not just an economy, and it is no exaggeration to say that when the buffalo herds died off, the traditional life that had been lived on the plains for seven or eight thousand years died with it. The proud, fierce, self-sufficient warriors and hunters of those formidable tribes — the Blackfoot, Cree and Assiniboine — were reduced to hunger and poverty. They could survive the long decades of crisis that followed the destruction of the herds only as the wards of an often unsympathetic and usually uncaring Canadian state. Canada was more intent on clearing the way for new inhabitants in the West than on caring for the indigenous populations, either human or animal.

CHAPTER
14

Possessing the West

DURING THE MID-NINETEENTH CENTURY the question of prairie settlement was raised by both the British critics of the Hudson's Bay Company and the expansionists in Upper Canada. The former, one of the last monopolistic chartered companies to survive from an earlier era, resented the idea. The latter, aware that land was becoming scarcer in the east, began to view with combined disapproval and envy the fact that such a vast territory as Rupert's Land and New Caledonia should be held under the suzerainty of an organization that merely collected furs from it. The fur traders had obstinately denied that the prairies were suitable for agriculture, but the experience of the Red River settlement, where farms were succeeding despite adverse physical circumstances, made it difficult to sustain such an argument. Meanwhile, events on the Pacific coast had shown how vulnerable and tempting to expansionist neighbours territory barely administered by a thin line of fur traders could be. The creation of the colony of Vancouver Island in 1849 had set the precedent for replacing fur-trading authorities with regular government.

Just after the middle of the nineteenth century, both the British Colonial Office and the government of the province of Canada began to actively investigate the settlement potential of the broad, wild lands of the prairies. In 1857, largely through the intervention of the Royal Geographical Society, the British government commissioned Captain John Palliser to explore the Canadian prairies north of the American border and to continue through the Rocky Mountains to the Pacific. Palliser and his scientific associates spent three years in the West. They concluded that there was only a remote possibility of establishing direct communication between Canada and the Red River across the Shield and they found the mountains of British Columbia a formidable obstacle. However, they did discover, outside the dry "Palliser Triangle" in southern Saskatchewan, a broad expanse of fertile land all the way across the plains.

In the same year, the government of the province of Canada sent out Henry Youle Hind, a geologist who was also an acute scientific popularizer, to assess to what extent Canadian interests could be served in the Northwest. Hind was the brother of the well-known early Canadian painter, William G. R. Hind, and he himself was a man of considerable aesthetic sensibility. After he had returned for a second time to the prairies in 1858, he wrote his historic *Narrative of the Canadian Red River Exploring Expedition of 1857 and of the Assiniboine and Saskatchewan Exploring Expedition of 1858*. Despite its forbidding title, Hind's *Narrative* is one of the most interesting travel documents of Canada in the nineteenth century. It contains illuminating details of settler life along the Red River, as well as remarkable lyrical passages that for the first time celebrate in adequate prose the visual wonders of the prairie landscape. Even more appealing to his Canadian contemporaries, however, was his positive assessment of the agricultural possibilities of the Northwest.

Although the potential for success was there, the question of access remained, and Captain Palliser was pessimistic on that issue. However, a different view was offered by another investigator. In 1858 the Scottish surveyor S. J. Dawson was employed to investigate the problems of establishing a line of regular communication across the Shield. The point was to avoid routing Canadian transportation through American territory. He concluded that it was indeed possible to create an effective all-weather transportation link by road, river and lake between Fort William and Fort Garry. Ten years later, in 1868, Dawson was called upon to give concrete form to his proposals when he was commissioned to construct the rough-and-ready route to the Red River known as the Dawson Trail.

In the meantime, in 1867, Canada and the Atlantic provinces of Nova Scotia and New Brunswick had become the Dominion of Canada, and provision had been made under the British North America Act of that year for the remaining British provinces and territories in North America to be incorporated eventually. Already a movement to join Confederation was afoot in British Columbia. Even the Hudson's Bay Company's attitude towards settlement had changed. In 1863 it had been acquired by the International Finance Society, whose shareholders were less interested in the dwindling profits of the fur trade than in what they anticipated would be a favourable market for land in the West if it were opened up to agricultural settlement.

IMMEDIATELY AFTER CONFEDERATION, three-sided negotiations began between the Canadian government, the Colonial Office, and the Hudson's Bay Company for the purchase of Rupert's Land, including the Red River settlement. The Company finally abandoned its domain to Canada for a payment of £300,000. The most profitable part of the deal so far as the Company was concerned was the retention of a twentieth part of the fertile areas that would be opened for settlement, as well as the lands on which its establishments were built, many of them in what later became important urban areas. Thus, the old fur-trading company was partly metamorphosed into a major real estate development enterprise. Many of its former posts were transformed to meet the needs of growing towns and cities, some of them becoming department stores to which the fur-trading posts that survived in the less developed areas became subsidiary.

Meanwhile, during the lengthy period of negotiations over the transfer of territory, the Canadian government and individual Canadians began to take affairs largely into their own hands. Encouraged by the propaganda of expansionist Toronto newspapers like the *Globe*, Canadians began to settle along the Red River early in the 1860s. Many of them presented themselves aggressively as the forerunners of a takeover by immigrants from Ontario. Their attitude, given expression by the Red River's first newspaper, the *Nor'Wester*, which demanded annexation by Canada, was characterized by religious and racial prejudice, encouraged by members of the fiercely Protestant Orange Order. In 1867 a group of Canadians who had gathered around a recently founded mission at Portage-la-Prairie defied the Hudson's Bay Company and set up a short-lived "republic of Manitoba." Even before the negotiations for the transfer of Rupert's Land were completed, Sir John A. Macdonald had authorized S. J. Dawson to start in 1868 the clearing of the trail from Lake Superior to the Red River, and a party under Colonel J. S. Dennis was sent out in the summer of 1869 to survey the Red River according to the system of square townships that had been followed in Upper Canada.

It was this action that brought to a head the apprehensions of the inhabitants of the Red River, and especially the Métis majority. None of them had been consulted regarding the future of the country they considered their homeland and over which they believed

they shared with the Indians rights of aboriginal title.
On November 11, 1869, Louis Riel, a young man educated in Quebec who had already emerged as one of the
leaders of the militant Métis, performed the symbolic act
of stepping on a surveyor's chain and preventing the
survey from continuing in the area where the riverside
strip farms were situated. Out of this incident emerged
the Red River rebellion, which was not strictly a rebellion, since with the virtual abdication of the Hudson's
Bay Company there was no constituted authority against
which to rebel.

The story of the Red River resistance, as it has also
been called by writers sympathetic to the Métis, belongs
to political, rather than social, history and in any case
has often been told. To sum up the essential elements, it
was an almost bloodless insurrection, though the one
notable death, that of the aggressive Orangeman
Thomas Scott whom the Métis unwisely executed for in-
subordination, had unfortunate consequences, particularly for Riel, whom it forced into a long exile. Basically,
the rebellion achieved its principal aim, which was for
the inhabitants of the Red River to have a say in their
own government. Instead of being administered as a territory, which the Dominion government had intended,
the old district of Assiniboia was admitted to Canada as
a province, and the Métis were given grants of land or
scrip convertible into money as an alternative.

Having acquired Rupert's Land, the Dominion government was faced with two problems, that of populating the country and that of administering and policing it
effectively so that it would no longer be a temptation to
American expansionists. A first attempt to attract settlers
was made with the passing of the Dominion Lands Act
in 1872. It offered free homesteads of 160 acres each to
settlers who would break, cultivate and live on the land.
However, even though settlers did begin to percolate
into the Red River valley and the nearby plains during
the 1870s, it was evident that the great expanse of the

prairies would not be settled until the construction of the transcontinental railway. The building of that transportation link had, in fact, been one of the conditions under which British Columbia entered the Dominion. But the railway was delayed for political reasons. The more urgent problem was to show the flag effectively throughout the newly acquired region. Beyond Manitoba, the new lands were now called the Northwestern Territory, and they had been given a governor and an appointed council, but little in the way of an administrative structure. Of particular importance was the matter of establishing good relations with the still-powerful prairie tribes to prevent an Indian war, which would have been a much more serious matter than the Red River uprising. Although their numbers had been reduced by epidemics, the Indians were still aggressive in defending their territories, and in 1870 there was a major battle over hunting grounds between the Blackfoot and the Cree. Several hundred braves were killed in that conflict.

The problem was aggravated by the fact that Americans from Montana and other frontier territories were beginning to penetrate the lands to their north, bringing with them the viewpoint that "the only good Indian is a dead Indian." American traders peddling a kind of hooch, well watered but laced with cayenne pepper to give it kick, were setting up their posts north of the Canadian border. One establishment in the Cypress Hills called Fort Whoopup became notorious for its half-poisonous brew and for the arrogant aggressiveness of its traders.

Even worse than the whiskey traders were the lawless wolfers who slaughtered wolves and bison indiscriminately for their skins. In the spring of 1873, after a dispute over stolen horses, a party of wolfers massacred a band of Assiniboine Indians, also in the Cypress Hills, and it was this inhuman act — a blatant violation of Canadian sovereignty — that provoked Sir John A. Macdonald into hastening the plans he had already formed for sending a paramilitary force to the prairies. A Manitoba Field Force had been established in 1870, but that merely operated within the province, and in 1872 a British officer, Colonel Robertson Ross, who toured the prairies, recommended that a mobile force, the Northwest Mounted Rifles, should be created to keep order in the plains and to restrain undesirable intrusions.

Macdonald thought that a body which was too openly military might seem provocative to the Americans, so instead he created in 1873 the force known as the Northwest Mounted Police. All the same he dressed his "policemen" in red coats like those worn by members of the British army to give a symbolic assurance to the Indians that they would not be dealing with a force like the blue-coated and generally hated American cavalry. Indeed, the original Mounted Police force was military in all but name. Its original three hundred officers and men had all served either in the British regular army or in active Canadian militia units. Its first commissioner, Captain G. A. French, had held a commission in the Royal Artillery, and he established a strict soldierly discipline. His men lived in barracks and were forbidden to marry during their early years in the force. They were subjected to intensive drills and to training in light cavalry guerilla tactics.

On June 10, 1874, 275 of the new recruits started on the Great March that was launched in order to show the Canadian flag in the new West, as well as to pacify the country. In the middle of the prairies they divided, and a small force set off northwestward to establish a post at Fort Edmonton. The larger party made its way through the vital border country in the direction of the Cypress Hills, relying greatly on the Métis and Indian guides and hunters who accompanied them. When they finally reached Fort Whoopup, they found that the whiskey traders had prudently retreated over the border, leaving an American flag floating defiantly over their stockade.

The police arrested a few straggling American booze
pedlars they met on the way, and poured into the
ground a few kegs of dubious whiskey. They proceeded
to the foothills of the Rockies, where they established
Fort MacLeod. Farther north they built another fort that
became the nucleus of the present city of Calgary.

As well as being frontier policemen and symbolic up-
holders of Canadian sovereignty north of the forty-ninth
parallel, the Mounted Police virtually administered the
territory until the late 1880s. At that time the Department of the Interior began to organize both immigration
and the allocation of lands, and the multitudes of Europeans who would eventually become Canadians began
to flood over the vacant prairies. When the police first
arrived, however, the plains were still the domain of the
hunting Indians and the Métis — apart from a few missionaries and fur traders and some small pioneer groups
of settlers in scattered places like Prince Albert and Portage-la-Prairie. For the time being only the Métis were
effectively challenging Indian domination. The Dominion government was still faced with the problem of se-
curing the lands of the prairies for settlement without
arousing the hostility of the tribes. At all costs the government wanted to avoid the kind of savage Indian wars
that had been going on south of the border for the
greater part of the century.

The only way to do this was to establish agreements
that both sides would honour. Precedents were found in
the treaties that the authorities of New France had concluded with the peoples of the *pays d'en haut* and in
treaties like those the Quakers had made with the Indians of Pennsylvania. Implicit in such treaties was the
recognition that the Indians had original title to the land
and that the title must be transferred by a treaty that
would be sealed by suitable payments. Only in British
Columbia would these precedents be ignored and the
land taken without treaty.

PERHAPS THE MOST IMPORTANT TASK OF THE Mounted Police
after they arrived in the plains was to establish the kind
of relations between Canada and the prairie tribes that
would facilitate the treaty-making process. In the Red
River area, shortly after the creation of Manitoba, a
treaty had been made with the Swampy Cree and the
local Ojibwa. There had been no great difficulty because
the Indians of this region were already in a state of economic deprivation. They had originally welcomed and
assisted Selkirk's settlers and had refused to join the
Nor'Westers and the Métis in attacking them. But they
had seen their land appropriated for farms and the bison herds driven out of their hunting grounds, so that
in the middle of the century their chief, Peguis, made
this famous lament:

> Before you whites came to trouble the ground, our
> rivers were full of fish and woods of deer. Our creeks
> abounded with beavers and our plains were covered
> with buffalo. But now we are brought to poverty. Our
> beavers are gone forever; our buffalo are fled to the
> lands of our enemies. The number of our fish is di-
> minishing. Our cats and our rats are few in number.
> The geese are afraid to pass over the smoke of our
> chimneys and we are left to starve while you whites
> are growing rich on the very dust of our fathers, trou-
> bling the plains with the plough, covering them with
> cows in the summer and in the winter feeding your
> cattle with hay from the very swamps whence our
> beavers have been driven.[23]

The government had expected to encounter difficulties with the prairie tribes, but since the Blackfoot-Cree
War of 1870 an unwonted peace had fallen over the
plains. This was partly because of the growing influence
of missionaries like Father Albert Lacombe among the
Blackfoot and the Methodists George and John McDou-
gall among the Cree. At the same time some of the leading Métis, notably Gabriel Dumont and his father

Isidore, had been active in promoting treaties among the
mutually hostile groups of the prairies — independently
of official initiatives. There was also the fact that the
more far-sighted chiefs were aware that the decline of
the buffalo was only one sign among many that the old
order in the West was coming to an end and that they
and their peoples would have to accommodate to the
new. Some of them even welcomed the arrival of the
Mounted Police as a stabilizing force in the plains, and
there was a strange mixture of resignation, diplomacy
and real gratitude in the statement which Crowfoot, the
paramount chief of the Blackfoot Confederacy, made at
the signing of one of the treaties:

> If the Police had not come to the country, where
> would we all be now? Bad men and whisky were kill-
> ing us so fast that very few, indeed, of us would have
> been left today. The Police have protected us as the
> feathers of a bird protect it from the frosts of the
> winter.[24]

The important treaties of the plains were No. 4, concluded in September 1874 with the Cree and the Ojibwa
of the southern plains from Lake Winnipegosis to the
present-day Alberta border; No. 6, concluded at Fort
Carlton in September 1876 with the Plains and Woods
Cree who lived in the basin of the North Saskatchewan
River; and No. 7, concluded in September 1877 at Blackfoot Crossing with the tribes of the Blackfoot Confederacy and the Stoneys or Assiniboines.

Under these treaties Indian rights over the land were
transferred to the Dominion. In return, the tribes received land reserves on the basis of 128 acres per head
and they were expected to settle there, giving up their
nomadic ways. Derisory annual payments of a few dollars a person were thrown into the deal, along with taw-
dry medals and uniforms for the chiefs, rations of
ammunition and fishing twine, medicine chests, and ed-

ucational and agricultural assistance aimed at turning
the proud hunters into good farmers like the incoming
settlers. Although they were still allowed to hunt freely
over unsettled land, this soon became a meaningless
privilege as the bison declined in numbers. No adequate
provision was made under the treaties for dealing with
the acute distress that many people in the plains already
foresaw would follow the disappearance of the herds.
The Indians had been induced to sell their birthrights
for trivial gifts and uncertain promises.

THE OLD WEST DID NOT DIE quietly. There were many
bands and chiefs, particularly among the Cree, that did
not accept easily the attempts made after the treaties to
force them to abandon their traditional ways. There was
also one important prairie people — the Métis — who
were not included in the treaties, though they had
served as mediators and interpreters during the treaty
negotiations. They now found themselves in the position of being forced to abandon their traditional hunting
life yet having no assurance of rights to land. The land
grants made in Manitoba after the Red River rising were
not extended to Métis in the Saskatchewan area, so that
from a legal point of view, they were squatters on the
strip farms they had staked out beside the South Saskatchewan in the area around Batoche. By the early 1880s
not only the Métis but also the English-speaking mixed
bloods and even the white settlers were becoming dis-
turbed by the fact that the Dominion surveyors were
moving through the prairies, laying out the land in
square townships without regard to existing occupancy.
Sir John A. Macdonald ignored the pleas and petitions
of the aggrieved groups, just as he ignored the griev-
ances of the Indians for whom the treaties were being
meanly interpreted by an economically minded government.

In their exasperation at not gaining even the semblance of a hearing, Gabriel Dumont and the other Métis

leaders in the Saskatchewan country called Louis Riel
back from exile to help their cause, and eventually, in
1885, having petitioned for years without satisfaction,
the Métis armed themselves and declared a provisional
government at Batoche. At the same time two of the
Cree chiefs, Poundmaker and Big Bear, led separate Indian revolts. Now, since there was a constituted government in the Northwestern Territory, the Métis were
technically rebels, and militia regiments were mobilized
in the first all-Canadian army, whose first campaign was
ironically not against the traditional American enemy,
but against other Canadians.

Batoche was captured, the Métis were broken as a
force in the plains and the Northwest rebellion was
over. Riel was tried and executed for high treason under
an obsolete mediaeval English statute. His death would
leave a festering wound on the Canadian conscience,
and he put the moral if not the legal position very
clearly in the speech he made in his defence during his
trial in a makeshift courthouse in Regina. His words still
echo in pleas for the rights of minorities in our society
today:

> I suppose the Half-breeds in Manitoba, in 1870, did
> not fight for two hundred and forty acres of land, but
> it is to be understood that there were two societies
> who treated together. One was small, but in its small-
> ness it had its rights. The other was great, but in its
> greatness it had no greater rights than the rights of
> the small, because the right is the same for everyone,
> and when they began by treating the leaders of that
> small community as bandits, as outlaws, leaving them
> without protection, they disorganized that
> community.[25]

For many decades after 1885 the Métis remained a disor-
ganized, marginal community in Canadian society and it

is only recently that they have re-established a kind of unity and cohesion as a people.

CHAPTER
15

The Flood of Settlement

EFFECTIVE TRANSPORTATION, THE SPREAD of population and the development of the country have always been interdependent in Canada. Settlement in New France occurred around the navigable waterways, the St Lawrence and the Richelieu. Across the continent, birchbark canoes opened up the land for trade and exploration. Steamboats, canals, roads and eventually railroads like the Great Western and the Grand Trunk took the settlement of rural Ontario to saturation point by the middle of the 1860s. And the settlement of the West depended on the great transcontinental railroads, for the first of which it had to wait until the mid-1880s.

Among the terms on which British Columbia agreed to enter Confederation was the promise that Canada would begin within two years, and complete within ten years, a railway connecting the Pacific seaboard with the existing railroad system in eastern Canada. It was an extraordinary promise: a country of fewer than 3,700,000 people in 1871, with an existing railroad mileage of less than 2,500, proposed to build a railroad 3,000 miles long across the rock and muskeg of the Shield, over the empty prairies, and through British Columbia's multiple ranges of mountains, in order to link up with a province whose population was less than 40,000 people, of whom three-quarters were Indians. And, since railways in Canada had become a matter of politics as much as of economics, the Canadian government soon encountered difficulties.

The Dominion was already burdened by the promise to build an intercolonial railway that for the first time would link Quebec and Ontario with the Atlantic provinces, and this one — seven hundred miles long — was not completed until 1876. In the meantime Parliament decreed that the western railway must be constructed by private enterprise, and since this would be a risky proposition for any group of financiers, the government decided to follow American precedent and offer subsidies. Arrangements were made provisionally for a syndicate headed by Sir Hugh Allan, the shipping magnate, to build the railway in return for a large grant of public funds plus generous allocations of land. But Sir John A. Macdonald's political opponents discovered that the prime minister had taken election funds from the Allan group, and in the ensuing Pacific Scandal his Conservative government was forced to resign and a Liberal administration came into power under Alexander Mackenzie. The new government refused to grant funds or lands to any railway company and made a mere token start by laying 160 miles of track in the easier stretches of the prairie. Angry British Columbians threatened to secede from Confederation and were only placated when Macdonald and the Conservatives returned to power in 1878 and made the construction of the railway a plank in their National Policy platform.

After many vicissitudes the Canadian Pacific Railway moved towards completion. In the spring of 1885 it carried into the prairies the little army that defeated the Northwest rebellion, and by using thousands of Chinese labourers its engineers completed the difficult British

Columbian stretches of the line so that the last spike
was driven in the heart of the Monashee range in November 1885. Regular passenger service across Canada
was established by the following summer. The country
was at last united by a bond of steel, not just one of ca-
pricious sentiment, and from this point on there was
very little talk in British Columbia of secession.

IN THE PLAINS THE IMMIGRANTS had not waited for the railway. During the 1870s they began to arrive, singly and
in small groups, carrying their belongings in convoys of
creaking Red River carts, often with livestock trailing behind, over the historic Carlton Trail to the northern
parkland. By 1875 the pioneers had reached Battleford
on the North Saskatchewan, where they founded a settlement that became the temporary capital of the Northwestern Territory. Also during the 1870s American
ranchers began to push northward from Montana into
the Alberta foothills, establishing the western Canadian
cattle-breeding industry.

In 1874 the first of the great collective settlements began. It consisted of 7,500 German-speaking Mennonites,
who had been allowed by Catherine the Great to settle
on the Russian steppes, and left that country because of
religious persecution. Because of their Russian experience, the Mennonites made a special contribution to the
settlement of the prairies. On the steppes they had
learned how to dry-farm successfully without being
close to a river, which the original Red River settlers had
believed was necessary. The next year, in 1875, 1,250
Icelanders arrived, in flight from the eruption of Mount
Hecla, and founded their settlement of Gimli ("the great
hall of Heaven") on Lake Winnipeg. There they combined farming with commercial fishing. At the same
time Swedish farmers began to move northward from
the Dakotas, and by the early 1880s English gentlemen
farmers were attempting to establish themselves in
southern Saskatchewan. Several hundred Jewish refu-

gees, fleeing the pogroms in Russia, arrived in Winnipeg, and while most of them remained in the city to become artisans, shopkeepers and sweatshop workers,
some of them tried homesteading, and a few Jewish settlements were established under the patronage of a European philanthropist, Baron de Hirsch. However, they
had little of the agricultural success that was later
achieved by the *kibbutzim* in Israel. But even with these
varied and sometimes large groups, the prairies were
populated slowly, and by 1880 there were still only
about 120,000 people in Manitoba and the Northwestern
Territory, of whom a mere 40,000 were newcomers from
abroad and from the rest of Canada.

As the railway moved across the prairies in the early
1880s, in the flatter stretches at the rate of as much as
three miles a day, it spawned villages and small towns.
Regina and Calgary, both children of the railway, were
populated mostly by land speculators, and soon had
their lawyers' offices, farm equipment warehouses and
newspapers. These were the same places where men
had once waited for months on end until the arrival of
the fur brigade would inform them of what had been
happening the previous year in the outside world. But
the flow of immigrants was still slower than either politicians or speculators had expected. This was in spite of
the fact that the Canadian government offered free
homestead land to all comers, and the Canadian Pacific
Railway sold at cheap rates the 25 million acres of choice
land it had received as a subsidy. By 1891 there were
still only a quarter of a million people living on the prairies, though by now well over half of them were newcomers.

The settlement of the prairies had become a prime
objective of Canadian governments, whatever their political complexion, since they realized the general economic development of the country depended on it. It
had been an essential part of Macdonald's National Policy, and it became one of the main goals of the Liberal

government under Wilfrid Laurier which in 1896
brought to an end the long period of Conservative rule
in Canada. Laurier appointed Clifford Sifton, an Ontarian who had already made a name for himself in Manitoba provincial politics, as minister of the interior, in
charge of immigration. Sifton set about his work in a
vigorous but not always popular way.

He recognized that the British Isles, which had contributed so much to the population of Upper Canada
and the Atlantic provinces, could no longer provide the
number of immigrants that were needed to fill the prairies, nor were British immigrants always the kind of
people who could face up to the rigours of prairie settlement. If the west were to be filled quickly with hard-
working farmers, he reasoned, he must attract people
from continental Europe, and he must do so by persuading them that Canada had something better to offer
than the closed societies of the Old World. This led to
the first in a series of major shifts in Canadian immigration policy, which up to this time had been dominated
by a narrow racism. Anglo-Saxons had been regarded as
the most desirable immigrants, followed by Scandinavi-
ans and Germans. Out of deference to Quebec, objec-
tions were not raised against the French, though in the
nineteenth century they were not an emigrating people
and few of them reached Canada. Other Latins were
suspect, and even more so were the Slavs of Eastern Europe.

But it was among the Slavs that Sifton saw the likeli-
est untapped source of hardy farmers he considered
necessary for prairie settlement. So in the face of a prejudiced opposition he directed his efforts to persuading
the subject peoples of the Russian and Austrian empires
that Canada could offer them not only land but freedom. He was particularly fortunate with the Ukrainians
(who in those days were generally called Galicians).
They were not only eager to escape the yoke of the Russian or Austrian overlords; they, like the Russian

Mennonites, were also used to farming the steppes. They were therefore unlikely to be troubled by the climatic extremes of the prairies. When he was attacked by racial bigots for bringing the Ukrainians in, Sifton made a classic reply: "I think a stalwart peasant in a sheepskin coat, with a stout wife and half-a-dozen children, is good quality."

Sifton had reached a decision that would change the whole demographic picture of Canada. It would add to the peoples of British and French origin a third current of people of other origins that eventually accounted for a fourth of the whole population of Canada and made it a multicultural if not a multilingual country. His solution changed the face of the prairies, for by 1911 the population of the plains had leapt from the quarter of a million who lived there twenty years before to more than 1,300,000. Sixty thousand of these people were born outside Canada, and they included not only Ukrainians but also Czechs and Slovaks, Poles and Hungarians, Serbs and Croats. All of them preserved something of their native culture, many of them retaining their native languages, publishing their own newspapers and carrying on their literary traditions, so that some of the finest Ukrainian, Icelandic and Hungarian poets of modern times have been Canadian residents.

As the southern prairies began to fill up along the track of the Canadian Pacific, the later groups of newcomers began to move into the parklands of northern Manitoba and Saskatchewan. The growing season there was appreciably shorter, but in 1907 Charles Saunders developed his fast-maturing strain of wheat called Marquis, which made it possible to grow large crops on the fertile lands along the North Saskatchewan. Here there was an even more intimate relationship than in the southern plains between railway building and settlement, for by the late 1890s a railway boom had developed in the West and two competing lines moved into this northern area. The Canadian Northern, which would eventually run through Edmonton and over the Yellowhead Pass to Vancouver, opening up the northern Ontario wilderness on the way, was incorporated in 1899. The Grand Trunk Pacific, an offshoot of the original Grand Trunk Railway, started to move westward in 1907, also using the Yellowhead Pass and then running down the Skeena River valley to reach saltwater at Prince Rupert. Most of the navvying work on these railways was done by East European immigrants for whom it provided a basic income until their homesteads began to produce crops. By 1914 Canada had more than thirty thousand miles of railroad, the highest ratio of track to population in the whole world.

The two competing northern railways soon proved uneconomical, and eventually, between 1919 and 1923, they were taken over by the federal government and incorporated into the Canadian National Railways. But they had completed their task of settling the prairies. During the years after they were opened to traffic new Canadians came in such numbers that, though there was no immigration during the Great War, by 1921 2,000,000 people were living on the prairies, almost a quarter of the population of Canada; 800,000 of them had been born abroad, and another 350,000 of them hailed from the more easterly Canadian provinces. During these final pre-war years, immigration was at its historic high point. Between 1910 and 1913 almost 1,400,000 people came to Canada, and many more stayed than in the past. They included a considerable surge of British immigrants, the largest since the 1840s, and also many Americans, who at this time were beginning to experience land-hunger in the Midwest. They were attracted by Canadian immigration propaganda to try their skills at dry-soil farming and open up the arid Palliser Triangle in southern Saskatchewan.

THE LAND ALL THESE PIONEER SETTLERS ENTERED bore little resemblance to the well-farmed prairie provinces of the twentieth century. The first settlers, who came before the railways arrived, had to set out over the open plains on journeys of hundreds of miles with their Red River carts or covered wagons, following deeply rutted trails, on which their vehicles would often mire down. Even the railways brought the homesteaders only part of the way. There were still many miles of roadless country to be traversed by wagon, with livestock following behind and nightly camps until the homestead was reached — and that would be a speck of land in an ocean of grass.

The wild prairie, with its abundance of flowers and migratory birds and its atmospheric extremes, could be extraordinarily beautiful, but the pioneers had no time for aesthetic pleasures. The thick pelt of grasses had to be broken, and often it provided material for the homesteader's first house. The sod house, or "soddy," was at least warm in winter and cool in summer, though it never kept out heavy rainfalls. Since he had to become as self-sufficient as possible, with stores far away and profitable crops several years ahead, the pioneer's first task after building his soddy would be to establish a garden. Then he would start the breaking of the tough tangle of prairie grasses, not only so that he could start sowing wheat as soon as possible, but also because the best protection against the lethal fires that often swept over the prairies was to plough a good firebreak around one's house. Water was often alkaline or otherwise polluted, or the land was marshy, and then the mosquitoes would be almost unendurable. But every homesteader was driven on by the fact that by the end of three years he must not only have his house built, but also have a substantial area of land broken and sown if he wished to gain title to his quarter-section of 160 acres.

Women shared fully in the toils and privations of prairie pioneering. They had to carry out all the tasks of a largely self-sufficient life in the same way as their predecessors in Upper Canada. They endured greater remoteness, however, and a far harsher climate, in which

it was possible to grow fewer items than in central
Canada. As for natural fuel, the turf was often all that
was available. Many necessities had to be bought, and,
thus, until the first crops came in, or when crops failed,
essentials were often in short supply. Sometimes the
women helped in breaking the land; Doukhobor women
harnessed themselves in teams of twenty to the ploughs
because they could not afford many horses. And always, in the early days, the women — and the children
— had to help in the harvest, which at first was reaped
with sickles and scythes. Only in later decades did they
use the combines that were now being made in the
Ontario implement factories. When the itinerant threshing crews began to travel from farm to farm with their
big steam traction engines, the women also had to cook
for them, for a farmer's reputation could rest on the
quality and abundance of the food his wife provided on
such occasions.

Out of this harsh life there developed an extraordinary degree of cooperativeness. As soon as there were
enough settlers to form local communities, usually
around the railroad stations, a social life and a great deal
of mutual aid developed, centred usually around the
churches and the tiny one-room schools. The prairie
people needed and helped each other during the crises
of childbirth and sickness and death. By 1905, when
Saskatchewan and Alberta were separated from the
Northwest Territories and transformed into new provinces, a more-or-less stable agricultural economy had
emerged, along with a vigorous and resilient local society distinguished by the virtues of endurance and cooperativeness. They were characteristics that stood prairie
dwellers in good stead when their economy faltered
during the Depression of the 1930s and drought turned
their farms into dust.

Before the discovery of oil in Alberta and of potash
in Saskatchewan, prairie life was in fact perilously dependent on one crop. As Stephen Leacock once re-

marked: "The Lord said, 'Let there be Wheat,' and Saskatchewan was born." But dependence on a single crop gave a grand simplicity to rural life in the prairies, and to the prairie year, which would begin with the late spring sowing, continue through a summer of work punctuated by picnics (political and otherwise) and reach its high point every autumn when the wheat was cut. During harvest season the threshing teams wandered over the plains of golden stubble, and the farmers took their wagons of grain to the clusters of grain elevators in the villages that were situated every twelve miles or so along the railway lines.

The harsh winters lasted five months, and during bad weather people endured long periods of isolation, which tended to produce a breed of thoughtful individualists. Prairie religion was inclined to be evangelical and fissiparous, providing a great variety of revivalist schisms and offshoots. Prairie politics tended to be populist and radical. When religion and politics combined, as they did in such characteristic prairie movements as the Progressive Party, the Social Credit Party in Alberta, and the mildly socialist Co-operative Commonwealth Federation, founded in Saskatchewan, they were capable of shaking accepted patterns and entrenched establishments. Nor was prairie radicalism the prerogative of men alone; the prevalent yearning for independence expressed itself also in an advanced attitude towards the emancipation of women. It was in the prairie provinces that, in 1916, women were first allowed to vote in Canada, while in Alberta women were allowed to become magistrates before they received such appointments anywhere else in the British Empire.

Political radicalism is usually the product of an urban society; on the prairies it developed out of the simplicities of a rural life where issues were clear and all men quickly realized, whatever their ethnic origins, that they shared the same enemies: the weather, the railways that

overcharged them and the grain merchants who underpaid them.

BEYOND THE MOUNTAINS, in the far western province of
British Columbia, the very configuration of the country
imposed a different pattern of settlement and development from that of the prairies. There were no vast, un-
broken areas of fertile land as there were on the central
plains of North America. Most of the province consisted
of mountainside fit only for growing forests. Where
open plateau areas did exist, as in the drylands of central British Columbia, like the Cariboo and Chilcotin regions, they were for the most part too arid or devoid of
soil for cultivation and so could be used only as ranch-
land. Except for the grain-growing Peace River country,
which was really an extension of the prairies, agricultural possibilities were confined to the valleys between
the mountains. Apart from the lower Fraser valley and
the Okanagan valley, these tended to be too narrow to
allow for much cultivation. Some river valleys, like the
Nass and Skeena, were too far north to allow for any diversity of crops. British Columbia has only 2 percent of
the agricultural land in Canada. The fact that it accounts
for as much as 5 percent of the agricultural production is
due to intense specialization in certain areas — such as
the fruit- and wine-growing Okanagan and the dairying
Fraser valley. Farming has always been the least of the
primary industries of British Columbia, trailing after logging, mining and fishing, and this has greatly affected
the province's patterns of settlement and population.

On the prairies, where farming was the principal industry until far into the present century, other activities
tended to be ancillary to it. In British Columbia the reverse was true. Farming began on southern Vancouver
Island and around the trading posts of New Caledonia
to provision the fur traders. In the second half of the
nineteenth century, it continued to provision the gold
miners. The first ranches of the interior, for instance,

supplied the miners of Barkerville, and in areas as far away as Kamloops cattle were being reared in the 1860s to be sold to those working the goldfields. Ever since that time the agricultural production of British Columbia — in ranching, dairying and truck gardening — has been devoted, never adequately, to meeting the needs of those who live by other industries in the same province. The exception is the Okanagan valley, whose orchards and vineyards, first planted by Catholic missionaries in the 1860s, produce fruit and wine that form British Columbia's only exported crops apart from Peace River wheat.

This situation has profoundly affected the social and demographic patterns in British Columbia. There was never the need, as there had been in both Upper Canada and the prairies, to encourage massive immigration in order to build up a farming population. When the migrant flocks of placer miners had skimmed off the immediately available gold deposits, little remained to encourage a rapid growth of population until the logging industry was commercially developed later in the century. Indeed, when British Columbia became a province of Canada in 1871 it had far fewer non-Indian inhabitants than at the height of the Cariboo Gold Rush nine years before, and it had the look of a community in decline. Even in 1891 the population of the province was a mere 98,000, and not until the end of the century did it begin to pick up, reaching about 180,000 in 1901, and coming just short of 400,000 in 1911.

THE ETHNIC ORIGINS OF THIS POPULATION were strikingly different from those of the population of the territories east of the Continental Divide. There had been no need to call on the men in sheepskins to fill the empty lands, though six thousand Russian Doukhobors did arrive in 1906. They settled as a community in the valleys of the Kootenay area after they had failed to agree with the Canadian government on the terms of their settlement on the prairies. As religious anarchists, the Doukhobors had refused to take the oath of allegiance under the Dominion Lands Act and had been evicted from their homesteads.

But the largest body of British Columbian immigrants, who were perhaps attracted by the province's name, had been British, and in 1911 the number of Britons actually exceeded the number of locally born inhabitants. They were of three distinctly different types: members of the gentry and upper middle class who often went in for fruit farming or ranching, lower-middle-class white-collar workers, and artisans who imported English trade union traditions and helped to sustain the confrontational pattern that began to characterize British Columbian society at this period. Friction was especially evident in the logging and mining industries, in which wealthy, autocratic entrepreneurs clashed with members of militant unions, often imported from the United States, like the strongly syndicalist Industrial Workers of the World. To this day the heritage of that turn-of-the-century confrontationalism lingers in British Columbian industrial relations and in class relations as a whole. The province has remained as it was at the turn of the century, a haven of snobbery unrivalled in Canada, but also, as in the years leading up to the Great War, the most industrially exploitive province in Canada. In recent years, however, British Columbia has shown nothing to rival the 1914 riots in the coal town of Nanaimo on Vancouver Island. Then the striking miners took over the town in protest against the employment of Chinese and Japanese strikebreakers. The British Columbia government mobilized the militia, which occupied Nanaimo for almost a year.

The presence of Chinese workers on this occasion illustrates another unusual feature of British Columbia's population. Since the turn of the century British Columbia has maintained the highest proportion of Asians in the country. Many of the Chinese who had come during

the Gold Rush remained, and during the 1870s a second
wave arrived, brought in directly from Canton province
by labour contractors. They worked for the mining syndicates, on farms, in the new fish canneries and as domestic servants. By 1880 there were four thousand of
them, compared to twenty thousand Caucasians, and
the labour unions of the time, especially the Knights of
Labor (whose constitution ironically included a clause
welcoming workers of all races), were militantly opposed to importing more of them for fear of depressing
the general level. Under pressure, the provincial government banned the employment of Chinese on public
works in 1878, and in 1879 Amor de Cosmos presented
to Parliament a petition from fifteen hundred British Columbian working men asking for an end to Chinese immigration.

By 1882, however, full construction had begun on
the Canadian Pacific Railway in British Columbia, and it
was evident that there was not enough local labour to
complete it. With the approval of Sir John A. Macdonald, the contractor Andrew Onderdonk imported ten
thousand Chinese coolies via Hong Kong. They were
scandalously underpaid, at a dollar a day, but they were
willing to accept dangerous tasks. We know that many
of them died in building the CPR; we do not know how
many. It was a wholly male migration; the Chinese
brought no women, since they intended to return home
when they had earned enough money, and many of
them did. But enough remained to offer sustained competition to white workers, and attitudes to them tended
to polarize along class lines. Employers like the mine-
owner Robert Dunsmuir found them helpful in combat-
ing militant miners; he first used them for strikebreaking
at Nanaimo as early as 1883. Merchants in Victoria and
Vancouver found them diligent and inexpensive servants, who made possible a lifestyle not unlike that of
the tycoons on the China Coast. But organized labour
feared them and racial prejudice in British Columbia was

for many years most rampant in the working class. The first anti-Chinese riots took place in Vancouver in 1887.

By the 1890s a further Asian element was added to the population by the arrival of the first Japanese, who entered the fishing industry in considerable numbers, and by their competition added the local fishermen to the ranks of the racially prejudiced. In 1907 there were serious anti-Asian riots in Vancouver once again, during which the Japanese fought back against their attackers.

The politicians tried in various ways to please their voters by inhibiting the entry of Asians. The provincial government began by trying to impose restrictions based on those used in Natal, South Africa, making language proficiency a test for entry. These regulations were disallowed by the federal government, which instead imposed a series of head taxes, beginning at fifty dollars in 1885, rising to one hundred dollars in 1901 (by which time there were almost fourteen thousand Chinese as well as six thousand Japanese in the province). The tax rose to five hundred dollars in 1905. When these measures ceased to work, they were replaced in 1923 by the Chinese Immigration Act, which kept out all Chinese apart from diplomatic personnel, and remained in force for many years. In the case of the Japanese, diplomatic negotiations with the government in Tokyo rather than laws made in Ottawa were used to regulate the situation, and after 1908 the flow of immigrants from Japan slowed down.

A further Asian element was added to the population of British Columbia and Canada in the early twentieth century by the arrival of Sikhs from India. Some came north over the border from the United States, whence they had been expelled by the immigration authorities. Others came from Hong Kong, where they had served as part of the British garrison. By 1907 there were over four thousand Sikhs. Like the Chinese they would work for any wages they could get — especially in the timber industry — in order to establish themselves in the small businesses they liked to conduct and enlarge, and this made them as unpopular with non-Asian labourers as the Chinese and the Japanese. But they were British subjects, and claimed a special status on that account. In 1908, however, orders-in-council were issued to restrict their entry, which then narrowed to a trickle, and by 1914 enough Sikhs departed for their numbers to be reduced to a hard core of about two thousand who remained.

In that year there occurred an incident that dramatized the growing restrictiveness of Canadian immigration policy. A Japanese steamer, the *Komagata Maru*, sailing from Hong Kong, arrived in Vancouver harbour with 376 prospective Sikh immigrants on board. They were refused permission to land, and for weeks the ship lay in Vancouver harbour as the immigration authorities sought deportation orders from the courts. A pitched battle was fought, with the Sikhs hurling volleys of coal, when 175 police and immigration officers tried in vain to board the ship and transfer its passengers to a liner leaving for Hong Kong. Finally, the recently created Royal Canadian Navy went into action for the first time when the cruiser *Rainbow* was called from Esquimalt on July 23, 1914, to escort out to sea this invasion of British subjects with the wrong skin colour. The incident brought to a somewhat discreditable close the era of settlement before the great wars transformed Canadian society.

PART
VI

CHAPTER
16

Canada and the Great Wars

THE GREAT WARS OF THE TWENTIETH CENTURY changed
Canada both socially and politically, not by introducing
new social developments but by accelerating those that
already existed. To use a biological analogy, they resembled the periods when the gradual processes of evolution suddenly take on the impetus of a dramatic
mutation, and changes that have been long developing
are all at once made evident and irreversible. During the
course of human history there have been many such periods of rapid change, which one discovers were actually
long in the preparation, when one traces their antecedents.

The first Great War, which lasted from 1914 to 1918,
tested the very structure of Canada as an emerging nation. The population of the country in 1914 was still
barely eight million, yet the strength of imperial sentiment at the time was so powerful that the country's political leaders, who were Conservative and English-
speaking, pledged half a million soldiers, out of a working population of at most three million. Recent English
and Scottish immigrants enlisted in large numbers. The

Canadian-born and immigrants from the continent of Europe were less enthusiastic, and the people of Quebec showed themselves the truest North Americans of all in their reluctance to sacrifice themselves in the quarrels of the imperial powers.

Indeed, they were so detached from European considerations that even the plight of a France (from which they had so long been alienated) did not move them. When an election was fought in mid-war on the issue of conscription, the French Canadians voted overwhelmingly against it. In English-speaking Canada, however, the opposition consisted only of an unorganized grouping of trade unionists, pacifists and farmers, many of whom were suspect because of their German ancestry. The conscription forces won the day, though their attempts to force French Canadians into the fighting lines were mainly unsuccessful. The result was a mutual bitterness between the two major ethnic groups in Canada which eliminated much of the goodwill built up between English- and French-speaking reformers in the years after the 1837–38 rebellions, and this acrimony laid the foundations for the epic disputes of the 1960s and 1970s between Canadian federalists and Québécois separatists.

In World War II the scenario would be repeated almost act for act, with a hesitant government (Liberal this time) deferring to majority English-speaking sentiment and once again passing a conscription bill bitterly opposed by French Canadian nationalists and largely evaded by the inhabitants of Quebec.

Yet while both wars exacerbated the cultural differences within Canadian society, they not only enhanced the role of Canada within the Empire and later the Commonwealth, but also established it as an independent polity. By the end of the Great War nobody seriously believed that the British Empire could be reconstructed as a federation of equals — a concept that had been widely discussed in the Edwardian era. There were too many differences between the interests of the various dominions and colonies and the parent country. On the other hand, Canada had made a major contribution to the war. A largely autonomous and militarily effective Canadian corps captured Vimy Ridge in 1917 and otherwise served well on the western front, and sixty thousand Canadians had died in battle. This gave the country a higher profile and allowed it to play an increasingly independent role in the years following the armistice of November 1918. At the end-of-war conference that culminated in the Treaty of Versailles, it appeared as a power distinct from the United Kingdom. When the League of Nations was founded in 1919, Canada became a member in its own right. And in 1922 it demonstrated that it was not willing to pledge unconditional support to imperial aims. In that year, during the Chanak crisis, Mackenzie King refused to commit his country to hostilities with Turkey at Britain's behest.

THE CUMULATIVE RESULT OF SUCH SHOWS of independence by Canada and the other dominions was the historic series of imperial proclamations between the wars recognizing first of all the virtual and then the actual independence of the already self-governing dominions. There was the declaration inspired by Lord Balfour in 1926, which declared Britain and the dominions constitutionally "equal in status." This was followed by the Statute of Westminster in 1931, an act of the British Parliament which finally ended the colonial status of Canada and the other dominions by giving them full local freedom except in such areas as they chose to remain subordinate. With the encouragement of such developments, Canada began to emerge as a full-fledged member of the family of nations. Sir Wilfrid Laurier had established a department of external affairs in 1909, but apart from appointing a high commissioner in London, the department existed in embryo until the 1920s. For the most part Canadian affairs abroad were still conducted through British missions in the appropriate countries. But in 1926 a Canadian embassy was established in Washington, to be followed by similar missions in Paris in 1928, in Tokyo in 1929, and in Belgium and the Netherlands in 1939. A full-scale diplomatic service with posts in seventy-five countries would develop later in the century, after World War II had further enhanced Canada's stature in the world community.

These, of course, were political and also largely military developments in a peaceful community uncharacteristically engaged in bitter warfare, but they had social consequences. Canadians began to look at themselves differently, and in some ways this countered the divisive aspects of both wars, which had tended to set the English against Canadians of other ancestries. During the wars, indeed, Canadians reverted to looking at each other in pre-Canadian ways, as British or French or German first of all, and therefore as potential rivals or even enemies according to the ways of the Old World. But the emergence of Canada as a separate entity within the Empire that was changing gradually into the Commonwealth, and as a nation among nations within the broader world context, caused people to think less of what divided them than of what united them. They shared a single, if immense, geographical terrain, a common historical tradition in which their various pasts intermingled of necessity, and an identity in which the sense of being colonial — and therefore being linked irrevocably to a land far away — metamorphosed into a sense of being Canadian.

The steadily increasing proportion of the population born in Canada also had its effect on developing a national rather than a colonial consciousness. The floods of immigrants that came after each of the great wars did not change the whole nature of Canadian society in the same way that previous immigration waves had done: the Loyalists in the 1780s, the British poor in the 1830s and 1840s and the "men in sheepskins" in the 1890s. The post-war immigrants played roles of enhancement and variegation, enriching what had now become a truly national community, self-contained and consistent within itself. The Citizenship Act of 1947 was of great symbolic as well as actual importance because it gave definition to the sense of being a Canadian. We were no longer in the era when our passports intimated that a Canadian was still a British subject. A Canadian was, by definition, a person born in Canada or who had elected to become Canadian by naturalization, and this entailed abandoning past allegiances; Britain was at last recognized as another country.

The Canada whose basic population the Citizenship Act defined, without rejecting the always considerable population of landed immigrants who had not made their final choice of allegiance, was a rural country that had become urbanized without abandoning the wilderness. It was an agrarian country that had become industrialized without cutting its links with the land, and it was a country that had gone through grave economic crisis and class struggles, as well as ethnic conflict. But Canada was already moving in the direction of a pluralistic society and towards the elimination of discrimination, both in regard to those already in the country and to those who sought to enter it.

CHAPTER
17

The Rise of the Cities

WHEN THE NINETEENTH CENTURY BEGAN, the colonies of
British North America were overwhelmingly rural, and
more than 90 percent of the people were country dwellers. Not all of them were farmers, since a considerable
number of the people who lived in Newfoundland and
the Atlantic provinces and along the shores of the St
Lawrence depended mainly on fishing. A smaller number were involved in the fur trade and in mining. Nevertheless, probably about 75 percent of the fewer than
four hundred thousand people dwelling in the various
colonies lived mainly by farming. (Some of these, however, did play a seasonal part in the emergent logging
industry or in the building of wooden ships in the varied economy of New Brunswick and Nova Scotia.) Quebec, already a city in miniature with the fine buildings
that were the heritage of New France, had about eight
thousand inhabitants, and there were four other places
that by European standards might be considered towns
because of their population and commercial importance:
Montreal and Halifax, St John's and Saint John. Other
places, like Fredericton and Charlottetown, Trois-

Rivières and Lunenburg, York and Kingston, may have had their importance as administrative or trading centres, but in terms of population and development they were hardly more than villages.

During the generations that followed, Canadian society became steadily urbanized. The great migrations of the mid- and late nineteenth century filled the rural lands of Ontario and the prairies, but a certain proportion of the migrants always stayed behind in the towns, finding employment in the growing commerce that fed in from the agrarian hinterland and from the mining areas. And so villages were turned into towns and towns into cities.

Yet the real trend towards urbanization in Canada did not seriously begin until the disparate colonies had become united in a single country. As separate colonies, none of which before Confederation contained many more than a million inhabitants, they did not have the social and commercial infrastructures that could produce large cities. On the Atlantic seaboard the Maritime colonies carried on their commercial activities more or less independently of the more inland provinces, to which they had no year-round transport links until the Intercolonial Railway was completed in 1876. They traded with the United States, Britain and the West Indies rather than with the two Canadian provinces, and acted largely as entrepôts for trades that were dominated by merchants in London.

BECAUSE OF THE TRANSPORTATION SYSTEM based on the St Lawrence, there was a necessary interconnection between Upper Canada and Lower Canada, which controlled the upper province's outlet to the sea. It was because of this fact that Montreal developed into the largest city in British North America, with a population of 115,000 at Confederation, more than twice that of Toronto, which had displaced Quebec as its principal rival.

Montreal had begun as a fur-trading centre, but after the union of the North West Company with the Hudson's Bay Company, it became the distribution centre at the junction of the navigable St Lawrence and the transportation system of the increasingly agriculture-dominated interior. Two developments at that time enabled Montreal to pull ahead of Quebec in both commercial importance and population. One was the exhaustion of the lower St Lawrence forests, whose timber had been exported from Quebec. The principal source of timber outside New Brunswick had become the Ottawa valley, and great timber rafts began to make their way down the Ottawa River to Montreal. From there the timber was loaded into the ships on which the poor immigrants had come to the Canadas. The other important development was the increase in steam navigation, which enabled ships to come without difficulty as far as Montreal, where they were halted by the Lachine rapids. Montreal thus became the unrivalled centre for the export of grain and other farm products from Upper Canada, and that trade rapidly increased when the Corn Laws were repealed in Britain. In addition, Montreal was the landing point of the majority of the immigrants coming from Europe from the 1830s until the death of the passenger lines after World War II. Many of those early immigrants, especially the Irish, stayed in Montreal to meet the growing demand for labour in this port city where industry began to develop early.

The influx of British newcomers of all classes, from merchants down to labourers, during the early part of the nineteenth century, meant that Montreal acquired a mixed population. Until the 1870s the majority were British, and because of its situation and its early start as a commercial centre, Montreal would become Canada's first metropolitan city. It would become the focal point of Canada's railroad system and the financial centre of Canada, as well as its principal seaport, rivalled only by Halifax, which had the advantage of a frost-free harbour during the winter. Montreal would hold this position well into the twentieth century.

As the nineteenth century went on and settlement covered the arable land, the inland towns began to grow, first as centres from which the produce of the countryside was distributed and which provided the farmers with the necessities they could not grow or make for themselves. Later they became the commercial focal points of settled regions, and towards the end of the nineteenth century, they combined manufacturing and commerce, and sometimes the industry of government. Later a few of them, as we shall see, would take on the cultural attributes of diversified metropoles.

A major shift in the direction of Canadian development was heralded by the National Policy which Sir John A. Macdonald introduced in the federal election of 1878, proclaiming that it would be appropriate to the continent-wide nation that Canada had become. Two of the elements of the National Policy related to the settlement era: the building of the transcontinental railroad and the populating of the prairies by immigrants from Europe. But a third element was directed towards bringing the Industrial Revolution into Canada and making it something more than a nation devoted to the primary industries of farming and fishing, mining and logging. This was the policy of protective tariffs, designed to foster Canadian manufacturing, for which the new farmers inhabiting the prairies were expected to provide an ever-growing market. The coming of industry, which will be dealt with in more detail in the next chapter, brought changes in the character of Canadian communities, and resulted in urban population increases that were disproportionately high, compared to the rural increases in population. Even at the time of Confederation, except for the major centres of Montreal and Toronto, Canada was still a country of small towns, even if some of them served as miniature capitals, of villages and above all of isolated farmsteads. Less than 20 percent of Canadians lived in urban centres, that is, places with one thousand inhabitants or more.

THERE WAS FAR MORE VARIETY among these mid-nineteenth century communities than there is among the Canadian towns of the late twentieth century. Many of them were marked by the characteristics of the urban cultures in the countries from which their inhabitants originally came. Quebec towered over the St Lawrence in the mediaeval solidity of its fortifications, greeting the traveller approaching up the river with an image of imperial might, but its streets of tall, stone-faced houses, like those of the older parts of Montreal, were likely to remind visitors of the old port towns of the French north coast: Le Havre, Honfleur and St Malo. Smaller Québécois towns like Trois-Rivières and Sorel and the lesser villages along the river were dominated by the steep-roofed fieldstone houses, modelled on Norman peasant homes, which Krieghoff immortalized in his paintings of *habitant* life. By now most of the original thatched roofs had been replaced by sheet metal, which dazzlingly reflected the sun mile after mile along the St Lawrence.

Halifax was a handsome stone and wood town that had not yet been defeated by the slums that came later in the nineteenth century as a result of the commercial recession following Confederation. Fredericton was elegantly Georgian, as it still is for the most part, and so were Kingston and other towns along the Ontario lakeshore. Even Toronto, which was about to enter its industrial age, had some of this air of a pleasant colonial backwater. Some of the lesser Maritime towns resembled those of New England from which many of their citizens had come. Berlin in Ontario and Lunenburg in Nova Scotia had German-style architecture and were surrounded by farms of Germanic neatness. In Ottawa, the capital of the province of Canada since 1857, the Gothic revival buildings of the Canadian Parliament had been going up beside the river since 1859, and by

Confederation they were ready for use. But the city was still a centre to which the great rafts of logs came down and were sawn into the squared timbers that were floated downriver to Montreal. The last great raft of dressed timber went down in 1901; by then the forests were stripped of saleable timber and Ottawa settled into its role as the national capital. Everywhere, as in Europe, the buildings were still low, and the profiles of towns and villages were dominated by the towers and pinnacles of churches, which were well attended, for Canada was still a demonstratively religious country.

Still beyond civilization, on Hudson Bay and in the prairies, were the stone and log forts of the traders and the first small missionary settlements, and along the Red River straggled the wooden farmhouses of Métis and Scottish settlers that later became part of Winnipeg. But there was no place that could fairly be called a town in the whole expanse of Rupert's Land, and even beyond the Rockies the gold-mining towns were in decay. The coastal tribes who still lived in their villages of large communal longhouses were still fishermen without a sense of urban values in spite of their artistic sophistication. New Westminster, which had been a temporary capital of British Columbia, remained a very small town, and would be rapidly overshadowed in the 1880s by the new community of Vancouver. Victoria was the only real city left over from the Gold Rush, with its massive San Francisco style warehouses near the waterfront and its elegant wooden mansions on the slopes behind.

The growth of the cities from this point in relation to the rural population was steady and relentless. By the end of the nineteenth century almost 35 percent of Canadians lived in urban centres, and the 50 percent mark was passed at some point in the 1920s. Curiously, the watershed of transition was marked by a brief but dramatic realization on the part of farmers that political power would soon slip out of their hands. After the Great War came to an end, social discontents were increasingly channelled into militant movements, and the farmers' groups, which had long complained of railways that kept rates high, tariffs that kept the price of implements high and merchants who kept the price of grain low, decided to become politically active. The United Farmers of Alberta and Manitoba, where the farming population was still in a majority, contested and won elections in 1921 and 1922, respectively, and they ruled in Alberta until they were replaced by William Aberhart's Social Credit Party in 1935. And the Social Credit also had rural roots. The prairie farmers also created a Progressive Party, resembling the agrarian populist parties of the American Midwest. In the 1921 election they swept the West, winning sixty-five seats and forming the second-largest party in the Canadian House of Commons. Mackenzie King played on their disunity, and the Progressive Party fell apart, but it had transformed politics in the Canadian West and shaken the hold of the traditional Liberal and Conservative parties.

Even more surprising was the fact that in 1919 the United Farmers of Ontario won the election in their province, which was already well advanced in industrialization, and briefly formed a government. But these manifestations of the power of rural communities were doomed as the urban population steadily increased, reaching the 60 percent level in the early 1940s. A sign of the times was that from the 1930s on, the farmers did not seek to form parties of their own; those who were politically militant joined with industrial workers and socialist urban intellectuals to form the Co-operative Commonwealth Federation in 1932. Today, in the 1980s, more than four of every five Canadians are urban dwellers, and only one in twenty still lives by farming.

CANADA'S LARGEST CITIES HAVE REALLY BEEN mercantile ones, characterized by the concentration of economic power and social function, not by the concentration of political

power. The capital of the country is the medium-sized
city of Ottawa, and of Canada's three real metropolitan
centres only one, Toronto, is even the capital of a province. Montreal may be the commercial centre of Quebec,
but the much smaller city of Quebec is its political capital. The same is true of British Columbia, where Vancouver, as the Pacific coast metropolis, concentrates the
economic power and leaves political authority to the
much smaller city of Victoria across the water on Vancouver Island.

Another special characteristic of Canada's urban pattern has been the absence of a single major metropolis,
like London in Britain or Paris in France, that draws
power and prestige and talent towards itself. From the
time when Upper Canada acquired its own English-
speaking population and began to develop its hinterland
economy, Toronto started to emerge as the potential rival of Montreal. Nevertheless, well into the twentieth
century, while it retained its financial power and remained largely an English-speaking city, Montreal
seemed to be an all-Canadian metropolis. Its role in the
English culture of Canada in the first half of this century
was more important than that of Toronto. Modern Canadian poetry in English, for example, was virtually
born in Montreal between the 1920s and 1940s, with circles of poets that included A. J. M. Smith, F. R. Scott,
A. M. Klein, John Glassco, Irving Layton, P. K. Page
and many others. These were the poets who published
the first anglophone modernist literary magazines.
Canada's first great English-speaking painter, James Wilson Morrice, also came from Montreal.

It was not until after World War II and the rise of
Quebec separatism that Montreal became so French a
city that national financial institutions began to withdraw into Ontarian territory. At the same time, Montreal ceased to be the culturally cosmopolitan centre it
had been in its wealthiest and most vital days. It became, essentially, the economic and cultural capital of

the French-speaking third of Canada, while Toronto fulfilled the same role for the English-speaking two-thirds, not only replacing Montreal as the financial capital of the country, but also becoming the leading cultural centre of anglophone Canada, though by no means the only one. By the 1970s it had moved ahead of Montreal in terms of population, though the two urban areas each stood near the three million mark, and considerably exceeded the other two cities that can be seen as metropolitan in their role.

Of these, Winnipeg, once the most important city in the West and still the cultural centre of the prairies, began after 1918 to fall greatly behind Vancouver, which has grown steadily since its foundation in 1886 as the terminus of the Canadian Pacific Railway. Now, with a Greater Vancouver population of about 1,300,000, it is Canada's third city, possessing all the attributes of a major metropolis. With the maritime decline of Montreal owing to the end of passenger liner traffic, it is also the principal Canadian seaport and the junction of three railways that probe down to the coast. It has the largest university in Canada (and also the newest of the major academic institutions, since it began only on the eve of the Great War) and a flourishing local literary and artistic culture.

A STRIKING FEATURE OF CANADIAN patterns of communication is the tendency for large urban areas to form into decentralized clusters of cities and towns rather than continuous urban areas. Geographers have pointed out that Canada's two largest cities, Montreal and Toronto, despite their linguistic and cultural differences, have close geographical and historic links, since both are situated in the Great Lakes-St Lawrence region. They also share a history marked by simultaneous economic rivalry and a kind of fraternity, a relationship which parallels the rivalry and fraternity that has always existed between the two Canadas. The cities have grown over the same period, and their power, with fluctuations, has moved towards equality over that period.

Along the corridor of transportation and communication links that bind the two major cities has grown up a complex of smaller but still considerable cities. Those which fall into Toronto's orbit include Hamilton, which began to grow with the farm implements industry and later became a major steel-producing centre; Windsor and Oshawa, which house much of Canada's automobile industry; and other cities like Kitchener and London, which have become minor centres of financial power because of the insurance companies, trust companies and other financial institutions they have harboured. All these places live in the commercial shadow of Toronto. Farther downriver, industrial centres like Sorel, Trois-Rivières, Shawinigan and even Quebec City (insofar as it is an industrial centre) fall into the financial and commercial sphere of Montreal. This lakeshore and river strip, approximately four hundred miles long from Windsor to Sorel, but hardly fifty miles wide, represents an unrivalled concentration of financial and commercial power. Its development was fostered from as early as 1878 when Sir John A. Macdonald's National Policy began to protect central Canadian industries, and it has continued ever since to concentrate and attract major manufacturing and financial interests. Today about 80 percent of Canada's manufactured goods are produced in this area; it is the centre of three-quarters of the country's major corporations and of five-sixths of its financial institutions.

Nor is the ascendancy within Canada of this thickly populated and highly industrious double-metropolis corridor merely an economic one. Toronto and Montreal have become the leading cultural centres in anglophone and francophone Canada, respectively. Publishing, broadcasting, periodicals and film making, all the so-called cultural industries, are mainly centred there, and Montreal and Toronto tend to have the same kind of centripetal attraction for artists and intellectuals that the great cultural metropolises do in other countries.

Yet Canada has remained, for geographical, historical and political reasons, a country where regionalism is an obstinately persistent force. This tendency has been strengthened by the dual governmental structure in which the provincial governments in recent decades have increasingly become coordinate rather than subordinate powers in their relationships with the federal government. It is also encouraged by the sheer differences in the experience of living in environments as unlike each other as, say, a Newfoundland outport, a southern Ontario industrial city, a prairie railway village, a small town in the mountainous interior of British Columbia and a seashore city on the Pacific like Victoria. The different economies and cultures of the various regions, as well as their political divisions, have encouraged the emergence of local centres of considerable importance, and even of economic regions on a smaller scale not unlike that along the St Lawrence.

ALL THE MAJOR CITIES OF WESTERN CANADA appeared late and grew rapidly. Winnipeg was a wretched cluster of houses and taverns when the province of Manitoba was created in 1870, and even when it was incorporated in 1873 it had a population of less than four thousand. Fur trading may have given birth to Winnipeg, but the city did not grow up until the arrival of the railways: first the Canadian Pacific and then its two later rivals, the Canadian Northern and the Grand Trunk Pacific, all of which went through the city and had their depots there. From 1885 to 1914 Winnipeg also served as a kind of population funnel, through which the great floods of immigrants fanned out to the prairies, mostly in the two decades between the early 1890s and 1913. Capital flowed in, largely soaked up by a notable land boom in the city, and local factories and mills, setting out to serve the rapidly growing demands of the prairie farmers, made Winnipeg for a while the fourth most important manufacturing centre in Canada, after Montreal, Toronto and Hamilton. Wholesale houses, mail order firms and local financial institutions flourished. The population became diversified as some of the immigrants of European stock, including many Slavs and Jews, lingered there and mingled with the Anglo-Scottish population that had replaced the original Métis majority. For a time this created bitter ethnic tensions, but by 1953 these had died down enough for the Ukrainian Steve Juba to be elected mayor, and Winnipeg is now the cultural centre and the unnamed capital of the quarter of the Canadian population that is neither French nor English in culture.

The Great War brought an end to the original boom on which Winnipeg had grown prosperous, and it went into a decline even before the Great Depression which lasted until the economy revived during World War II. Since that time Winnipeg has grown steadily, though not so spectacularly as the cities farther west. Nevertheless, its expansion showed that urbanization had conquered even the once agrarian prairie provinces. Today almost 60 percent of the population of Manitoba lives in Winnipeg, and it dominates the region to such an extent that its only rival, Brandon, has a population of less than forty thousand.

West of Manitoba, in the younger provinces of Alberta and Saskatchewan, striking twin-city combinations once again sprang into being. The two prime cities of Saskatchewan are the capital, Regina, in the flat prairie, and Saskatoon, a more attractive city, about 150 miles northwest of the edge of the parkland. Their populations are as close as those of Toronto and Montreal, though much smaller. Regina has 160,000 inhabitants and Saskatoon about 155,000. A similar situation exists in Alberta, where the two major cities, Calgary and Edmonton, lie about two hundred and fifty miles apart, the first with a population of over 600,000 and the second with almost 700,000; together they account for more than half the province's population. Until comparatively recently Alberta and Saskatchewan were among the most rurally oriented provinces in Canada, but now almost 80 percent of Albertans live in towns, and even in Saskatchewan the rural population has fallen to 40 percent.

The origins of the paired cities in both provinces can be explained simply. Regina in Saskatchewan and Calgary in Alberta were created to serve the Canadian Pacific Railway, and in the same way Saskatoon and Edmonton appeared on the northern route, which is now part of CN Rail. The unexpected fertility of the northern areas, together with the introduction of Marquis wheat, made it inevitable that such independent centres should develop, first as raw new frontier towns to provide for the needs of the incoming immigrants, and later as complex commercial centres. Their growth was given official impetus when Edmonton was named the capital of Alberta and Saskatoon became the first centre of higher education in Saskatchewan when the provincial university there was established in 1909.

The striking difference in population between the main cities of these neighbouring prairie provinces — a ratio of four to one in favour of those in Alberta — is explained by the different patterns of development that occurred after the two provinces were formed out of the Northwest Territories in 1905. Saskatchewan became a textbook example of a one-crop economy. It not merely grew more wheat than any other Canadian province; it became one of the most productive wheat-growing regions in the world, which was advantageous when wheat was in demand but detrimental when the world market was glutted. Yet Saskatchewan was too far from the main centres and had too few natural raw materials to encourage manufacturing, and it was only in the 1950s that minerals — notably potash — were found there in any quantity. But even potash is an uncertain commodity in world markets. Saskatchewan has consequently remained mainly dependent on wheat, which still accounts for half of its production, and the cities have failed to grow rapidly because of the lack of a varied and resilient economy. The image of the prairie man driving his combine over the broad fields to reap the golden crop in the long days of summer still applies in Saskatchewan more truly than in any other Canadian province.

From the beginning Alberta had a more varied economy than Saskatchewan. In the southern parts of the province and in the foothills of the Rockies Texas cattlemen were already moving in during the 1870s, so that ranching began to complement grain growing, with Calgary figuring as the rancher's city and Edmonton as the wheat-grower's city. With the coming of the railway in the 1880s, coal mines opened in the Crowsnest area in the southern part of the province. During the same period the new resorts in the mountains, especially Banff and Jasper and Lake Louise, began to attract considerable numbers of tourists. But it was the rich strike of oil at Leduc in 1947 and the discovery of other oilfields that transformed the Albertan economy. For a long period the province was the most prosperous region of Canada. Its cities boomed, the population of both Edmonton and Calgary doubling during the 1950s, with people coming in from all parts of Canada and even from the United States to find work connected with the oil industry. Yet in the end oil seemed no more certain than grain or potash, and a recession in the oil industry in the early 1980s put an end to the boom and terminated two decades of rapid urban expansion in both Edmonton and Calgary.

URBANIZATION WAS NOT THE ONLY REASON for the decline of small communities in many parts of Canada and especially in the prairies. The growth of the cities was fed partly by natural increase and partly by immigration;

many of the groups who arrived after World War II, notably the Italians, Portuguese and Greeks, and later the Vietnamese boat people, were little interested in settling on the land and naturally gravitated to the cities. They transformed the life patterns of those urban centres, turning Toronto, for example, from a dull, Sabbatarian, Anglo-Scottish city into a lively, cosmopolitan one.

Changes in farming methods and in patterns of transport were just as important in depopulating the countryside as the pull of the cities. During the years after World War II farming became considerably less labour intensive, and its increasing mechanization meant that the 160-acre quarter-section of homesteading days became unprofitable and virtually obsolete. Small farms were joined together into big farms, land that did not lend itself easily to mechanized farming was often abandoned and the number of people actually engaged in farming shrank perceptibly. At the same time the building of the Trans-Canada Highway across the prairies during the 1950s and the general improvement in the road system of the farming areas made obsolete the little communities that had sprung up, with a hotel and a Chinese restaurant and a couple of stores, wherever there was a station and a cluster of grain elevators. Farmers found it more convenient to drive into the nearest large town where there was a greater variety of stores, and travellers on the highway no longer called in at the little villages they had once driven through on the older prairie roads. Many of the small communities disappeared; others survived as ghost villages inhabited by a few retired farmers and the people who operated the grain elevators. A whole pattern of smalltown prairie life that had entered into Canadian mythology through the novels of Margaret Laurence, W. O. Mitchell and Sinclair Ross, virtually came to an end, having existed for less than a century. To a lesser extent the death of the small communities was repeated in other parts of Canada. Even in those that survived there were changes. In particular, the populations aged as the young departed because of the lack of employment opportunities.

However, in recent years there have been signs of a revivification of the countryside, even of a degree of de-urbanization. This trend stemmed partly from the counter-cultural movement in the 1960s, when large numbers of young people left the cities to set up idealistic communes, and in the process bought up deserted farms and often reactivated abandoned land. Most of these migrants eventually abandoned the countryside, but some remained to reinforce the farming population. At the same time less ideologically motivated city people began to return to the country for a variety of reasons. Some were retired people who went to live in small towns because they could live more peacefully and economically there. Others were young married people who wanted to bring up their children in a healthier environment and therefore took to living in the country and commuting to their work in the towns. This has been particularly the case in southern Ontario and in the lower mainland of British Columbia, where the small communities of the Fraser valley have been revived and transformed into dormitories for Vancouver workers.

The result has been the emergence of a new kind of rural community, not as closely tied to farming as in the past, but dedicated to preserving what are seen as the values and virtues of a rural life. All this is unlikely to change the fact that Canada is now an urbanized country, where most people live in cities or clusters of cities, and where the vast countryside is less populated than it was in the high days of settlement during the earlier part of the twentieth century. But it does mean that rural life has once again acquired some meaning beyond mere agribusiness and is no longer seen as an obsolescent factor in Canadian society.

CHAPTER
18

Workers and Workplaces

INDUSTRIALIZATION HAD EFFECTS IN CANADA that went far beyond the encouragement of urbanization and the growth of the cities. It changed occupational patterns, living patterns and the class structure of society; it introduced new economic problems and new social tensions that led to conflicts of a different kind from the political ones that had been projected in the rebellions of 1837–38 and in the prairie uprisings of 1870 and 1885.

Canada came late into the Industrial Revolution. Under the French and for long under the British regime, it remained the kind of colony that had been envisaged by seventeenth century mercantilist philosophers, acting as both a source of raw materials for the Old Country and a market for its manufactures. If the colony produced its own manufactures the equation would be defeated. The most extreme example of such a situation was the fur trade, in which all the trade goods offered in exchange for furs were made in the imperial centre and benefited its industries.

In New France this arrangement was modified by the fact that the *habitants* in their subsistence economy rarely had enough cash to buy large quantities of French-made goods. A parallel economy therefore developed, in which home industries flourished, while imported goods were used mainly by the officials and officers living in the few towns that existed. The *habitant* women wove cloth from their own wool and linen, out of which they made their own clothes and those of their families, and in this modest way the Canadian textile and garment industries first appeared. Bulky articles like furniture were also made locally, and rural industries arose to process local raw materials using primitive mechanisms. Small flour mills were established on the seigneuries, and sawmills were set up at various points along the St Lawrence, all operated by water or, more rarely, wind. By the 1730s the Forges St Maurice near Trois-Rivières had begun to make iron from local bog ore. They also manufactured charcoal to supply the blacksmiths who made bayonets for the Troupes de la Marine, fashioned farmers' tools, shod horses and provided wheelwrights with iron tires.

The French guild tradition largely governed these early industries in New France. Blacksmiths, furniture makers, silversmiths, masons and church painters would all be recruited by apprenticeship, though in the country districts there were many *habitants* who picked up a craft and practised it outside the guild pattern. The mills and foundries and the considerable building works that went on in New France, especially under the patronage of the Church, developed a small class of labourers — men without land or skills who fitted uneasily into the New French pattern.

NOT A GREAT DEAL CHANGED in any of the British North American colonies until after the War of 1812–14. Manufactured goods of any quality were imported, and fur and fish indirectly paid for them. Wind and water still operated mills of various kinds, though the mill buildings often became impressive stone structures, some of which survive to this day. Even in the first foundry of Upper Canada, the Marmora Ironworks near Peterborough, the hammers in the forge were powered by water. The first steam engine in Canada had operated in John Molson's little ship, the *Accommodation*, in 1809 (many of its parts were made in local workshops), but so abundant was water power that in industry steam power would be introduced slowly and late.

Apart from iron and steel manufactures, the Industrial Revolution in Britain had been built up mainly through the textile industry, which had undergone rapid technological change during the eighteenth century. But the British textile industry was based on a growing export market which was not available for colonials, and everywhere in British North America the local production of textiles was for long carried on mainly by farm women at their looms. They produced material for family use and sometimes for sale, though a degree of mechanization did enter into the industry through the proliferation of small rural carding and fulling mills, also water-powered — like the fulling mill that figures in *Don Quixote*. In some small towns and villages in the Canadas and Nova Scotia, Scottish hand weavers, who had been thrown out of work after machines began to be used in Britain, actually set up their looms once again. These were the first professional textile workers in the country, usually processing the yarn that the housewives had spun. The earliest actual textile factory, which manufactured woollen cloth, was established at L'Acadie in Lower Canada in 1822, but the first cotton mill appeared in Canada West only in 1860, and the first silk-weaving enterprise started in Montreal as late as 1876.

Perhaps the most ambitious industry of early Canada before the appearance of the railways was shipbuilding. It was carried on at Quebec City during the French regime, where commercial as well as naval vessels were made. In the late eighteenth century, the shipbuilding that was going on in the Maritimes led to the development of a shipping industry as well. Shipbuilding played a part in the development of the Upper Canadian economy through the construction of warships at Kingston during the War of 1812–14.

Industry in Canada followed a process of development long influenced by the original preponderance of the primary industries, first fur and fish, and then logging, farming and mining. It was not until the late 1940s that the number of people employed in the secondary industries of manufacturing and construction exceeded those employed in the primary industries, and by that time those employed in the tertiary service and communication industries had already exceeded both of them. Until as late as 1891 more than 50 percent of Canadians worked in the fields or the woods or the mines or took their fishing boats out to sea. Even the manufacturing industries of that time were still largely ancillary to the primary industries or to transport undertakings like the railways, whose first function was to serve the primary industries by transporting the raw materials they produced.

Consequently, early Canadian manufacturing industry consisted of two types of enterprise. There were many craft workshops employing relatively small numbers of workers and producing a variety of goods for local consumption in the towns and the countryside. In addition, there were a few large enterprises devoted mainly to providing the equipment needed in the rapidly growing transport and primary industry sectors. The establishment of heavy industry in Canada really dates from the first railway boom, which took place in the 1850s. Equipment for the earliest Canadian railways (built in the 1830s) had been imported, but in 1853 the first Canadian locomotive was manufactured in Toronto for the Ontario, Simcoe and Huron Railway. Soon after this almost everything needed on a railway was being manufactured in Canada, from the rails to the cars.

From the mid-1860s on, railway building boomed, and the industries that supplied it, as well as the ones that produced tools and equipment for farmers, loggers and miners expanded rapidly. By the last quarter of the nineteenth century the factories employed more men than the craft workshops and contributed more to the national product.

MEANWHILE, THE GREAT IMMIGRATIONS of the nineteenth century had created a steadily growing consumer market. It was not so evident in the early years of the 1830s and 1840s, when pioneer farms were largely subsistence operations and people in large areas of both Upper and Lower Canada lived in a barter economy. But as the land was cleared and the farmers began producing cash crops, the situation changed rapidly. From the 1850s and 1860s onward Canadian manufacture diversified notably, with agricultural equipment in great demand in Ontario, and the first paper as well as the first textile mills coming into operation. Pottery and furniture also began to be produced on a broad commercial scale, replacing some of the local craftsmen who had had a more limited market.

This upsurge in secondary industry led to a revolution in retail practices. Up to this time the custom had been to operate specialty stores in the towns and general stores in the villages, where merchants and customers haggled over the prices of the goods that were purchased, where barter sales were as frequent as cash ones, and where quality standards were at best uncertain. In 1868 an Ulsterman named Timothy Eaton changed the whole pattern of trading. Eaton had been in partnership with his brothers in a general store in a small Ontario town, and there he had come to believe that the crucial element in running a good and profitable business was to inspire the trust of one's customers by fair dealing. In 1869 he opened a store in Toronto and announced that he was going to do business on new principles. In his stores everything was to be sold for cash; prices would be fixed to eliminate the bargaining then customary in the retail trade. Goods would be guaranteed for quality, and any customers not satisfied with their purchases would get their money back. By eliminating bad credit risks and working on the basis of cost plus a reasonable profit, Eaton was able to keep his prices low. On the basis of his success he built up a network in English-speaking Canada that eventually included more than sixty department stores. When settlement began in the prairies, Eaton turned to mail-order sales. In 1884 he published the first *Eaton's Catalogue*, which became an illustrated Canadian classic of its own kind, known among settlers as "the homesteader's bible," and among Indians as the "wish book." It eventually featured fifteen thousand items, from clothes pegs to prefabricated barns, and over the decades it documented the steady diversification of Canadian industry.

In a parallel development, the Hudson's Bay Company found that the new settlers in the prairies were buying goods at its posts, and began to change the stock to suit new demands. Eventually it began to build separate stores unrelated to the fur trade, so that a rival system of department stores emerged, also bringing cheap mass-produced products to the people, either over the counter or by mail. In this way real changes were made to the quality of Canadian life, and the pioneer's dependence on homemade or farmgrown commodities came to an end. By the later decades of the nineteenth century, the days of homespun and of domestic soap and candle making were drawing to a close except in a very few small and isolated communities.

The changes which took place at this time in the lives of consumers corresponded to changes in their lives as producers. The work patterns of farmers, of loggers, of fishermen, of fur traders, of placer miners, had been determined by the seasons rather than by the clock. Farmers, fishermen and miners worked hard from spring to autumn, often as long as the sunlight lasted, but they went through extended winter periods during which there was nothing to do. Loggers worked most in the damper, cooler parts of the year, for the woods were perilous places in high summer when forest fires could easily start. Perhaps in reaction to their months of lonely toil, the gatherings of such people often became tumultuous collective releases of frustration or trapped energy. Theirs was the culture through which messianic Methodism ran like wildfire in the nineteenth century in successive waves of emotional camp meetings. It was also the culture of the great binge, in which men would come in from the wilderness or the backwoods to spend their earnings in extravagant sprees. There were places on the western frontier known as "Saturday night towns" because each weekend they would be turbulent with the celebrations of men arriving from the forests or the mines or the ranches.

Even in the settlements, despite the overt puritanism of the Methodists and other zealots, and despite the well-filled churches, many people lived irregular, drunken lives, and the great land-clearing and barn-building bees, despite their social virtues, were often deplored because they were accompanied by a great consumption of cheap whiskey. In nineteenth- and early twentieth-century Canada there often existed a curious symbiosis between puritanism and libertinism which one finds in many frontier societies. To give one example among many, at the height of the Klondike Gold Rush, the Mounted Police in Dawson City insisted on the strict observance of Sunday, even fining people who cut their firewood on that day, but at the same time they tolerated the presence of a red-light district where the brothels did a brisk trade every other day of the week. Perhaps the most revealing — because the most cynically frank — remark about Canadian moral ambivalence was made by the famous mayor of Montreal,

Camillien Houde, when he was criticized for running a wide open town: "As long as we keep a good balance between prayer and sinning, I know my city is not going to sink into wickedness."

This kind of life rhythm was not inconsistent with hard work. A Canadian pioneer clearing a farm had no alternative but to toil hard during the time the weather gave him, and many of the occupations I have mentioned were equally demanding. Loggers in the early nineteenth century worked long hours while they were in the woods and lived in remarkably harsh conditions. As places where comparatively large numbers of men worked together, the logging camps of New Brunswick and Upper Canada actually preceded the factories. In the 1820s and 1830s large gangs were also employed in canal construction. These labourers worked in often very bad conditions, as was shown by the high death rate from fever during the building of the Rideau Canal through the swamp country between Ottawa and Kingston. But the job would end, the labourer would spend his savings if he acquired any, and then go on to the next job, in many cases a casual labourer to the end of his days.

Where regular employment existed in those early days it was in the small establishments then typical of Canadian society. The store or workshop that was often a family business might also employ a couple of journeymen workers and some apprentices, who would be bound for long periods and often much exploited before they were considered skilled in their crafts. This pattern did not apply only to hand crafts like blacksmithing and cabinet making; most of the flour mills, sawmills and carding mills were small establishments of this kind, and so were even the distilleries, the breweries and the foundries in the less important towns. The actual craftsmen who worked in such establishments would carry out every stage of the work in which they were occupied; the division of labour so praised by the Scottish economist Adam Smith had yet to reach Canadian industries. The craftsmen were paid good wages and were usually men of standing in the communities to which they belonged. If they wished, they could often rise quickly through the mobile colonial society; the second prime minister of Canada was the former stonemason, Alexander Mackenzie.

THE RISE OF THE FACTORY SYSTEM and the emergence of time-oriented methods of transport like the railways immediately put limitations on the less disciplined aspects of Canadian life. Trains and factories ran according to the clock and not to the season. That great Victorian slogan, "Time is money," began to dominate the workplace, because time wasted was wages wasted. Employers regulated times and patterns of work so as to get as many hours of toil from the workers for as little money as possible. Ways were sought to increase the pace of work so that the maximum production could be obtained from men or women or even children and the machines they operated. The operations of manufacture began to be divided into a series of mechanical acts so that the multiple skills of the old craftsmen, learned over the years, became unnecessary.

By mass producing goods in this way, with machines and with workers whose operations became almost as automatic as those of machines, the large manufacturers were able to crowd out of the market the smaller undertakings whose skilled workmanship made their products more expensive. And so more and more workers were forced into the factories. In some industries, like garment making, in which a great deal of handwork was still needed, small workshops remained, but these tended to be transformed into sweatshops, which flourished greatly in Montreal and later in Winnipeg. In such establishments people would work for minimal wages, often crowded together in unhealthy conditions. The sweatshops were notorious for their exploitation of recently arrived immigrants, whose ignorance, insecurity and poverty made them easy victims of the system.

Canadian factory owners and managers imitated their British counterparts of the Industrial Revolution by introducing strict supervision and discipline into the workplace to ensure effective coordination and the most economical production. In the larger factories discipline was so strict that workers were often forbidden to talk lest that should distract them from their work, and they were fined or dismissed for being late or for other breaches of discipline. Often they had little protection while working with dangerous machines, and compensation for injuries was almost nonexistent. Job security was virtually unknown; a worker could be sacked on any pretext or none at all. Working under such conditions was not only physically unhealthy; it was mentally degrading. The situation was made even worse by the fact that the housing of the factory workers was often wretched (the mining slums of Cape Breton were notorious even in the nineteenth century), the air they breathed in their few unworking hours was often polluted, and few people, except the churches in a sporadic way, did much to make the leisure of working men or women at least a little more meaningful than their work.

In a way the crowding together of the workers in such adverse conditions eventually produced its own remedy, for here were people in considerable numbers, united in the same predicament for large parts of their lives. Originally they had nothing to unite them, but now they had a shared locale, the workplace where so much of their life was spent, and a common enemy, the boss. Necessity — the need to protect themselves from further assaults on their fragile freedom and to gain positive improvements in their condition — created a sense of unity. A single worker could do nothing, but the employees of a factory, acting together, could bring its operations to a halt. It was a lesson already learned by workers in Europe, and some of the first workers' organizations in Canada were branches of English unions established by immigrant English workers. The Amalgamated Society of Carpenters and Joiners and the Amalgamated Society of Engineers were two of these organizations. Union branches began to appear during the 1830s in Upper Canada and in Montreal. However, some kind of industrial organization seems to have begun earlier in Nova Scotia, probably among the shipwrights, for in 1816 the colonial legislature, dominated by the merchants of Halifax, passed a law forbidding workers to bargain collectively over hours or wages and specifying prison terms as penalties.

THE FIRST UNIONS WERE CRAFT organizations of skilled workers, no longer protected by the old guild system, who found it necessary to unite in order to maintain their status now that the old workshop system was breaking down. Masons, tailors, shoemakers, bakers, barrel-makers, all had formed unions by the 1850s, though their memberships were small and they represented only a tiny proportion of the growing body of working men and women. These pioneer unions were mainly local ones, but about the middle of the nineteenth century, already established American unions began to recruit members north of the border. With organizations like the National Typographical Union, what is known pretentiously as "international unionism" began to enter Canada; it was really subcontinental unionism, for the organizations rarely had members outside the United States and Canada.

In these early days there was no organization of unskilled workers, though this did not prevent large strikes from taking place during the building of the Lachine and Welland canals in the 1820s and 1830s, in which Canada had its earliest taste of industrial violence. As industrialization spread, the general mass of the factory workers remained unorganized, but craft workers who had become involved in the factories used their organizations to repel attacks on traditional work routines or wage levels. Before Confederation few unions existed outside the area of skilled labour, and those unions moved on insecure ground. This was because, under old English laws against "combinations," still unrepealed in Canada, their legality was dubious. Nevertheless, they realized that their only strength lay in solidarity, and they began to establish local assemblies of unions, the equivalent of modern trades councils.

The dominant labour issue in Canada during the 1870s and 1880s, as in the United States, was not wages, but hours of labour, which in many cases had been pushed up as high as twelve hours a day. The first real show of labour strength took place in 1872 when the unions in Montreal, Toronto and Hamilton united in the Nine-Hour Movement. The workers marched through the streets in large demonstrations with bands and banners, as they had never done before, and a number of strikes took place, the most important being that of the National Typographical Union against the *Globe*, which was owned by the bitterly anti-unionist Grit leader, George Brown. Brown invoked the obsolescent anti-combination legislation, and the union leaders were prosecuted, but Sir John A. Macdonald seized on the issue to discredit his great political rival and introduced measures to repeal the laws that forbade unionization. An immediate result was the founding of the first general labour organization in Canada, the Canadian Labour Union, which was created in 1873, survived for a few years like a sickly child and then expired from lack of enthusiasm.

A needed impetus was given to labour organization by the first appearance of industrial unionism — the organization of workers not by specific trade but by industry, so that all workers in a factory or mine would belong to the same organization and be able to bring more effective pressure on the employer. The first North

American group to advocate such industrial organization was the Knights of Labor, a semi-secret order, bound by oaths and rituals, which was founded in Philadelphia in 1869. The Knights stood for the organization of all workers, regardless of skill, sex or race, and they revived an old idea formulated by Robert Owen and advocated by the famous British group, the Grand National Consolidated Trade Union of 1834. According to Owen, labour organizations should not merely concern themselves with day-to-day issues but should work towards a social system that was more just than one based on monopoly capitalism.

The old craft unions, which in their own way were defenders of privilege, regarded the Knights with distrust, but at first the movement was highly successful. The Knights reached Canada in the late 1870s, and dominated the union movement there during the 1880s and 1890s. They penetrated large towns and small ones, and though they were strongest in Ontario, Montreal and British Columbia, they also spread into the Maritimes and the prairies. At their peak of influence they had 450 "assemblies," bringing together the workers of a locality regardless of trade, and a total membership of 20,000. Small by present standards, it made the Knights for the time being the most powerful labour organization in Canada. Unlike the old craft unions, the Knights became politically active, supporting labour candidates in the elections; a Knight was elected to the Ontario legislature as early as 1874, and another to the federal Parliament in 1888. Even more important, it was largely through their efforts that a successful central organization of unions was at last created, the Trades and Labour Congress of Canada, out of which emerged in 1956 the still flourishing Canadian Labour Congress.

The craft unions did not accept the temporary ascendancy of the Knights of Labor. Supported by the powerful American Federation of Labor across the border they organized actively during the 1890s, and by 1902 they were strong enough to expel the Knights of Labor from the Trades and Labour Congress. Interunion struggle of this kind did not greatly further the cause of labour, particularly as the unions, though at last legal, had few of the privileges they now enjoy. No law made it obligatory for an employer to bargain with a union his workers had established or chosen to represent them, and employers could and did sack workers for union membership. And there were many occasions during strikes when the government called out the militia at the behest of the employers, as much to intimidate the workers as to protect property.

Through this period of ascendancy on the part of the craft workers, the unskilled went unorganized, and particularly the exploited itinerant workers who became known as the Bunkhouse Men. They were the successors in the 1890s and the early years of the present century to the Irish labourers of the canal building era and the Chinese coolies of the CPR days, and they were treated no better than their predecessors. Usually single men and often immigrants, they moved about the country working as navvies on railway building and other construction works, providing rough labour in mines and logging operations, working in grain harvests and fruit harvests. They lived largely in work camps — hence the name they were given — and they wandered from one end of the country to the other, seeking work. They were brutally exploited, and the craft unions, anxious to maintain the privileges and status of their own members, did nothing to help them. Only a few isolated industrial unions, like the United Mine Workers, would even accept them for membership.

They were ripe for radical leadership, and it came with the importation into North America of the doctrines and practice of revolutionary syndicalism. Revolutionary syndicalism carried to its logical conclusion the philosophy of the Knights of Labor, declaring that the role of the trade unions should go beyond negotiating such matters as wages, hours and working conditions. Arguing that the distress of the workers was due to faults inherent in the capitalist system, syndicalists sought its transformation into a society where the community through the workers' organizations would control the economy. Revolutionary syndicalism, which originated in France and quickly spread to Spain and other Latin countries, was closely linked to the anarchism that flourished in Europe before the Great War. This meant that syndicalists made greater demands than the Knights of Labor, who had advocated political action within the existing state to further the interests of the workers. The anarchists and many of the syndicalists argued that the state itself was as corrupt as capitalism, and that workers should have no truck with the politics of elections and parliaments. Instead, they should struggle for the overthrow of a doomed order — if necessary by violence — and fight to replace it with a cooperative community that had no form of authority.

REVOLUTIONARY SYNDICALISM CAME TO NORTH AMERICA with the 1905 Chicago founding of the Industrial Workers of the World (IWW), better known to history as the Wobblies. The appeal of the Wobblies was less to the factory workers of the eastern side of the continent than to the workers of the West, who were still living in a frontier society where extreme attitudes could flourish. The Wobblies quickly spread to British Columbia, where their radical views appealed to the workers in the primary industries, such as logging, fishing and mining, as well as to the men who were building the second wave of railroads across the West. They gained particular fame for a hard-fought strike they organized — and lost — among the workers building the Canadian Northern railway through the Fraser Canyon in 1912.

Militant unions like the Wobblies and the mineworkers' unions faced a highly exploitative and ruthless type of employer in the forests and mines, and they also faced governments and municipal authorities who were more than willing to aid the employers in repressing labour activities. Their struggles left a lasting heritage of confrontationalism in the West and particularly in British Columbia, where politics as well as relations within industries tend to be highly polarized.

Resolutely anti-militarist, the IWW declined during the Great War largely because of governmental persecution, but other unions flourished because of the expansion of industry that the war created. By the end of the hostilities, union strength had risen to almost 400,000 members, who showed a high degree of activity as soon as wartime restraints were lifted. In 1919 alone there were four hundred strikes, breaking out all over the country, and reaching a climax in the Winnipeg General Strike of that year. That strike was fought as much to establish the principle of collective bargaining as to gain better wages and working conditions. The strike — which brought the city to the edge of violent class warfare — was lost, largely because the federal government sent in the Mounted Police and units of the army, and it would take another generation to win broad acceptance for collective bargaining in Canada. A heritage of the Winnipeg General Strike was the establishment of yet another revolutionary syndicalist organization, the One Big Union, which gained support among the very workers who had formerly provided a following for the Wobblies. It soon lost ground, however, to the craft unions, which were given covert support by employers and the government, and industrial unionism declined once again, to repeat its phoenix rise during the late 1930s.

By the 1920s the boom days had ended, and the later 1920s were a period of retrenchment for the unions; they tended to concentrate on holding what they had gained rather than struggling for more. But the Great Depression, which began in 1929, added another problem for the workers: that of unemployment on a far vaster scale than ever before. In the worst times a quarter of Canadian workers were without jobs in a country where unemployment insurance did not yet exist and where relief was stingily administered if it was given at all.

The situation led to an outburst of militancy among the unemployed, and violent clashes with the authorities, particularly in western cities like Vancouver and Regina. It also led to a spilling over the border of the next and final wave of industrial unionism, represented by the Congress of Industrial Organizations in the United States, which set out to organize the factory workers in the industries neglected by the craft unions. Canadian workers joined American industrial unions like the United Automobile Workers, and when they won a highly publicized strike in 1937 against General Motors in Oshawa, the future of industrial unionism was assured. True, it led to a split in the Canadian union movement, since the craft unions of the Trades and Labour Congress expelled in 1940 those unions that were affiliated with the Congress of Industrial Organizations; the latter immediately formed their own rival Canadian Congress of Labour. But a trend had begun that carried on through World War II, so that by the end of the 1940s a million workers were organized in Canada and the principle of collective bargaining was increasingly accepted.

But there were areas other than industry in which Canada was moving to more just, more civilized and more democratic ways during the vital decades between Confederation and World War II.

CHAPTER

19

Mingling Currents of Change

IN ANY DYNAMIC AND GROWING SOCIETY the social issues tend to intermingle, and change in one area can help to precipitate change in another. Urbanization and industrialization were two such trends that stimulated each other and led workers to become increasingly organized in order to preserve the quality of their lives. Other developments interacted with equal intimacy. The gradual universalization of education had profound effects on the status of women, while the struggle for women's rights that acquired such urgency in the early twentieth century became mingled with other social issues, like the temperance movement. In this and in other directions it also mingled with the emergence inside the churches of a consciousness of social issues and a conscience relating to them. In the end the churches' social conscience would combine with farmers' and workers' discontent with existing political parties to produce a third force in Canadian politics specifically directed towards social reform, though not to revolution.

Revolutionary reform has remained the concern of relatively small if vocal minorities, like the Wobblies early in
the present century and the Communists in the 1930s.

WE HAVE ALREADY OBSERVED the beginnings of education
for the more privileged young people in the clerically
dominated institutions of New France, in private schools
in Upper Canada like the one operated by John Strachan
in Cornwall, and in the earliest institutions of higher
education in the Maritimes. And one can fairly say that
though by World War II education of a kind was available to every child in Canada except for a few of the remoter native groups, higher education would still
remain a matter of privilege to a much greater extent
than it had become by this time in the United States.

In New France, outside the towns where only a
small minority lived, there was very little formal, academic education. Children learned farming from their
parents and began at an early age to work on the family
farm, a situation repeated in the other pioneer areas as
settlement spread across Canada. Some boys would become apprentices and learn trades, but often without becoming literate, and the catechism classes which some of
the parish priests organized did little to raise standards
of literacy. By the Conquest of 1760, and for long afterwards, the majority of the *habitant* population of Quebec
could neither read nor write.

In the towns of New France the religious orders provided an elementary education for local children based
principally on the three Rs and a little religious training,
and the missionaries tried, though with no great success, to disseminate a similar kind of training among the
children of the Indian tribes they set out to convert. The
Jesuits were the first to establish anything resembling
secondary education in Canada with the school they
founded in Quebec in 1635. It was the first of the traditional Quebec colleges, combining classical studies and
grammar with a good dose of theology.

Higher education emerged in 1660 when Bishop Laval founded the Séminaire de Québec, intended primarily to train priests, but open to young men who wanted the kind of training that would allow them to follow other professions. In the sense that it was intended to train a local ruling group, whether lay or clerical, it was — as Strachan's school was and Upper Canada College would later become — an elitist institution. However, the tradition of upward mobility that had characterized the mediaeval church still survived in New France and it was possible for a bright *habitant* child to find his way into the Séminaire and get a good education and a fair start in life. In 1852 the Séminaire would spawn Université Laval, the first francophone university in Canada. Though the Ursulines and other religious sisterhoods like the Congregation of Notre Dame provided some schooling for females, it did not go far beyond embroidery, reading and the catechism, and anything approaching higher education for women just did not exist. The church continued to dominate education in Quebec for the greater glory of God until education was almost completely secularized during the 1960s.

BEFORE THE 1840s THERE WAS LITTLE public education in the Maritimes or Upper Canada. Provincial governments tended, at best, to subsidize efforts by primarily religious groups to establish schools. Outside such efforts, which were largely concentrated in the towns, rural townships would raise money by local contribution to establish schools, but in the beginning there was no means of regulating curriculum or establishing teaching standards. The teachers were often men who had acquired a little education serving in the army and who were unfitted by health, age or inclination for any other occupation but that of underpaid schoolmaster.

On a higher level, education was one of the areas in which religion and government came together and often clashed. It was, after all, a highly religious age, and by the time of Confederation thirteen out of the seventeen degree-granting institutions were affiliated with various churches in Canada and controlled by them. Anglicans, Presbyterians, Methodists and Baptists, as well as Catholics, had their schools of university status, and the only non-denominational institutions at that time were Dalhousie, McGill, the University of New Brunswick and the University of Toronto.

In fact, the non-denominational universities, few though they then were, projected the future direction of higher education in Canada. The case of the University of Toronto was an especially interesting and important one, since it was closely linked with the attempt to create an established church in Upper Canada. The history of the University of Toronto began with the creation of King's College by royal charter in 1827, under the inspiration and control of Archdeacon Strachan, as he then was. King's College was seen as a bastion of loyalty to the Crown and as a symbol of the ascendancy of the Church of England. But only a minority of the inhabitants of Upper Canada were Anglicans, and opposition showed itself in two ways: in agitation to secularize King's College, and what would seem on the surface an inconsistent program of establishing colleges under the aegis of rival sects, such as Queen's University, which the Presbyterians established at Kingston, and Victoria College, which the Methodists established at Cobourg, both in 1841. Eventually the opposition to a state-supported university affiliated with the Anglican Church grew so strong that in 1850, under a Reform government, King's College was secularized and became the non-denominational University of Toronto. Bishop Strachan, as he had now become, retaliated by founding an Anglican university no longer financed by the state, Trinity College, in 1851, but in the end all the sectarian colleges of the time in Ontario, except for Queen's, became affiliated with the University of Toronto. Even Trinity finally joined in 1904.

The University of Toronto set a pattern for subsequent provincial universities as the West opened up. The University of Manitoba, founded in 1877, was a non-denominational degree-granting institution to which three previously established colleges belonging to various churches were affiliated. The University of Alberta (1906), the University of Saskatchewan (1907) and the University of British Columbia (founded officially in 1908 but not in active operation until 1915) were all provincially funded secular institutions, and all of them from the beginning were co-educational, which represented a notable advance since the earlier days of higher education in Canada.

There are other ways in which the University of Toronto can be considered a prototype of the Canadian university. One of the most striking is its steady diversification. By World War II the University of Toronto had added to its original faculties of arts and sciences others in law, medicine and dentistry, in home economics, education and forestry, in social work, nursing and hygiene. The Conservatory of Music and the Royal Ontario Museum had become its affiliates. It had established its own university press in 1911 and in 1931 had founded the *University of Toronto Quarterly*. (A rival institution had entered this field first, however: Queen's had established *Queen's Quarterly* in 1893.) The same pattern of adding professional schools to the traditional academic disciplines and of entering into the broader cultural field through publication and extension activities was to be followed by other Canadian universities, so that institutions of higher education became the principal centres of Canadian intellectual life, though not the only ones, as we shall see later.

A SIMILAR TENDENCY TOWARDS THE SECULARIZATION of teaching developed in the broader fields of elementary and secondary education. During the second quarter of the nineteenth century, the emphasis quickly shifted from

private to public and (except in Quebec) from denomina-
tional to non-denominational education, with the ultimate aim of making education universal and uniform in
its standards even if not necessarily in its content.
Among the most active agents of this shift in emphasis
and indeed in philosophy were the leading dissenting
sects and especially the Methodists, who believed that
state and church must be separate and that education
should be a responsibility of the community rather than
the churches. True, they had established their own Victoria College, but this they regarded as having been
forced upon them by the state's support of the Anglican
King's College.

Therefore it was appropriate that the prime architect
of the secular, provincially controlled and funded educational system that came into Canada during the mid-
nineteenth century should have been Egerton Ryerson,
who already had a great reputation as a Methodist
preacher. Ryerson had become convinced as early as the
1820s that education, while it should be based on a
Christian morality, should not be attached to sectarian
dogma and should be administered by public bodies
raising funds from property owners. When the united
province of Canada was established in 1840 a School Act
was passed by a reform-minded government which envisaged a uniform educational system for the province.
The Act remained a dead letter in Canada East, where
the priesthood continued to control the school system
and to use it in support of the Catholic faith. But in
Canada West, where he was appointed Superintendent
of Education in 1844, Ryerson set about establishing a
system that combined local responsibility for financing,
providing and running the schools with a centralized
control of curriculum and of teacher training, so that
both textbooks and the level of teaching would be uniform. Taxes on property to be collected by local boards
of trustees would finance the schools, and education
would immediately be free for children whose parents

chose to send them to school. Compulsory attendance was envisaged as the ideal goal, which was more or less achieved everywhere but in Quebec by the end of the nineteenth century.

The deficiencies of such a system when it reached the village level are part of the stuff of Canadian fiction, where the one-room schoolhouse figures frequently as a scene of early experience and sometimes romance. In the diaries and memoirs of those who served their time as teachers the view is usually less rosy. The buildings provided by local school boards were usually spartan, and teachers and students often had to carry out the tasks of keeping the schoolhouse warm and clean that would now be performed by janitors. Because of the lack of accommodation in rural districts, teachers were often grudgingly welcomed as guests in the houses of parents, but since the burden would usually be shared by several households, it meant that the teacher became a kind of nomad, moving from house to house several times within a single term.

Achieving real universality was also a slow process. The better-off and more ambitious parents were the most assiduous in making sure their children attended school. The children of the poor were more often kept at home to help with the housework and with earning money. Everywhere attendance was low during the harvest, which in the western provinces determined the shape of the school years. Nevertheless, by the time education did become compulsory, most parents were conscious of its advantages and most children were already receiving some schooling.

The great advances in the new teaching programs devised by Ryerson in Ontario and by other reforming educators like John Jessop in British Columbia and Alexander Forrester in Nova Scotia were those that assured a common curriculum, an accepted standard of texts and something like a universal level of competence among teachers. The school board might hire the teachers, but the provinces — to whom the control of education was assured under the British North America Act of 1867 — undertook the training of educators by the establishment of Normal Schools through which teachers had to pass before they could be certified employable in public schools.

THE UNIVERSALIZATION OF EDUCATION was in many ways the beginning of the movement to improve the status of women that occurred during the Victorian era. Before Ryerson's reforms the range of occupations for women outside the home, farm and family business was virtually limited to domestic service, which was really a kind of low-paid and ill-regarded extension of the woman's role as homemaker. Some women earned money in cottage industries like weaving, dressmaking and laundering, but their entry into the manufacturing work force did not start until factory production began to spread in the years after Confederation. Then they were invariably paid less than men; there were cases of young girls earning a dollar for a sixty-hour week. For this reason working men tended to oppose the employment of women — as they opposed the employment of Chinese — lest they undercut the standard of wages, and even by the end of the century only an eighth of the labour force consisted of women.

Teaching began to provide an alternative occupation to domestic service and factory work, and it gave those who followed it a certain social status. Everywhere women teachers were paid less than men, and they worked under male superintendence. Most women taught in the elementary schools, and before World War II very few of them were found on university faculties. Yet teaching provided a first step into the professions, apart from the literary activities by which a very few Canadian women were earning a living. And teaching provided the stimulus that led women to seek not only a greater role in the professions but also liberation from

the disabilities under which they laboured in a patriarchal society.

Emily Stowe, the first woman to practise medicine in
Canada, had her training in the Normal School and
taught in Ontario communities before she decided that it
was demeaning for women to have no alternative but to
be attended by male doctors. There was no provision for
training women doctors in Canada, so she attended the
New York Medical College for Women and returned to
Canada in 1867. She started practising without a licence,
which the male-dominated local profession would not
grant her until 1880. Other women followed her example, training in the United States until the growing demand for medical education in Canada resulted in the
foundation, both in 1883, of the Women's Medical College in Kingston and the Woman's Medical College in
Toronto. Shortly afterwards, medical training for women
was offered in the Maritimes at Dalhousie and in 1891 it
was offered at the University of Manitoba in the West,
but it would be many years before any medical school in
Quebec would be open to women.

The legal profession was slower to recognize women
than its medical counterpart, and not until 1897 was
Clara Brett Martin admitted to the Law Society of Upper
Canada. Even then women were not quick to enter the
legal profession, and at the outbreak of World War II,
there were very few women lawyers in Canada. In 1916,
however, the province of Alberta had set a precedent by
appointing two women magistrates, Emily Gowan Mur-
phy and Alice Jamieson, in Edmonton and Calgary respectively, the first of their kind in the British Empire.

The churches were even slower to follow the other
professions. In the regular churches there was as yet no
place for women to enter a religious vocation except in
the Catholic sisterhoods devoted to teaching and nursing. Even among the evangelical sects, those that encouraged women to take an active preaching role, like
the Salvation Army, were very few, and even in the Sal-

vation Army the number of Canadian Major Barbaras was never large.

In journalism, on the other hand, women did begin to gain a foothold in the 1880s, even though they might sometimes have to write under male pseudonyms, and at least two celebrated Canadian women writers, Sara Jeannette Duncan (whose original by-line was "Garth Grafton") and Lucy Maude Montgomery, entered literature by way of the Normal School followed by the newspaper office. Literature remained the profession in which women were, if not more numerous, at least more prominent than they were in other callings. A woman, Frances Brooke, wrote the first novel about Canada, *The History of Emily Montague* (1769), and in succeeding generations women played a leading role in the creation of an emergent Canadian literature. Among them were Anna Jameson, Susanna Moodie and her sister Catharine Parr Traill, Rosanna Leprohon, Isabella Valancy Crawford, Agnes Maule Machar, as well as Duncan and Montgomery.

During the nineteenth century a greater consciousness of the important social role of women emerged in Canada, largely as a heritage of the pioneer situation in which women had shared with men in the clearing of the land and the creation of communities. One of the results of this consciousness was the spread of organizations in which women could not only meet to discuss their mutual concerns but make an effective voluntary contribution to the bettering of society. Some of them were religious, though interdenominational, in orientation, like the Young Women's Christian Association. Others, like the Women's Institute movement, were directed towards rural wives. The Woman's Christian Temperance Union began as a group dedicated to ending the abuse of alcohol that was widespread in nineteenth century Canada, but later it took on wider social and political dimensions. The National Council of Women was a broader group, possibly the most powerful of all, to which many lesser organizations were affiliated. The fact that Lady Aberdeen, the governor general's wife, was instrumental in creating it gave it great prestige and even a quasi-official flavour.

Not all women's groups were in fact sympathetic to the movement to improve the status of women through gaining political rights, which centred on the fight for women's suffrage. This struggle lasted for almost exactly forty years after Dr Stowe founded in 1876 the Toronto Women's Literary Club as a front for suffragist activity. Seven years later the club was transformed into the Toronto Women's Suffrage Association, and then in 1889 it became the Dominion Women's Enfranchisement Association, though in fact it was far from dominion-wide in membership. A national movement really came into existence when the members of the Woman's Christian Temperance Union came to the conclusion that prohibition would never be achieved while only men voted. They therefore threw their energies and their considerable resources, as well as their influence in many of the Protestant churches, into the fight for women's suffrage. The National Council of Women did not give its powerful support until 1910, and the Women's Institutes stayed aloof, concentrating on their chosen task of helping women to become effective homemakers.

There is no doubt that the suffrage movement gained momentum during the Great War when women in considerable numbers took the places of factory workers who had joined the armed forces and helped to keep the country's farms going. The Woman's Christian Temperance Union had always been strong in the prairies, where its leaders, like Nellie McClung, also became dedicated campaigners for the vote, and it was the three prairie provinces, Manitoba, Saskatchewan and Alberta, that led the suffrage breakthrough when they all granted women the vote in the 1916 provincial elections. British Columbia and Ontario followed in 1917, the Atlantic provinces between 1918 and 1922, and Newfoundland, still a self-governing dominion, in 1925. Quebec women did not vote provincially until 1940, though, like all other Canadian women, they had been voting in dominion elections since 1918, when the federal vote was given to women. A lengthy legal battle fought by five Alberta women led to the granting in 1929 of the right of women to sit in the Senate, and in 1930 the first woman senator was appointed.

Gaining formal political equality was not the end of the struggle for women's rights. Indeed, as the women's movements of recent decades have shown, great areas of discrimination between the sexes remained and still survive to this day. Certain basic reforms were indeed carried through during this period, including the various Married Women's Property Acts of the late nineteenth century, which took away from men the control over their wives' property, but there was no provision for the equal division of assets at the break-up of a marriage, and the ending of marriage by divorce remained difficult in most parts of Canada until after World War II. In terms of employment, the numbers of women in the workforce gradually increased, but they continued to be paid less than the men.

THIS DID NOT MEAN THAT THE MEN WERE, by present standards, well paid. The standard of living and expectations of people were generally lower in those days, even though as early as the Great War the technological infrastructure of change was falling into place. By that time the first automobiles were being made in Canada, the first planes were flying in its sky, Marconi had made his experiments in wireless telegraphy from a stormy cape in Newfoundland, the typewriter was already creating a new occupation for women, and the telephone, invented by the Canadian Alexander Graham Bell in 1876, was combining with the earlier telegraph to put Canadians in complex communication with each other, if not in constant agreement. The possibilities of production were growing, but very little attention had been paid, at least by governments and industrialists, to the problem of increasing the power of consumption. Though skilled workers very often lived reasonably well, unskilled workers were universally poor and often ill-treated, and there were areas — notably on the reserves where the majority of Canada's Indians now vegetated in neglect, and on the coast of Labrador where the "livyers" existed as virtual slaves to the fish merchants — where poverty was extreme and hope was in very short supply.

As we have seen, certain sections of society, such as the industrial workers and farmers, were already seeking ways to better their situation. Like the suffrage movement, they envisaged political change, the workers by supporting labour election candidates independent of the large parties and the farmers by forming their own short-lived political movements. A further impetus came from an unexpected direction, the Protestant churches. On one level Canadian Protestantism was moving towards reunification after the sectarian struggles in earlier decades, and in 1925 the United Church — the largest Protestant body in Canada — was formed by the merging of the Methodists, the Congregationalists and a majority of the Presbyterians. At the same time, within the constituent churches — and particularly among the Methodists — a ferment had arisen whose manifestations in argument and example became known as the Social Gospel. It began in the 1890s when a number of younger Protestants, laymen and ministers, largely inspired by the teachings of John Ruskin and Henry George, began to declare that faith was not enough for the Christian life, that the Church must abandon its otherworldliness and play its part in the creation of a just and more compassionate society.

The movement clustered around the city missions that were set up to minister to the urban poor, and a group of social gospel protagonists arose, including Salam Bland, J. G. Shearer, and, the best-known of all,

J. S. Woodsworth. They directed the attention of church members beyond such familiar social-religious issues as temperance and Sunday observance towards the health and housing of the poor, the care of their children and the plight of destitute immigrants. Radical farmer leaders, the men who created the United Farmers movement, were attracted, as were labour leaders in the prairie cities. In this way the embryo of a potent alliance was formed, and when the force of the social gospel movement declined within the churches, leaders like Woodsworth withdrew from their ecclesiastical connections and gave the alliance a secular aspect. At the height of the Depression when social action seemed urgent, the secularized alliance formed the first viable third party in Canada.

By this time socialism had appeared as a political philosophy, represented by a number of rather dogmatic and sectarian groups like the Socialist Party of Canada (1904) and the Social Democratic Party of Canada (1911). These groups tended to reflect the doctrinaire socialism of Europe rather than North American experience, and there was room for a movement that reflected real Canadian urges for reform. A number of socialistically inclined academics, among whom the poet-lawyer F. R. Scott was prominent, moved out of the era of feuding factions and founded in 1932 the League for Social Reconstruction, modelled largely on the Fabian Society in Britain. At the same time a group of radical labour and farmer members of the House of Commons had formed themselves into a "Ginger Group," operating as a kind of guerilla band on the verges of the established parties; J. S. Woodsworth was one of them.

In 1932, not long after the foundation of the League for Social Reconstruction, the idea of a coalition of all these disparate forces began to emerge. During that year the concept of a new party that would embrace all the varying points of view gained shape. The founding meeting took place in Calgary. In 1933 the new movement, which had called itself the Co-operative Commonwealth Federation, to avoid an obvious emphasis on socialism and also to avoid the appearance of a political party on the established Liberal-Conservative model, met in Regina. The manifesto it adopted was mildly social democratic, calling for the nationalization of key industries, including that old farmers' enemy, the Canadian Pacific Railway, but otherwise envisaging a mixed economy. A fairly elaborate welfare system was also proposed, which called for universal pensions, children's allowances, workmen's compensation, health insurance and unemployment insurance. In the 1930s all these proposals seemed almost utopian, but in later years they were to be adopted and implemented by other parties and to become an accepted part of Canadian life.

In spite of its social democratic proposals, which reflected the view of the intellectuals of the League for Social Reconstruction and of some of the labour leaders, the CCF as it developed during the 1930s did not abandon its social gospel or its agrarian roots. Its first president was the old social gospeller, J. S. Woodsworth, and when the party picked up seven seats and gained 9 percent of the popular vote in the 1935 election he became its leader in the House and remained so until he resigned in 1939 at the beginning of World War II. His resignation was necessary because his pacifist principles did not accord with the view of the majority of the CCF MP's, who supported Canada's entry into the war. And when in 1944 the CCF won an election in the province of Saskatchewan, it came to power thanks to the support of the prairie wheat farmers, not of the urban workers. It formed that unusual political creature, a rural-based social democratic government. To complete the pattern of an alliance of strange bedfellows, the leader of the provincial party who became the premier of Saskatchewan was another old social gospeller, the former Baptist minister Thomas Clement Douglas.

With the election of the CCF to power in Saskatchewan in 1944, a new era of pluralist politics began in
Canada, putting an end to the Tweedledum-Tweedledee
dualism of Liberal-Conservative rivalries. And the new
era was one in which political and social issues would
be constantly intermingled.

PART
VII

CHAPTER
20

The Cultural Upsurge

Canadians entered World War II in a sombre mood, compared with the enthusiasm that had filled the recruiting stations in the early months of the Great War. British-born Canadians made up a much smaller proportion of the population, imperialist sentiment had died away and even English-speaking Canadians were affected by the isolationism that in the 1930s was strong in the United States. And Québécois and Acadians were as reluctant as ever to become involved in the quarrels and causes of Europe. Almost as a symbolic gesture of reluctance, the Canadian government delayed a week after Britain had entered the war before making its own declaration. Leader of a party that depended so much on Quebec to stay in office, Mackenzie King was not eager to impose compulsory military service, uttering one of his famous equivocations: "Not necessarily conscription, but conscription if necessary." Once again, the needs of war and pressure from the English-speaking provinces forced the government into adopting conscription, and once again Quebec protested and evaded. Canada's population in 1941 was approximately 11,500,000, not counting Newfoundland, which did not join the dominion until 1949. Almost 1,100,000 men and women served in the armed forces, roughly the same proportion of the total population as in the Great War, but there were far fewer deaths than in the earlier conflict.

With the advent of war the problems of the Depression immediately dissipated. Unemployment vanished almost overnight, and many women, including married ones, joined the labour force. The manufacturing industries were strengthened and diversified, and despite the cost of the war a strengthened economy emerged that kept expanding for decades. In national and political terms Canada emerged as a power among others. So many great powers, notably those of the Axis, had been temporarily paralyzed by defeat and so many other countries were in the process of reconstruction after enemy occupation that Canada stood out at the war's end as one of the world's most stable and prosperous countries. It had one of the highest standards of living in the world and a large merchant marine that was afterwards allowed to decay. The country was in good financial health and strong enough in resources (in spite of its still relatively small population) to flourish for a while in the councils of the nations as a "middle power" and an "honest broker" in international disputes, though as other countries recovered, Canada's relative position declined. Nevertheless, its independence was assured, and it had ceased to be regarded as a "colony" of Britain, though as the Canadian economy became more linked with the American, there would soon be Canadian nationalists who would claim that Canada had escaped from one colonialism to fall into another.

It was clear that the expanding economy had need of many new Canadians, and the 1950s especially were years of high immigration, contrasting with the extremely low entry rate of the Depression years. The Great War had also been followed by a surge of immigration, though never so ample as in the first years of the century, but the economic crisis of 1929 created a situation in which immigrants would only add to the numbers of unemployed, and there were years when more people left the country than entered it. Even compassionate considerations failed to move the bureaucratic hearts of immigration officials, and Jews and other people fleeing from Nazi persecution were refused entry even when this meant sending them back to certain death.

This may have been partly due to the political innocence of Canadians in the 1930s. Certainly by the end of World War II they were more aware of the realities of life in totalitarian countries and of the circumstances that had created so many homeless people in the world. From the early 1950s onward "displaced" persons from Eastern Europe were welcomed, and Canada reacted positively to a whole series of refugee-creating situations, admitting large batches of people fleeing from regions as various as Hungary, Czechoslovakia, Uganda, Latin America and Southeast Asia (the famous "boat people").

Gradually, racial discrimination wore away; the different waves of post-World War II immigrants showed the steady opening of Canada's doors to people who in the past would have been summarily denied entry. Immediately after the war came a great British immigration, differing from those of the past because a considerable proportion of those who came were highly educated professionals and people involved in the arts or skilled workers, who soon found employment in the rapidly expanding factories. The next wave consisted of the highly acceptable Dutch, whose government deliberately encouraged emigration to ease population pressures in a small country. Then, as wartime resentments died down, Germans were admitted in large numbers, well over three hundred thousand of them arriving, as well as seventy thousand Austrians. Next came the turn of the southern Europeans, Italians, Portuguese and

Greeks (and a very few Spaniards). During the mid-1950s the rapid expansion of Canadian colleges and universities attracted an inflow of American academics, which aroused a vocal opposition on the part of Canadian nationalists, who feared the Canadian education would be Americanized. During the 1960s, as a result of the Vietnam War, there was an even more substantial flow north over the border of people who opposed American actions, of young men who resisted the draft, and of those who found the Canadian pace of life more sympathetic than that of the American cities. In all, almost half a million Americans came to Canada between 1946 and the 1980s, and many of them settled into Canadian society and remained.

Finally, also during the 1960s, the Canadian government began to relax the colour barriers of a more prejudiced age, so that considerable numbers of West Indians, East Indians, Chinese coming via Hong Kong and Southeast Asians have entered Canada. Even this relaxation of the barriers was not without its discriminatory elements, however, for within these groups Canadian immigration officials have been selective in their choice of immigrants, choosing where possible the young, the healthy and the better-educated. Exceptions have occurred in the case of family reunification programs, which have allowed a proportion of older and less skilled people to enter the country, sponsored by the working members of their families. There has also been discrimination against potential immigrants suspected of radical political views or connections. Though Canadians in general have deplored the kind of American red-baiting associated with the names of Senators McCarthy and McCarran, their own security officials have been largely affected by the American fever, and left-wing refugees from countries like Chile and Guatemala have experienced particular difficulty in finding refuge among Canadians.

Because of the increasing restrictions on entry into the United States after World War II, a far higher proportion of immigrants to Canada have remained to make their lives here than was the case in earlier generations. The result was a rapid increase in population, of more than 20 percent in the decade from 1941 to 1951 (when it reached 14,000,000) and about 30 percent in the following decade (it reached more than 18,200,000 in 1961). After this the increase gradually slowed down as the economy grew less expansive and rates of immigration were reduced. The retention of the newer Canadians also contributed notably to the diversification of Canadian social and cultural life. Culturalism became politically fashionable during the early 1960s in the hope of preserving Canadian unity by promoting complete and nationwide equality between French- and English-speaking groups. By the end of the decade we were hearing more about multiculturalism, by which it was hoped that the recognition of many immigrant cultures would prevent their representatives from forming themselves into ghettoes of grievance.

In fact, there was surprisingly little ghettoisation, since Canadians began to show themselves far more receptive than in the past to new ways of living, of feeding, of entertainment. Northern cities that had originally been populated by quarrelsome and often xenophobic mixtures of English, Scots, Irish and their descendants, all at once became cosmopolitan centres in which restaurants offering Asian and Mediterranean foods would flourish alongside multinational markets, and life began to take on at least a measure of Southern ease and vitality. The effects were most striking, not in cities like Montreal and Vancouver which already had a touch of the cosmopolitan, but in those like Toronto, which so long had been despised for its Sabbatarian dullness and moralism, and now began to present a rich and variegated range of lifestyles. The traditional moralism was driven underground if not wholly expelled.

THE GREAT POSTWAR IMMIGRATIONS coincided with the coming of age of literature and the arts in Canada and the development of a recognizable national culture. It was a naissance rather than a renaissance, for anything that existed before in Canada was not revived but transcended. While it would be wrong to suggest that artists and cultural entrepreneurs coming from abroad were alone responsible for this cultural upsurge, since one can find in Canadian life the roots of everything that happened, there is no doubt that they played a leading role in realizing the possibilities of the situation.

To understand what happened during the crucial period of change between the 1950s and the 1970s in the artistic life of Canada we must look back at the past of literature and the other arts in the country. The two major cultures in Canada, the French and the English, have remained largely separate, though they show similarities of development, since each of them falls into two phases: a colonial era in which the old country traditions were adapted rather uneasily to a new environment which most people regarded as hostile, and a national era when the culture took on a distinctive character that its artists sought to express, abandoning irrelevant traditions.

The early French immigrants, like the English, Irish and Scots who reached Newfoundland and the Atlantic colonies during the seventeenth and eighteenth centuries, brought with them living peasant cultures. These were manifestations of a village existence, however, and survived only in early pioneer communities. They had little influence on the literate urban culture which the nascent colonial towns and cities tried to perpetuate as they sought to create in a strange environment a replica of the old worlds from which their peoples had come. It would be a long time before immigrants recognized that in their efforts to subjugate the environment, they were in fact creating new societies for which new forms of expression were appropriate.

In consequence, as the poet Louis Dudek once said, English Canadian poetry "begins with decadent romantic lyric and with the lees of late-eighteenth-century sentimental poetry imported from Europe." Early English-language poets, up to the late nineteenth century, like Oliver Goldsmith the younger, Charles Heavysege and Charles Sangster, showed no originality of form and very little response to the special nature of the Canadian environment. Early French Canadian poets, like Octave Crémazie and Louis Fréchette, are somewhat more interesting because they show at least the passionate resentment of a people proud of their past and anxious to redress the humiliations of their defeat in 1760.

As for early Canadian fiction, its tone was already set shortly after the Conquest by Frances Brooke's *The History of Emily Montague*, which, significantly, is concerned with garrison life. It is a novel of manners that might easily have been written about a small town with a nearby military camp in eighteenth-century England if it were not for a few French characters and the Canadian winter, which the English lady, Mrs Brooke, had clearly experienced with a horror she did not attempt to disguise. "The rigour of the climate suspends the very powers of the understanding; what then must become of those of the imagination?"

And, indeed, in what passes for literature in Canada until near the end of the Victorian era, the imagination does seem to be paralyzed, and the best writing is descriptive and narrative, the vigorous, functional prose of explorers like Samuel Hearne in the late eighteenth and David Thompson in the early nineteenth century. Such writers were so involved in the pressures of experience that they made use of literary conventions rather than being dominated by them. In the same way, the best writers that came out of the early nineteenth-century settlements was that which set out to portray factually or satirically the realities of Canadian life at the time.

Prominent among them were the English sisters, Susanna Moodie and Catharine Parr Traill — members of the famous bluestocking Strickland family — whose hopes of duplicating the life of the English squirearchy in the woodlands of Upper Canada came to nothing, and who wrote their books out of a bitter experience of trying to sustain gentility in an alien environment. Because of this intense involvement, Susanna's *Roughing It in the Bush* and Catharine's *The Backwoods of Canada* seem to give a more authentic portrayal of life during the 1830s on the pioneer verges of Upper Canada than any novel written during the same period. In the Maritimes it was satire rather than documentation that brought authenticity. Thomas Chandler Haliburton in *The Clockmaker; or, the Sayings and Doings of Sam Slick of Slickville* (1836) and Thomas McCulloch in *Letters of Mephibosheth Stepsure* (1860) were frustrated reformers who tried to laugh their neighbours out of their follies and prejudices by creating in sketches for periodical publication, a comic yet very realistic picture of the Atlantic provinces just before the Victorian era.

LIKE EARLY CANADIAN LITERATURE, MOST early Canadian painting, apart from the work of peasant *naïfs* in Quebec, is that of uninspired imitators of European academic styles. When Queen Victoria's son-in-law, Viscount Lorne, then governor general, founded the Royal Canadian Academy in 1879, the paintings exhibited showed a conventionalized perception hardly distinguishable from that of the Royal Academicians in London. The most interesting early painters in Canada were a small group of British army officers trained as topographical artists in the days before photography, who used their excellent training in drawing and watercolour to paint the landscape in their spare time, and they did so with direct and fresh perceptions. The best of them was Thomas Davies. His clear-coloured sketches of Canadian landscape in the late eighteenth century are interesting as historical documents and also capture something of the mythical resonances of the northern wilderness. It is to the topographers and to a few *plein air* enthusiasts like the immigrant pre-Raphaelite William G. R. Hind that we owe the first real attempts to inter- pret the landscape, which was later to become so much the abiding preoccupation — one might almost say ob- session — of writers and painters in Canada.

But many potentially good painters of this age were destroyed by their subservience to academic conven- tions. One was that very interesting man, Paul Kane. In 1845 Kane travelled across the prairies to the Pacific coast with the aim of studying and recording the native Indian cultures before they died out. When he returned he painted a series of vast canvasses that portrayed In- dian life in an artificially heroic manner. Only recently have the actual sketches which Kane painted on small pieces of board come to light; they reveal a far more original painter than one would have imagined from his finished work. He had a sharp eye for mood and move- ment and a fresh sense of colour, but he subdued all this to please a Victorian public in Toronto and Montreal that was accustomed to academic painting and to a false image of the "noble savage."

In literature the consciousness of landscape setting first began to appear with the group of writers generally known as the Confederation Poets, a somewhat mislead- ing title, in view of the fact that only one of them, Charles G. D. Roberts, began to write even as early as the 1880s. The other three, Bliss Carman, Archibald Lampman and Duncan Campbell Scott, were men of the 1890s, and in many ways they were typical of their dec- ade, with its neo-romanticism and its sentimental rebel- lion against the Victorian conventions. Their models were Keats, Rossetti and Matthew Arnold, whom they followed skilfully, but all of them occasionally rose above mere derivativeness, and Duncan Campbell Scott did so frequently. It is to them — and particularly to

Lampman and Roberts — that we owe the first effective evocation in literature of the forms and moods of the Canadian countryside. Scott, who worked for many years in the Department of Indian Affairs, expressed in often very moving verse his observations of the native peoples, at this time of their greatest decline.

This was also the period when the influences of Baudelaire and the poets who followed him first became evident in Quebec with the work of the group of poets known as the Montreal School. Its members absorbed rather eclectically the rapidly changing French fashions of the 1890s, from the Parnassians to the Symbolists. Among them was the first Canadian poet who might conceivably be regarded as great: the golden boy Emile Nelligan, who produced his whole work in his teens, lost his reason at the age of twenty, and survived for more than forty years, unproductive, insane and almost unrivalled up to the time of his belated death.

From France also came the influences that helped to mould the perceptions of the first two major Canadian painters, Ozias Leduc and James Wilson Morrice. Leduc, a self-taught Quebec church decorator, was probably the best of the painters who learned from the Impressionists. He produced — in an obscure Laurentian village — still lifes as glowing and splendid as those of Chardin, and landscapes where the Impressionist light gains an otherworldly limpidity. Morrice, son of a rich family of Montreal merchants, became a truly cosmopolitan painter, passing from the orbit of the Impressionists into that of the Fauves and moving as an equal among the painters of the School of Paris.

On the experiments of Leduc and Morrice the most famous school of Canadian painters, the Group of Seven, based their practice. There were really eight painters involved, for Lawren Harris, A. Y. Jackson, Arthur Lismer, Frederick Varley, Frank Carmichael, Francis Hans Johnston, and J. E. H. Macdonald were closely associated between 1913 and 1917 with Tom Thomson. He shared their preoccupation with a visual re-exploration of the Canadian landscape, using the techniques of the Impressionists, of Cézanne and of Art Nouveau. Thomson, perhaps the most talented, drowned in 1917; A. Y. Jackson, the movement's best-known master, survived until 1974. Pushing far into the wilderness, these men observed and recorded the forms and colours of the Canadian landscape as had never been done before by painters; they established a colour range so vibrant and an interpretation of natural form so compelling that most educated Canadians are still inclined to see their country with a vision shaped by these remarkable men.

But the Group's influence on Canadian painting was heavy and lingering. Only a few other painters of importance emerged from their shadow in the early part of the century — notably Emily Carr and David Milne — and it was only in the late 1930s that a group of French Canadian painters broke away from local influences and figurative traditions to embrace the modernist experimental trends that flourished in Paris and later in New York. Notable among them were Alfred Pellan and Paul-Emile Borduas, Jacques de Tonnancour and Jean-Paul Riopelle, the only contemporary Canadian who also enjoyed a great reputation as a leading painter in France.

In the modern age literature in Canada has followed a development rather like that of the English and American traditions, beginning with the vivification of poetry, proceeding to fiction, going on to criticism and culminating in drama. The vital period for poetry was the 1930s, with the emergence of the Montreal school dominated by Smith, Scott and Klein and of Toronto poets like E. J. Pratt and Dorothy Livesay. Smith, Scott and Livesay were influenced by the English poets of the 1930s and given to an original combination of satirical social criticism and lyrical celebration of the wilderness landscape. During the 1940s, the American influence of Pound and Williams became important, but later poets would move out into a distinctively Canadian idiom.

Modernist Canadian poets in the 1930s tended to be rather self-consciously nationalist, and nationalism was also one of the components of the new fiction that began to appear in the late 1930s. In fact, this early period seemed to be dominated by the contrast between the undifferentiated North Americanism of Morley Callaghan, whose *They Shall Inherit the Earth* appeared in 1935, and the nationalism of Hugh MacLennan, whose *Barometer Rising*, a resolutely Canadian novel with a message of unification, appeared in 1941.

IN THE YEARS AFTER WORLD WAR II, Canadians became conscious for the first time of the importance of a vigorous and characteristic artistic life to a nation emerging into self-awareness. Native writers and artists grew in vigour, talented immigrants provided stimulation and the community intervened directly through official channels in patronage of the arts.

In the 1950s official support came in two different ways. The Canadian Broadcasting Corporation had been founded in 1936 as a Crown corporation, modelled largely on the English BBC. Along with its mandate to provide a unifying voice in Canada, it had what its directors and producers then interpreted as a duty to foster the literary arts. It was a period when writers still found it hard to earn a living by their work, and the CBC helped them by commissioning scripts of many kinds. More than that, it fostered radio drama, and kept both acting and dramatic writing alive at a time when Canadian live theatre had been in eclipse for a long time. CBC programs provided an outlet for short stories and poems when there were few literary magazines, and encouraged criticism, helping to make up for the poverty of Canadian periodicals and publishing until these began to develop in the 1960s. The CBC is now, in the 1980s, a negligible cultural force in Canada, but its importance at a vital period of development in Canadian literature was great.

But official intervention went much further when the Royal Commission on National Development in the Arts, Letters, and Sciences was set up in 1949 under the chairmanship of Vincent Massey, later the first Canadian governor general of Canada. In 1951 the Commission issued a report charting the almost total official neglect of the cultural life of the country. As a result, in 1957, the Canada Council was established to provide patronage, not only in the form of grants to individual writers, artists, musicians and other creative people, but also to support the theatres and the performing companies that began to appear in the decades after the war, largely under the direction of dedicated immigrants. To list some of the institutions that now began to illuminate the darkness of the Canadian cultural world is to indicate only a fragment of the wealth of new endeavour: The Royal Winnipeg Ballet, the National Ballet of Canada and Les Grands Ballets Canadiens; the Shakespeare Festival at Stratford and the Shaw Festival at Niagara-on-the-Lake; the Citadel Theatre in Edmonton, the Neptune Theatre in Halifax, the Playhouse in Vancouver, and Tarragon and Passe Muraille in Toronto. Orchestras and opera companies began springing up all over the country, along with local festivals of the arts. For the great naissance of the arts in Canada reconfirmed emphatically the strong regionalism of the country — the fact that, try though they might, Toronto and Montreal have never succeeded in drawing all artistic activity towards them.

Not only did the post-war period produce a great upsurge in the performing arts; it also produced a corresponding creative surge among dramatic writers and composers, which reflected the general literary and artistic vitality of the period. As the various arts moved into maturity one of the most striking features of the period was the shedding of the overt nationalism of the 1930s and 1940s, and the remarkable variation in styles and preoccupations that emerged. Writers and painters no longer felt they had to tell themselves and the world that they were Canadians; they could take that for granted and go ahead with developing their techniques to give expression to their imaginative visions of Canadian life. There are too many names to mention them all, and perhaps it is sufficient to remark that by now novelists like Robertson Davies, Margaret Atwood and Margaret Laurence and poets like Earle Birney, Al Purdy and Michael Ondaatje have ceased to be merely Canadian names. They are recognized abroad as representatives of a distinctive national tradition, and so, in their own fields, are painters like Jean-Paul Lemieux, Alex Colville and Jack Shadbolt, and architects like Arthur Erickson.

Patrons never create artists, and it would be pointless to attribute to official institutions the surge in the arts that has taken place during the past three decades in Canada. Yet it was fortunate that a national sense of urgency produced the Canada Council when it could be most useful, not merely in giving artists time to work, by awarding bursaries and fellowships and by sustaining theatres, art galleries and performing companies, but also by helping Canadian publishers and magazines to survive in a competitive world, thus offering adequate opportunities for Canadian writers to reach Canadian audiences.

For Canadian culture — and especially anglophone culture — is perpetually rendered precarious by the presence below the border of mass organized cultural industries operating in the same language. The power of the American film industry has made it difficult for Canadian film-makers to reach audiences even in Canada; magazine racks are filled with American publications and drugstore shelves with American paperback novels. Canadian schools and colleges often have to put up with American textbooks because it is not profitable enough to publish Canadian counterparts. American television stations beam their programs over the whole length of the international border. Canadians are divided three ways: between those who are indifferent to the steady Americanization of the media, those who feel that Canadian culture is strong and individual enough to stand up to the competition, and those — including many of the writers and artists — who feel it is imperilled and must be defended. Up to the present, for all their limitations, institutions like the Canada Council, which give individual artists and cultural institutions the means to keep on working, to survive against continental odds, seem to have been the best protection for the arts in Canada. But one day soon, if the nation's culture is to have any validity, it will have to depend, as all great cultures have done, on the power of its own creativity.

CHAPTER
21

Work and Play

THE GREAT DEPRESSION AND THE WAR that followed it
brought about profound changes in the way people
worked, in the general condition of the working population and in the welfare of the non-working population.
The nature of industry continued to change, with the
hitherto dominant primary and secondary (manufacturing) industries yielding place to the service industries,
including the growing number of public servants who
were needed to administer increasing government intervention in many sectors of social life.

This occurred partly because the Depression had
shown the great vulnerability of a society which, in a
major economic crisis, depended for its welfare on private charity. It is true that the state had already moved
to intervene on behalf of the underprivileged even before the Depression, when the first old age pension was
instituted, under pressure from J. S. Woodsworth and a
number of other radical MPs; it was a meagre concession
to the idea of public responsibility, for it allowed a mere
$20 a month, granted only after the applicant had
passed a strict means test. But during the Depression

even the old-line parties were sufficiently alarmed to think in terms of a radical intervention on the part of the state, and in January 1935 R. B. Bennett, the Conservative prime minister then in office, attempted to follow the example of Franklin D. Roosevelt by proposing a New Deal for Canada whose outline anticipated in a remarkable way what subsequent governments would actually do after the war. He proposed legislating a maximum work week, a minimum wage and better regulation of working conditions. He called for unemployment, health and accident insurance and promised to offer a more generous old age pension and to institute agricultural support programs.

All Bennett actually succeeded in doing was to establish the Canadian Wheat Board to help the farmers sell their grain; he was voted out of office later in 1935 before he could begin to implement the rest of the program. In any case his proposals were declared outside the competence of the federal government in 1937 by the Judicial Committee of the Privy Council in Westminster, which was then the ultimate court of appeal as far as Canadian laws were concerned. As a consequence, the provision of relief for the unemployed and destitute was thrown back on the provinces and the municipalities. There was no uniformity in the relief programs, and a family of five in Nova Scotia might receive $20 a month, while a similar family in Alberta would receive three times as much. When thousands of young unemployed rode the rails from eastern Canada to the west coast because at least the climate was more endurable there, the local governments in the West restricted their aid to families.

The federal government, using the army, established Unemployment Relief Camps for single unemployed and homeless men, paying them twenty cents a day for working in the bush, a program that caused great bitterness among the men who felt that, because of their misfortunes, they were being treated as if they were criminals. The result in 1935 was a mass strike in the camps; the strikers converged on Vancouver, where they started the On to Ottawa Trek, hundreds of them riding the freight trains east to lay their claims before the government in the capital. They were intercepted by the Mounted Police in Regina, where one of the most violent riots of a bitter period took place.

Finally, in 1940, when the Depression had ended and the war was creating almost full employment, the federal government introduced the first of the series of programs which led to the present Canadian welfare state when it passed the long overdue Unemployment Insurance Act.

After the Great War, the leaders of the Allied countries had made great promises, typified in Lloyd George's call in Britain to make that land "a fit country for heroes to live in," but the Depression everywhere had revealed the hollowness of those promises, and during World War II politicians began to think more seriously of creating a society where the means of something more than a meagre life of toil could be made available to all.

Canada, with its alternating Liberal and Conservatve governments, was slower than Britain — where a Labour government gained power in 1945 — to meet such expectations. In 1944, however, a family allowance program was instituted and in 1952 the Old Age Security Pension was universalized and means tests were abolished. Later, in 1967, a Guaranteed Income Supplement was introduced for people who had no other income than the Old Age Security Pension, in 1963 a contributory Canada Pension Plan was started and in 1969 a countrywide medicare program was instituted to bring uniformity into the patchwork of provincial medical assistance programs that already existed.

All the social legislation of the 1960s, which virtually established the Canadian welfare state, was passed or prepared by Lester Pearson's Liberal minority government that lasted from 1963 to 1968. The Liberals moved left of centre because social legislation brought Pearson the support he much needed in Parliament from the New Democratic Party, the new social democratic group into which the Co-operative Commonwealth Federation had metamorphosed in 1961, and which was now led by T. C. Douglas, the former CCF premier of Saskatchewan.

One of the important factors which distinguished the New Democratic Party from its predecessor was that now this avowedly socialist party had the active support of the Canadian Labour Congress, which itself had been formed by the union in 1956 of the two rival labour organizations, the Trades and Labour Congress and the Canadian Congress of Labour, and which represented about 70 percent of organized Canadian workers. The Confederation of National Trade Unions, situated mainly in Quebec and originally established as Catholic organizations under church influence, was the principal body remaining outside the CLC. The deliberate involvement of the CLC in politics, mirroring the participation of the Trades Union Congress in the British Labour party, was a reflection of the growing strength of the Labour movement in Canada and of its acceptance as part of the changing socio-political structure of Canada. Capital, Labour and the State had moved nearer to an uneasy accommodation.

UNION MEMBERSHIP EXPANDED RAPIDLY during World War II, when the decline in unemployment created a tight labour market, of which the international unions, helped by funds injected by the American headquarters, took advantage to build up their memberships in Canada. In the decade from 1939 to 1949 union membership grew from 360,000 to over a million, and there was a further rapid surge in the late 1960s and the early 1970s, when large numbers of white collar workers and public employees became organized, bringing many women into the labour movement, and by 1981 membership was nearing a peak of three and a half million. This was about 37 percent of Canadian workers, leaving many industries and undertakings unorganized and agricultural workers almost entirely so. The balance of allegiances has changed, for the new white collar and public service unions have tended to be exclusively Canadian, and this has shifted the balance of strength against the international unions. This development has pleased Canadian nationalists, particularly since it has led the Canadian memberships of some of the international unions, like the United Automobile Workers, to insist on autonomy.

During the 1960s and 1970s the unions were able to make considerable advances not only in membership, but also in winning favourable contracts, which notably improved the economic position and working conditions of Canadian employees. The benefits tended to spill over to unorganized workers, many employers being willing to pay fairly good wages, provided they escaped the restrictive practices often insisted on by the unions. At the same time there remained a notable discrepancy in wage levels between various regions, with the Atlantic provinces remaining the lowest paid, Quebec the next lowest, and British Columbia the highest. In 1983 the average weekly earnings of workers in the Atlantic provinces were $347 and those of workers in British Columbia, $424, a reflection of the continued depression of the eastern Canadian economy, where unemployment is habitually the highest in Canada. The position of the unions was strengthened by the creation of a federal Labour Code and a Labour Relations Board to administer it, with similar bodies in the provinces, which give official certification to the unions and administer the regulations regarding minimum wages and maximum hours of work that most provinces as well as the federal government now sustain.

Nevertheless, in spite of this protective framework, relations between workers and employers do tend to reflect the economic situation. Since the slowing expansion of the economy in the 1980s, which produced unemployment running as high as 15 percent in some regions of Canada, the tendency has been for unions to fight to keep their past gains or at best to accept less generous settlements than they would once have demanded.

THE FACT REMAINS THAT WITH ALL THE ADVANTAGES offered by the welfare state, the average worker, the average old person, the average unemployed person is far better off than before World War II, when only the slightest of safety nets was provided for the unfortunate. There are still many poor people, though what we regard as poverty and what we regard as an adequate standard of living have changed over the decades, and many people now officially classed as poor would have seemed relatively well off during the Depression and in earlier generations. (Recent statistics place an eighth of all families and three-eighths of unattached individuals in the category of poverty.) But there remain situations in which poverty becomes distressing or degrading because it involves a permanent dependence on welfare agencies. Old people, disabled people, families headed by women, and native people living on unprosperous reserves all tend frequently to fall into this category. One does not encounter in Canada distress like that to be seen daily in the streets of Calcutta or Dakka, and death by starvation is rare. However, malnutrition does occur frequently, with long-term consequences, and real psychological patterns of distress come from poverty and dependence on government or private charity. In an upwardly mobile society still dominated by the myth of the self-made man, those who are left behind in the race tend to be ignored.

Still, for the majority of Canadians, life has improved in material ways since as recently as the early 1950s, even though they are far more regulated and bureaucracy-ridden than their forefathers were. The Canadian standard of living is one of the highest in the world; Canadians are, in comparison with workers in other countries, reasonably well protected against unsafe working conditions, though the environment in which they live has deteriorated. They also enjoy reasonably adequate medical services, which are available to everyone; their children are assured of an education commensurate with their abilities (even though not so many Canadians as Americans attend universities); an unprecedented number of people own their own homes and most families have cars and often more than one; most Canadians enjoy far more leisure than their ancestors.

The argument that most people now enjoy more leisure time applies particularly to employed workers who operate on a regular time schedule. With the self-employed it is somewhat different. Farmers, unless they are engaged in dairying or ranching, still work according to the seasons rather than the clock, as they did in the past. A prairie wheat farmer still has a long work-free winter. The prairie summer, on the other hand, is a time of long working hours on the farms, and equipment is often used in the fields by floodlight after dark, with the whole family working hard during harvest time. In construction work there have always been layoffs during hard winter weather in the prairies and central Canada. The logging industry is particularly susceptible to climatic interruptions, not only in the depth of winter but also at the height of summer, when lack of rain can lead to the woods being closed for long periods because of the fire hazards. Fishing in British Columbia, which is dominated by the annual salmon runs, has always been a highly seasonal occupation, as it was when the Pacific coast Indians could store enough preserved food from their summer's catch to give them a winter of leisure and ceremonies. Thus, in the primary industries, the old seasonal patterns survive, and though people working in them take their leisure in a different way from factory or office workers, they experience it according to what many regard as a more natural rhythm, which is why many people choose to continue in such occupations.

Another category, of course, are the self-employed, who also work far less by the clock than factory or office workers, since they are free to set their own time patterns. They include the owners of small businesses, professionals of various kinds, artists and craftspeople. Often, to establish their businesses, or because they find their work absorbingly interesting, they work far longer hours than people who work for others. Yet one can hardly say that they enjoy less leisure, since, especially among artists and craftsmen, their work is of a creative kind that brings its own pleasure. In general, artists work harder for smaller financial gain than most people in Canada. In the categories of incomes that the tax authorities prepare, "Self-employed Entertainers and Artists" regularly rank second-lowest, just above "pensioners." In 1981, for example, their average income was $8,284, as compared to an average income for "Self-employed Doctors and Surgeons" of $57,553. A few highly publicized artists and best-selling writers are rich, but most are poor. The same applies to craft workers. During the 1960s one aspect of the so-called "counter-culture" was a rebellion against the imposed working patterns of factories and offices; many people took up crafts of various kinds that both satisfied their creative urges and freed them from the working patterns of outside institutions, and a considerable craft community still exists in Canada. Once again, it is difficult in such cases to make a clear division between creative work and leisure.

The Canadian employed by others is no longer involved in struggles to reduce a twelve-hour day to a nine-hour day. He or she is likely to work only five days a week and between thirty-five and forty hours. Workers receive at least ten days' paid leave a year, usually more, and enjoy the statutory holidays which vary from province to province but which average about nine days a year. Christmas and Good Friday are religious holidays everywhere in Canada. American historic links are shown in the October observance of Thanksgiving, introduced by the Loyalists, and the early September celebration of Labour Day — as distinct from the European celebration of May Day as a workers' holiday. Canada's strong links with Scotland are shown by the fervent celebration of New Year's Day, while holidays that have a more political flavour are Canada Day — formerly Dominion Day — held on the 1st of July to celebrate the implementation of Confederation on that day in 1867, and Victoria Day in May, commemorating the British monarch who played the greatest personal role in Canadian history. In addition, most of the provinces have public holidays of their own, like St Jean-Baptiste Day in Quebec, St George's Day in Newfoundland, and Discovery Day when the people of the Yukon celebrate the finding of gold on the Klondike. With all these holidays it has been estimated that all employed Canadians enjoy a minimum of 124 days annually, or more than a third of the whole year, which they can spend as they wish.

CANADIANS FIND AS MANY WAYS as other peoples of spending their leisure productively or enjoyably. Some use it to improve their material situation, moonlighting in various ways. Many spend a great deal of their leisure working on their houses (a fair number of Canadians even build their own wooden dwellings), or on their boats if they happen to live on the east or west coast, or in their gardens. The English-style gardens of west coast cities like Vancouver and Victoria, blessed with mild winters, are among the most beautiful in the world.

But many also, in one way or another, follow the life of the arts. Before the arrival of cinema and radio, Canadians were much inclined to make their own music, publicly in connection with the churches and privately around the parlour piano, and to organize amateur theatricals, particularly in small and remote communities that the American or British professional touring companies did not reach. In those days there were few Canadian professionals in any of the arts, though the church organist would often serve as the nucleus around which musical activities might develop in a small community.

In recent decades, after a hiatus when various media — the cinema, radio and later television — seemed to be turning them into a captive and passive audience, Canadians are participating in the arts as they have never done before. They flock to live presentations of various kinds, or to art galleries, in such numbers that some statisticians have estimated more Canadians attend arts events than sports events. Classes in the arts flourish, as well as creative writing schools, on a community level and in academic institutions. Although most students in these classes remain at best amateurs, they do represent a wide public involvement in the arts, which is reflected in the popularity of small-town arts festivals. On a more passive level there is also a steadily growing readership for Canadian books, so that each year more writers make a living by their publications, and more publishers can survive by printing Canadian books.

Many Canadians are enthusiastic followers of sports and more people are active in amateur sports than attend professional sports events as spectators. Millions of Canadians do become spectators vicariously, however, by watching their favourite sports on television.

Some Canadian sports are indigenous, developed by earlier generations as they coped with the problem of filling in time during long, workless winters. Lacrosse is the oldest Canadian game still being played. It was based on an Indian ball game called baggawatay that was seen by the French when they arrived on the St Lawrence in the sixteenth century. By using this game as a ruse, Pontiac's warriors gained entry into the fort of

Michilimackinac in 1763 and massacred its defenders. Lacrosse became popular among the settlers of early Canada, and when the Dominion of Canada came into existence in 1867 it was adopted as the national game, but it soon began to wane because another Canadian game that may originally have been borrowed from the Indians came into vogue.

Ice hockey, which Canadians now regard as their national game, is said to have first been played in something near its present form by British soldiers in Quebec seeking to relieve the boredom of winter garrison duty. It was slow in being accepted as an authentic sport, and the first enduring team, the McGill Hockey Club, was established in 1880. Ice hockey leagues came into existence, and in 1893 the governor general, Lord Stanley, bestowed an official blessing by presenting the Stanley Cup, since then the leading competitive award in ice hockey. No game more deeply arouses Canadian passions than does this fastest of all team sports.

The other games that Canadians follow with commitment have their origins elsewhere, like the American game of baseball, which as a summer game has greatly outrivalled the English game of cricket. Canada is the only Commonwealth country not to have adopted the English ball game with enthusiasm. English forms of football — soccer and rugby — are played, but here again the more boisterous American football is more popular. In sports, in fact, Scotland has made a greater mark in Canada than England, since golf is very popular in Nova Scotia and British Columbia, where the mild winters allow it to be played almost the whole year round, and curling is a great sport in the winter provinces and even in the Arctic.

MUCH CANADIAN LEISURE ACTIVITY, as befits a country with a small population and much land, tends to be unstructured and is often solitary. Here the wilderness, which has dominated the Canadian consciousness in so many

ways, is important. The vast spaces of this largely un-
tamed environment provide a setting for many outdoor
activities that are almost sports. Skiing is most popular
in the mountains of British Columbia and Alberta and in
the Laurentian hills of Quebec, and in recent years
many people have been deserting the crowded and commercialized slopes of the resorts for cross-country skiing.
The Rockies and the Selkirks lend themselves especially
to mountaineering, and some of the great contemporary
climbers in the Himalayas have trained in the ranges of
British Columbia. The Rideau Canal in Ottawa is almost
as thickly populated by winter skaters as the canals of
Amsterdam, and tobogganing and sleighing are favourite pastimes in Quebec. In that province an air of event
and leisurely ritual is given to such domestic late winter
occupations as "sugaring off" in the maple groves (testing the first maple syrup of the season).

Thanks to an unparalleled abundance of fresh waterways and lakes, as well as the intricate salt-water channels of all its coasts, Canada offers remarkable facilities
for boating. Sailboats and speedboats figure largely in
the leisure patterns of communities along the British Columbia coast, in the Maritimes and on the Great Lakes,
while canoe tripping is popular in the Shield country
with its networks of lakes, small rivers and portages.
Thanks also to the great waterways, fishing is a sport
pursued in all parts of the country from the Arctic down
to the American border, and although millions of Canadians and many thousands of tourists go fishing every
year, the country still has untouched lakes full of fine
fish. However, the number of such lakes is declining because of the plague of acid rain caused by the emana-
tions of American and, unfortunately, Canadian
industrial plants, while the salt waters have become depleted by the commercial fishing that in western Canada
has been going on for almost five centuries. It is no
longer possible, as it was in Cabot's day, to catch cod
merely by dipping a bucket over the boat's side.

Hunting is an occupation less favoured than fishing and seems to be declining in popularity, for many people, conscious of ecological problems, now content themselves with observing and photographing animals and are concerned with ensuring the preservation of the many threatened wild species, in the hope that the disaster of the bison's virtual extermination on its native prairies will not be repeated. Groups seeking this end vary from the militant Canadian-founded organization, Greenpeace, which favours dramatic direct action to save whales, seals, mountain sheep and other imperilled species, to the less dramatic Nature Trust in British Columbia, which systematically acquires and protects the habitats of rare animals and plants. Yet if hunting tends to be more restricted by law as well as less popular, many thousands of people still do hunt, from rich American trophy collectors who travel expensively with guides and much equipment and are probably the greatest peril to wildlife in remote areas, to the prairie farmer who drives out with shotgun and dog for a day shooting wild ducks and wild geese along the local sloughs.

Fishing and hunting, the serious occupations of the first Canadians, are part of the mystique of the wilderness that is strong in the modern Canadian mind. Having lost the dread of the wilds that was part of the settler syndrome, Canadians have tried to recapture the experience of the Indians, fur traders and explorers who once moved through the forests, mountains and tall buffalo grass of the roadless prairies as if passing through their natural habitats. Not that all Canadians are willing to replicate the actual journeys or the wilderness living conditions of the fur traders, though some on occasion do. But in summer cottages fringing most of the accessible lakes in the Shield country and the northern parts of the prairie provinces, in cabins on the shores of islands off Nova Scotia and British Columbia, and in summer camps where Canadian children are sent for an annual toughening-up, the past is romantically evoked by direct contact with nature, accompanied by a modicum of pioneer hardship.

In this Canadian wilderness mystique the park systems of the country play an important role. The federal system began when hot springs were discovered in 1885 at Banff during the construction of the Canadian Pacific Railway. Now more than fifty thousand square miles are reserved in representative ecological areas. They range from the series of great mountain parks that includes most of the Canadian Rockies, to seacoast parks on Vancouver Island, Prince Edward Island and Newfoundland (including the historic L'Anse aux Meadows with its Norse relics); from Wood Buffalo National Park in Alberta where the last sizeable herd of bison lives in natural conditions, to Arctic parks on Baffin Island. The most recent addition is an area of primeval forest on Moresby Island in the Queen Charlottes, which was the site of a protracted struggle by environmentalists allied with local Indian bands against the logging interests that wanted to fell the ancient first-growth trees. In their role of preserving still unspoiled natural areas, the national parks are supplemented by the 115,000 square miles of provincial parks, the best known of which is Algonquin Park in Ontario, where Tom Thomson and the Group of Seven painted some of their best work.

Such parks allow people to travel through areas that are in an almost natural state and to see in their appropriate habitat wild animals that elsewhere have fled before encroachments on their environments. Many people can see mountain sheep and goats with no more effort than that involved in driving the mountain highway from Banff to Jasper. But some areas are preserved as wilderness where even roads cannot penetrate and only *bona fide* naturalists are allowed to observe the otherwise undisturbed patterns of wild nature.

Environmental groups have flourished in recent decades as never before in Canada and have achieved some notable successes, often working in alliance with groups of native peoples whose traditional hunting or fishing grounds have been threatened. Governments have been persuaded to introduce measures of stricter environmental control and, to varying degrees, have enforced them. At least some industrial enterprises in ecologically sensitive regions have been halted. The principle of environmental protection has in general been accepted.

But in a country still as economically dependent on natural resource industries as Canada, there are inevitable conflicts of interest where environment issues emerge. In devoting more of their leisure to exploring their wilderness heritage, Canadians have become more conscious of the perils that threaten it, and here sometimes their work and their leisure interests have clashed. Often the person who spends his or her leisure travelling in the wilderness is dependent for a living on industries that are in the hands of corporations whose primary interest lies in exploiting and therefore changing the environment, usually for the worse. Environmental controls are often opposed not only by industrial corporations but also by the labour unions who tend to accept more than they did in the recent past the argument that where jobs are threatened environmental damage has to be accepted.

Canadians at work and at play are indeed faced with a testing problem as the 1980s draw to a close. What ways can be devised to prevent the industries and technological advances that make life easier for us from destroying the environment that gives meaning to our increasing leisure?

CHAPTER
22

Reasons for Revolt

I<small>N MANY PARTS OF THE WORLD</small> and on many levels of society, the 1960s were years of revolt, re-evaluation and change. These manifestations often had special and local causes. In the United States the unpopularity of the Vietnam War helped trigger widespread student revolt, but revolt was also linked with the Civil Rights Movement, in which whites and blacks, young and old, joined together to fight racial discrimination by widespread passive resistance. In China differences within the ruling Communist party opened the way for the anarchic revolt of the young known as the Cultural Revolution. In France a student strike in 1968 created a situation of near-revolution in Paris, which almost toppled the government of Charles de Gaulle. And in Canada a movement of self-assertion among the people of Quebec led at its most extreme to the terrorist acts of the violently separatist Front de libération du Québec (FLQ) and to an equally extreme reaction on the part of the Canadian government, headed by Pierre Trudeau, when it suspended civil liberties by the application of that essentially totalitarian law, the War Measures Act.

These, of course, were the extreme manifestations of a widespread movement of change in lifestyles and social attitudes that took place during the 1960s and the years immediately following. Central to the revolution was the youth revolt that arose from a complex group of causes. It was caused partly by the phenomenon of the baby boom — the large numbers of children born in the years immediately after World War II who began to demand a place in the universities in the sixties. In Canada before World War II, higher education had still been regarded as a matter of privilege, to be enjoyed only by a minority. By the 1950s it had come to be regarded as a right for any capable young person, and there had been a steady growth in enrolments, so that by the early 1950s the student population was double that of 1940, and by the early 1960s it had doubled again.

By now the proportion of Canadian youth attending universities was higher than in any other country except the United States and Sweden, and the proportion of women students was steadily growing (it reached 47 percent by the 1980s). Existing universities were expanded to their utmost capacity, and from the late 1950s new universities were established, such as Carleton (1957), York (1959), Waterloo (1959) and Trent (1963), while former two-year colleges blossomed into full-scale universities. The University of Victoria (1963) and the University of Calgary (1966) were among these. The rapid expansion of facilities led to an equally rapid growth in academic personnel with an inevitable dilution of the quality of teaching and scholarship. Unconvinced of the relevance to real life of what they were being taught, the students also became discontented with the traditional restrictions on student behaviour outside the classroom, and began to press for participation in the operation of the universities, emphasizing their various demands by strikes, sit-ins and other demonstrations.

Such student unrest took on a political edge because of the emergence in the United States, partly as a result of discontent with the Vietnam War, of the New Left, an ill-defined and ephemeral movement of radical revolt that included elements of both traditional anarchism and heretical Marxism. It found most of its following among radicalized students, spreading into Canada with the immigration of Americans who voted with their feet against the state of war.

The New Left was in fact the political expression of a wider social movement, mainly among middle-class youth, that challenged the values and moral standards of the prosperous society that had come into being during the 1960s — an expansive period not yet threatened by the economic crises that would shadow the later 1970s and the 1980s. Attempts were made to create what was variously called a "counter-culture" and an "alternative society," based on a relaxation of moral imperatives manifested in the broader use of hallucinogenic drugs and in the "sexual revolution."

The counter-culture swept up young people from outside the universities as well as students, and created a whole social class or tribe of "hippies" or "flower children," with its own speech patterns and language, its own increasingly uniform styles of dress and coiffure. But it was not entirely a matter of libertinism, of breaking free. The New Leftists and their less overtly political associates proposed a new arrangement of social and political relations that would be based far more than existing arrangements on participation and consensus. As working models of the world they envisaged, the proponents of the counter-culture established urban and rural living communes, collectives devoted to publishing their characteristic literature and consumers' and producers' cooperatives that tended to reflect a return-to-nature philosophy, stressing organically grown foods and handmade products. Whole districts of Canadian cities, like Kitsilano in Vancouver and Yorkville in Toronto,

became suffused with the hippie ethic and loosely knit
ideology, stressing pacifism, decentralization and direct
protest through "be-ins," "love-ins" and "sit-ins." Neglected areas of the countryside, like the remote Slocan
Valley in British Columbia were partly repopulated by
counter-cultural communes that bought up deserted
farms, brought land back into cultivation and established craft workshops and health food stores, thus
helping to revive moribund local communities.

THE HIPPIE MOVEMENT FADED AWAY in the 1970s as a more
conservative generation of young people appeared, directed once again to more material goals. But it had
acted as a kind of spearhead, as the extreme manifestation of libertarian attitudes that to some degree permeated Canadian society during this period of
increasing national consciousness, of Expo '67 and its
own special euphoria. Certainly, by the time the 1960s
had come to an end, our system had become less restrictive in its regulation of individual behaviour. Amend-
ments had been made to the Criminal Code which
reflected Pierre Trudeau's view that "there's no place for
the state in the bedrooms of the nation." Divorce proce-
dures had been relaxed and common law unions had
lost their stigma except among religious fundamental-
ists, while the broad acceptance of homosexual relationships was a sign of growing tolerance within an
increasingly pluralistic society.

But there have perhaps been two important heritages
of the revolt of the young, of the now-vanished New
Left and of the more bizarre aspects of the counter-cultural revolt of the 1960s. First of all there has been the
lingering concern for an imperilled environment which
we have already noted. Second, yet perhaps more important, there has been a widespread sense that democracy must become more participatory than our present
parliamentary system allows. Society in recent decades
has become permeated with a profound distrust of

professional politics and politicians. This results partly from the fact that the media, and especially television, have made them more closely observable than they ever were in the past, and they have fallen victim to the contempt that comes from familiarity. At the same time the movements of the 1960s and afterwards brought a renewed sense of the power of public protest, especially when the protesters were willing to carry their actions to the point of dramatic civil disobedience. Here again the media played their part, for a demonstration that might seem unimpressive when described in a paragraph of print suddenly becomes dramatic when it is enacted visually and audibly on the television screens in the living rooms of a nation.

The recognition of the possibility and the acceptability of protest in present-day society has helped to draw attention to surviving injustices and inequalities, and in many areas has resulted in dramatic changes, even though there are areas in which much still needs to be done to redress the wrongs caused by past histories of discrimination and neglect.

At least three important Canadian movements have arisen out of unjust and inequitable situations, and have had varying degrees of success in modifying the obstinate fabric of Canadian society. One, in which the outcome was generally successful, was that of the French-speaking Canadians, and especially the Québécois, to establish their own culture and their virtual autonomy as an equal community within the general structure of federal Canada. The second movement had only a moderately successful outcome. After the women of Canada achieved political gains with their equal voting power, they struggled to translate that equality into its social and economic equivalents. The third, even more modestly successful movement, was that in which the native peoples reasserted themselves after generations of silence, trying to revive their ancient and half-vanished cultures, and laying claim not only to their lost lands but also to self-government according to their traditional patterns.

CLAIMING ALWAYS TO OCCUPY a province "pas comme les autres," the Québécois have been engaged for more than two centuries in the struggle to adjust the balances created by the Conquest of 1760. Immediately after the Conquest, the British officers who were the first governors of Quebec very wisely acknowledged the separate cultural identity of the people of Quebec by allowing them to keep their language and their religion. On the whole the *canadiens* accepted the settlement effected under the Quebec Act, which confirmed the seigneurs in their traditional rights and left the clergy even more powerful than they had been in New France, since to a great extent they played the vital role of mediating between conquered and conquerors.

The *canadiens* were unused to democratic government, so that they did not immediately take offence at the rather autocratic form of administration, under military officers acting as civil governors, which the British set up. It was the British merchants in Montreal who objected strongly to the absence of an elected assembly, which they imagined they would control, since in the eighteenth century the British Parliament and other assemblies deriving their powers from it were closed to Catholics. But when the Constitutional Act was passed in 1791, and Canada was divided into the Lower and Upper provinces, provision was made for rule by a governor assisted by an appointed legislative council and an elected assembly, the qualification for voting being based not on religion but on property. French Canadian Catholics could vote their own people into the assembly, and did so with enthusiasm, so that the English-speaking inhabitants of Montreal and the Eastern Townships were in a permanent electoral minority while Lower Canada existed. The fact that they themselves suffered no political disadvantage because of their religion did not make the *canadiens* sympathetic to those who did. In 1807 and again in 1808 the merchant Ezekiel Hart was elected to represent Trois-Rivières in the assembly, and on each occasion he was prevented from sitting by the French-speaking majority because of his Jewish religion.

The governor and his advisors held executive power in Lower Canada, and, except for certain money votes, the Legislative Assembly could legislate very little on its own account. The result was a deep division within the community along racial and social as well as political lines. The British inhabitants of the province tended to support the governor in his autocratic acts, and the French landowners and professionals who dominated the assembly embraced with zeal the democratic rhetoric that had never been heard in autocratic New France. (It had only appeared in Quebec during the American Revolution when the rebels in the Thirteen Colonies sent their emissaries into Quebec and sowed the first seeds of republican sentiment.) When the extreme radical Patriote movement developed in Quebec in the early nineteenth century, led by the Speaker of the aggrieved Legislative Assembly, Louis-Joseph Papineau, it was Jeffersonian democracy from south of the border that they took as their model rather than Jacobin republicanism as it had been developed in revolutionary France. The rebellion of 1837 was defeated, to be followed by another in 1838 which was heavily repressed, with the Church standing aside and giving tacit support to the British authorities, who, even if they were Protestant, were still, in the eyes of the bishops, the duly constituted government of the country.

The Union Act that followed the rebellion and brought Upper and Lower Canada into the single province of Canada, was manifestly discriminatory against the French-speaking population. Although the population of Lower Canada at that time was much greater than that of the sparsely settled Upper province, the number of representatives sent to the assembly was the same for Canada East as for Canada West, and the financial arrangements of the union were so contrived that the Lower Canadians had to help pay off the large public debt incurred by Upper Canada, to a great extent as a result of the War of 1812. Nevertheless, as we have seen, a *modus vivendi* was worked out between English- and French-speaking reformers so that there was a semblance of political equality. However, the people of Quebec went through periods of anxiety as the English-speaking population in the 1850s moved into a majority position, and it was not until they could manage their local affairs as a province under Confederation that they began to feel politically secure. Even then there were many, particularly of the radical party called *les Rouges*, who mistrusted the continuing link with the English-speaking provinces; these were among the ancestors of present-day nationalists.

The economic even more than the political situation kept alive the banked-up fires of Québécois resentment. The economy of New France had been a backward one, based on subsistence farming and on a cash flow dominated by the fur trade. Apart from small-scale shipbuilding and iron founding, manufacturing hardly existed and commerce other than the fur trade was ill-developed.

At the Conquest this rudimentary commerce and industry fell into the hands of aggressive British and American merchants who followed hard on the heels of the armies and took over business in Quebec and Montreal, making the latter city their commercial domain until far into the twentieth century. They built it into the transport and financial centre of Canada, and held the control of its local and also its national trade firmly in their own hands. The situation was complicated by the educational system and the social attitudes that the Québécois had developed. Early nationalist leaders and their priestly allies often taught that all that was valuable in Quebec society was based on attachment to the land, and that true *canadiens* should not seek to become immersed in the materialistic society of the English-speaking world. At the same time, the classical colleges operated by the Church were ill equipped to train industrialists or financiers or technicians. The sons of the *bourgeois* and the *habitants* who went through their classes either joined the priesthood or became teachers themselves or swelled the large and somewhat parasitical professional population of the province, becoming doctors or lawyers, or more often notaries. It was out of this professional class that the Québécois politicians most often emerged.

The result was an ill-balanced and divided society in which the Church controlled education, the French-speaking lawyers controlled local politics and played their part on the national level and virtually all business other than petty trade was in the hands of English-speaking entrepreneurs. There was not enough land to sustain the agrarian mystique, for by the mid-nineteenth century, when the seigneurial system came to an end, most of it was under cultivation, and the younger sons of the *habitants* began to flock either south to the New England mills or west into the slums of Montreal, where they formed a French-speaking proletariat, working in the factories and competing with the Irish for work on the docks and in the railway yards. Catholicism formed no bond between the two working groups, and there was in fact a long-standing feud between the Irish and French hierarchies and congregations in Canada. Both the local factories and the great financial and transport undertakings that developed in Montreal were owned and operated almost entirely by anglophones, and in that city of French origin English had become the operative language of business. The rich English lived in their own enclaves, notably in Westmount, which they ran as an anglophone municipality distinct from Montreal. Although no one cared to define it in that way at the time, it was a typically colonial situation in a country that was already aspiring to be independent, for "les Anglais" in Westmount seemed to the francophone inhabitants of Quebec remarkably like the sahibs inhabiting their cantonments on the edge of Indian cities and waited on by the "natives." Westmount was an enduring and painful reminder of the Conquest.

There were other reasons for the Québécois to believe that they were being treated in Canada as citizens on sufferance. While the British North America Act guaranteed the status of English in French-speaking Quebec, the only English-speaking province in which French was guaranteed was Manitoba, and the provincial authorities there quickly went back on their promise to assist French-speaking schools. There was strong social pressure on French-speaking Canadians outside Quebec to assimilate into the anglophone population, and while a person speaking English would be widely understood in Montreal, a Québécois who spoke no English would be like a bewildered foreigner in Calgary or Vancouver. Even in the Canadian government service, which legally and theoretically was bilingual, the nation's business was conducted almost entirely in English; francophones were almost as scarce as women in the federal civil service before the 1960s.

IT WAS SMALL WONDER that at the beginning of the 1960s, when Jean Lesage, René Lévesque and a group of Quebec intellectuals coined the slogan, "Maîtres chez nous," a majority of Québécois should agree that the time had come to liberate their society from its subservience to alien influences. For practical purposes, those influences included not only the anglophone financial and industrial establishments, but also the intellectual ascendancy of the Church, which, while claiming to maintain the spiritual integrity of French Canadian life, had so often encouraged its material subordination.

Traditional Quebec nationalism, in spite of *les Rouges*, had more often been conservative and even reactionary than liberal and innovatory. Its protagonists in the early twentieth century, like Edmond de Nevers and Jules-Paul Tardivel, had deliberately turned their backs on the modern age, as Tardivel did when he declared:

> It is not necessary that we possess industry and money. . . . Our mission is to possess the earth and spread ideas. To cling to the soil, to raise large families, to maintain the hearths of intellectual and spiritual life, that must be our role in America.[26]

The Abbé Groulx, one of the most revered of clerical nationalists, actually coined the phrase, "Notre maître, le passé," and in doing so had implied a rejection of progressive politics and economics, even though he sustained an obstinate kind of populism. Even the greatest of the early nationalist leaders, Henri Bourassa, who sought hard for a way of reconciling the two major cultural traditions of Canada during the period of the Great War and gave some of the best definitions of a workable federalism, adhered to conservative ideas. He was as distrustful of the modern industrial world as he remained dedicated to re-establishing the worship of God in a Catholic way as the dominant aim of Canadian society.

Old-style conservative nationalism eventually sank into a political muskeg under the long government of Quebec by the Union Nationale under Maurice Duplessis, which lasted, with a war-time interruption of five years, from 1936 to 1959. Corrupt and autocratic, that government operated one of the most intricate patronage machines in Canadian history. Duplessis gave expression to his conservatism in battles against the labour unions and in an intolerance of political dissent which led him to pass the notorious Padlock Act, allowing the police to seal premises whose owners were suspect of left-wing activity. Duplessis allowed the Church to keep its power at the price of running his hospital and school systems, and far from turning Quebec into an agrarian paradise, he encouraged even more outside investment, achieving a *modus vivendi* with the Anglo-Celtic establishment that left its power intact while bringing greater economic growth to Quebec. Yet, socially, the province remained backward, its workers badly paid, its farmers poverty-stricken, its schools and hospitals inadequate, its social services scanty.

Strong resistance, especially among intellectuals and labour leaders, had arisen by the time Duplessis died. There was even a bizarre populist movement in the rural areas called the Ralliement des Créditistes that sought to revive rustic life by preaching the monetary reform ideas of Major C. H. Douglas, which had already sparked off a similar movement in Alberta twenty years before. But the main current of change was embodied in a revivified Quebec liberalism. It took two forms, involving groups of Quebec intellectuals who eventually took very different paths, though both were dedicated in their various ways to enhancing the role of Quebec and Quebec people in Canadian life.

On one side were those like Pierre Trudeau and Gérard Pelletier, who detached themselves from the idea that Quebec was a province "pas comme les autres" and sought instead to universalize the French Canadian presence in Canada. The Royal Commission on Bilingualism and Biculturalism worked for six years (1963–69) and eventually produced a many-volumed report detailing the ways in which the French language and French culture were given subordinate status in Canada. As a result, the use of both English and French was decreed in many areas of public life, arousing considerable opposition. Serious, but not always successful, attempts were also made to teach French to elderly and reluctant civil servants. Trudeau and his associates interpreted their task as giving equal rights to individuals all over

Canada, whichever language they spoke, but they remained politically centralist, and resisted any suggestion that Quebec should have a special status within Canada or any kind of autonomy greater than that of the other provinces.

The provincial Liberals who came to power in 1960 after the death of Duplessis, including not only federalists with strong local loyalties like Jean Lesage, but also those like René Lévesque who would later become separatists, saw the situation in a different way as they developed a progressive, as distinct from a conservative, nationalism. They recognized that a great change in social attitudes had taken place in Quebec, based on a final realization that it was no longer an agrarian, village-based society and could not return to that state.

Out of this realization, which they shared with many of the people, emerged what has been called the "Quiet Revolution," reflecting the many changes that were taking place in Quebec life. The emphasis on the family declined, and young Québécois were so little interested in the *revanche du berceau* that the birthrate fell from the highest in Canada to the lowest. Even so, the pressure of children on the schools and colleges in the 1960s was as great as in the rest of Canada and a reform of the antiquated educational system became imperative; it was finally secularized and taken out of the hands of the Chruch. The Labour Code was revised to give more freedom to the unions and to regulate working conditions, a pension plan was introduced for the first time and the social democratic inclinations of the new Quebec nationalism were revealed when René Lévesque as minister of national resources made a first attack on the anglophone business establishment by nationalizing the private electricity companies.

But the social reforms were not enough for the more radical nationalists. They were concerned about the survival of French culture in Canada, which they equated to the survival of the French language, and a growing number of them believed that both the culture and the language could be securely protected only if Quebec became a separate country, the true home of a people who had so obstinately maintained their distinctness throughout two centuries of subjugation. Out of this concern arose a whole series of separatist groups, some of which antedated the Quiet Revolution. They ranged from the violently radical and short-lived Front de libération du Québec, whose terrorist tactics provoked the October Crisis of 1970, to the reformist but still separatist Parti Québécois, which René Lévesque founded in 1970 and led to electoral victory in 1976.

The Quiet Revolution had already helped to change the shape of Quebec society through the creation of new classes of teachers and reform-minded bureaucrats, and through changing the relationship between the state and organized labour in the direction of collaboration rather than mutual confrontation. The Parti Québécois presided over the completion of this process of social change even if it did not achieve its ultimate goal of a separate French-speaking state under the guise of "sovereignty-association." That concept was resoundingly defeated in a 1980 referendum in which the majority of the people of Quebec indicated their desire to remain in Canada.

Paradoxically, that willingness to accept the political status quo was probably encouraged by Bill 101, the controversial *Chartre de la langue française*, which established French not only as the official language of the province of Quebec, but also as the language of workplace, school, communications, commerce and business. No longer forced to work in what they regarded as an imposed language, and encouraged by the withdrawal of a number of all-Canadian business headquarters from Quebec, French-speakers entered into business and industry in unprecedented numbers and seemed to reverse the anti-commercial bias of their past. Undoubtedly the referendum vote of 1980, which would be followed shortly by the electoral defeat of the Parti Québécois, showed that the people believed they had substantially gained their objective of cultural and social independence and could postpone the more problematical gains of political independence. As so often before, they showed the essential pragmatism that underlay their passionate defence of their cultural identity.

JUST AS THE QUÉBÉCOIS DISCOVERED that the early Reform alliances and the provincial autonomy they had gained under Confederation did not lead to their real equality as a cultural community in Canada, so Canadian women quickly found that being able to vote and to sit in Parliament and in the Senate did not give them a genuine equality, either economic, social or cultural. Assumptions of male primacy tended to dominate literature, the media, advertising and social intercourse, from the unthinking use of the word "man" to designate humanity in general to the systematic exploitation of the woman considered as sexual object by advertisers and their photographers. Legal disabilities relating to women's property rights remained; as late as 1973 many Canadians were shocked by the Murdoch Case, in which a divorced Alberta farm wife was denied the half-share of a farm she had worked a quarter-century to build up. Such features of the Criminal Code as the provisions forbidding abortion and until recently limiting instruction in birth control militated against women more than against men.

During and after World War II, Canadian women entered the labour field in such numbers that while in 1951 some 20 percent of them were at work outside the home, by 1981 more than 50 percent were working, and these included 52 percent of married women. Women now make up more than 40 percent of the Canadian working population. Yet in spite of this great incursion into the labour force and in spite of recent moves to gain equal pay for equal work, the average woman still receives less than 64 percent the average pay for men. Moreover, by a substantial ratio, women are more often unemployed than men.

This chronically unfavourable position is due largely to the fact that by coming fairly late into the labour market women have tended to crowd into the expanding but precarious service industries. Only in a few manufacturing industries like textiles were women traditionally employed, and here they were always hired as cheap labour. The poorly organized service industries are a stronghold of part-time employment, which many women prefer because of their family responsibilities, but such work is usually ill-paid and leads nowhere in terms of mobility in the workforce. Other areas, like office work, retail sales, teaching and the medical field have traditionally attracted large numbers of women; 95 percent of nurses and 96 percent of telephone operators are female. But even in those fields women usually occupy the lower and less remunerative positions. Altogether, women hold 75 percent of the jobs in the medical and health field, but they include only 21 percent of physicians and surgeons; less than a third of medical students are now women, so that this situation will not change greatly in the short run. In education an extraordinary pyramid structure exists. Fifty percent of teachers are women; they include 95 percent of kindergarten teachers, 70 percent of elementary school teachers, 33 percent of secondary school teachers, less than 16 percent of university instructors, and, at the apex of the pyramid, less than 5 percent of full professors. Law is still a heavily male profession, while engineering remains almost completely closed to women, with one female engineering student to every twenty males. The vast majority of judges, school principals, high civil servants, broadcasting executives and business executives are men, and all too often the women in these fields are seen — in W. H. Auden's ironic phrase — as "the beautiful dullards / Inspiring their bitter ambitious men."

The situation in Parliament is especially significant, in view of the fact that Canadian women have now been actively involved in politics in various ways for the past seventy years. The present Parliament (1988) contains the highest number of women MPs on record — twenty-eight — and the Cabinet contains the highest number of women ministers — six. But that means only a tenth of the members of the House and less than a sixth of the Cabinet — and all but two of those in minor positions. This is partly a reflection of slowly changing attitudes to the role of women. Most men and many women still think, as recent polls have revealed, that the woman's real place is in the home. Most men resent women being in positions of control, and even in politics women of real ability are often willing to content themselves with the roles of good and loyal but clearly subordinate campaign workers.

It is mainly in the free world of the arts and particularly in literature that women have moved into positions of real influence and prestige, their gifts recognized and their opinions heard. Anglophone writers like Margaret Laurence, Margaret Atwood, Alice Munro, Phyllis Webb, Mavis Gallant, P. K. Page, Dorothy Livesay, Marian Engel, Audrey Thomas stand or have stood (for two have recently died) at the height of their profession, as do Marie-Claire Blais, Anne Hébert and the Acadian Antonine Maillet in the francophone world. The broad recognition of their talents has given them a hearing for their ideas. Even if they have often avoided close identification, they stand near the head of the loosely structured combination which emerged during the great ferment of the 1960s. Such writers and the feminist groups that appeared in the sixties are more militant and less bound by religious and social conventions than the women's organizations that appeared earlier in the century.

Rather like the youth movement, the contemporary women's movement, in Canada as elsewhere, has brought together people with a wide range of attitudes. There are liberal feminists and radical feminists, Marxist feminists and anarcho-feminists; those who fervently advocate lesbianism and those who offer it as one of a number of permissible lifestyles for women. And there has been a corresponding variety in the issues such women's groups have espoused. Some have concentrated on the issue of abortion, regarding choice in such matters as a vital element of a woman's freedom. Some have devoted themselves to situations in which women are especially prone to be victims — wife battering and rape. Others have concentrated on the special problems that arise from the broader employment of women, such as daycare for young children. Yet others have drawn attention to the fact that single mothers and elderly women are among the poorest people in Canada, victims of the discrimination of neglect rather than that of prejudice. Feminist academics, contending that history and social studies have always been male oriented, have launched programs of women's studies. And always the large issues of equal pay, equal working conditions and equal property have been matters of high consideration.

The focus for all these activities was provided by the formation in 1971 of the National Action Committee for the Status of Women, which now brings together 280 groups, often with different approaches and different strategies, varying from demonstrations and marches to petitions and lobbying. In many areas, like the legalization of abortion and the revision of family laws to prevent further incidents resembling the Murdoch Case, progress has been made, as it has in such areas as the introduction of maternity benefits into labour codes and agreements relating to women. The labour movement, so long male-dominated, has changed as more women have entered the workplace; it now lobbies for equal pay for work of equal value. But many areas of inequality remain. The majority of women who stay in the home give their work for scanty gain, and little has been done in the dark areas where women work at low-paid or part-time non-unionized jobs, or live poorly with their families on welfare, or survive into a lonely and impoverished old age. And from what has been achieved it is younger, middle-class, better-off and better-educated women who have mostly benefited. Canadian society is still a privileged one, as women and native peoples have discovered.

THE NATIVE PEOPLES, THE FIRST peoples of Canada, almost vanished out of the public eye at the end of the nineteenth century after all the treaties taking away their land had been concluded and the pathetic rebellion of 1885 had been lost. Restricted to reserves that were often unsuitable for farming even if the Indians had been inclined to pursue that occupation; deprived except in the remote north of their traditional hunting grounds; educated often in residential schools where they were taken out of their environment and discouraged from speaking their own languages; treated as second-class citizens who could not vote in federal elections until 1960; forbidden to continue ceremonies like the potlatch and the rain dance, which were central to their cultures, the Indians of Canada seemed by the early twentieth century to be dying out from disease, malnutrition and a sheer failure of the will to continue. Into the 1920s their numbers continued to decline, until there were hardly more than one hundred thousand of them left in the country. Their extinction was generally assumed to be near, and Diamond Jenness's classic work, *The Indians of Canada*, published in 1932, read like the threnody for a dying group of peoples and cultures.

The Indians survived, and from the 1930s on, they began to increase; more astonishingly, they survived as distinct peoples, with their traditions remembered and their languages retained, even though many individuals had drifted away from the reserves where the Indian Department and its successors tried to impose a regime that would prepare them eventually for what was called "enfranchisement." This really meant severance from the tribe and assimilation into white society; it was hoped that the tutelage of Indian agents, missionaries and teachers within the reserve would turn them into good Christian farmers and fit them to emerge as imitation white men.

Just how many Indians there now are in Canada is not certain, since the authorities seek to diminish their numbers and the Indian militant leaders to exaggerate them. Apart from about 25,000 Inuit in the Arctic regions, the official estimate of Statistics Canada in 1981 claimed 293,000 status Indians, meaning those who were attached to reserves and came under the care of the Department of Indian Affairs and Northern Development, 93,000 Métis, and about 75,000 non-status Indians, falling outside the reserve system, which made a total of almost half a million people, or about 2 percent of the population of Canada. Some native leaders claim that the numbers of Métis and non-status Indians has been grossly underestimated and that there are as many as a million of them. The truth seems to lie somewhere in between, with a probable total for all categories of native people of about 750,000, several times their numbers sixty years ago, and about 3 percent of the total population of Canada.

There are some prosperous groups of Indians, like the residents of the villages that carry on profitable fishing operations on the British Columbia coast and some of the successful prairie farmers, but the majority are very poor in comparison with the average Canadian. There are many reserves where the land is unproductive, the game has vanished, the opportunities for employment are scarce, and sickness and drunkenness are widespread. Often the young people leave such places and become disastrously involved in a city life for which they are not prepared, with its temptations of drink and drugs and prostitution. On the other hand, many

Indians are attached to the land where their ancestors lived and to a more leisurely existence, remaining close to nature and following traditional occupations like hunting and fishing, which can still be carried on there. They do not always demand the conveniences and luxuries that ordinary North Americans seem to need, and will accept a different, non-urban way of living. And that is why, from the beginning of the native rights movement in Canada, the stress has rested mainly on land, on the space in which to live one's chosen kind of life.

The struggle to assert Indian land claims began in British Columbia. In that province there were never any comprehensive treaties like those entered into elsewhere by the 1870s. There had been a few small early treaties, but in general the provincial authorities had taken the land arbitrarily and assigned small areas to the Indians as reserves, often with the excuse that they were fishing peoples and had no need of land. At the time of Confederation Sir John A. Macdonald accepted this interpretation uncritically, which means in effect that the Indians of the westernmost province never surrendered by treaty their aboriginal rights to the land over which they had hunted, fished and gathered berries since time beyond memory.

The first Indians to lay claim to lands they asserted they had never surrendered or sold were the Nishga people who live on the Nass River in northern British Columbia. In the 1890s, encouraged by sympathetic missionaries, the Nishga made their first claim for confirmation of their right to large areas of land where their ancestors had hunted. In the late 1980s, more than ninety years after the claims were originally made, agreement with the Nishga has not yet been reached.

But other important land claims have been settled, notably that with the Cree, which had to be reached before the giant James Bay hydroelectric development in northern Quebec could go ahead. Their negotiations with the Quebec government resulted in a considerable financial settlement that the local Indians have been able to use to capitalize money-making schemes and employment-creating initiatives in their own villages. Undoubtedly there will be other economically beneficial agreements of this kind.

Another important development in the Indian communities is the revival of the arts and ceremonials of the various peoples. The law against potlatches and other traditional ceremonies was repealed in 1951. Since then, there has been a considerable revival in both the ceremonial life of the Indian peoples and in the arts that have been traditionally associated with it.

The principal centre of such activity has been British Columbia, the home of the great Coast Indian cultures, where the potlatches and some of the winter ceremonials are once again being performed. Many of the Indians who take part in these revivals are also Christians more regular in their churchgoing than most of their white neighbours, and we must assume that the religious significance has leached out of the ceremonials and that they are now more important in terms of community identification; the traditions have become more significant than their meanings. The same probably applies to the notable revival of West Coast Indian art, led by a partly Indian carver, Bill Reid, whose slick adaptations of ancient designs and motifs to please non-Indian patrons say more than he intends about the present cultural dilemma of the Indians, living materially in the white man's world but detached from it through memory of the past and resentment of the present.

The final issue between the Indians of Canada and the non-Indian majority that occupies their former homeland is that of self-government. At one time, during the 1960s, the federal government showed signs that it wanted to shed its embarrassing suzerainty over the native peoples. In 1969 it proposed to abolish the Department of Indian Affairs and allow the provincial governments to take over the affairs of the native peoples. There were immediate protests by chiefs and leaders all over the country and also by the National Indian Brotherhood and the Native Council of Canada, the main native rights organization of the time, so the proposal was shelved. Since then there have been negotiations regarding Indian self-government, which the native leaders seem to envisage as the creation of a number of separate autonomous tribal states within the political framework of Canada. During a conference on this issue in the mid-1980s government and native representatives failed to reach agreement, so that, in theory at least, the native person remains a ward of the Canadian state, sometimes prosperous, more often poor, and usually aggrieved. Clearly, some kind of autonomy and responsibilty for their own affairs is necessary for the native peoples, as it was for Quebec, if their cultures are to revive, if they are to adapt themselves to the modern age, and if they are to find an economic base on which to achieve whatever degree of prosperity they desire and deserve. Undoubtedly, as in the past, many individual Indians will want to make their way in the wider Canadian world. But for others the maintenance of their traditions, which are also Canada's most ancient, will always be important to remind them — and to remind the rest of us — of the origins of human society in our country more than ten thousand years ago.

EPILOGUE

A history that ends in the present always ends provisionally, on the moving edge of change, and that applies to this book as to any other. I have ended the story in the late 1980s when some of the ancient themes are returning in a new guise, when the Canadian racial mosaic seems still to be steadily changing as new people enter the country in flight, like the Tamils or Sikhs, or in expectation, like other immigrants, and when world economic trends have made our country seem a less important place than we imagined in the earnest 1950s. In those days Canada seemed the perfect mediating middle power, and in the euphoric times of the sixties the centennial of Confederation and Expo '67 seemed to irradiate our country, past and present, with historic interest and contemporary colour.

Perhaps we are once again our good grey Canadian selves, assuming the protective colouring appropriate to a land with so long and testing a winter. But though the St Lawrence and the Great Lakes may freeze over annually, the movement of history is not subject to any such congealment, and already, as I write, we see about us some of the events, often political and economic as much as social, that will have incalculable effects on Canadian society in the decades ahead.

When the new Canadian Constitution came into being in 1982, it seemed a lacklustre document, inspired mainly by Pierre Trudeau's vain pursuit of the will-o'-the-wisp of national unity, and offering us little new.

But the Charter of Rights and Freedoms appended to it provided an agent of change all the more potent because it could be applied to any law, and could reinterpret it according to certain basic concepts of justice and liberty. Only now are the cases beginning to work through the Supreme Court that will suggest how far the Charter may change our society; the Morgentaler case, with its vindication of the right of choice in the case of abortions, is the first of them.

Then there is the Meech Lake Accord between the federal government and the provinces, which brought Quebec into the Constitution at the price of recognizing its cultural individuality, and at the same time, of course, recognizing the cultural individuality of all the other provinces. With this document the potential for widened pluralism in Canadian society is incalculable. And finally there is the free trade agreement recently concluded with the United States. One does not have to take any political stance, either for or against the agreement or the government that brought it into being to recognize that its implementation can change not only Canada's economic prospects but also its social patterns, perhaps Americanizing them in some ways, but in other ways — which nationalists do not wish to recognize — stimulating the Canadian community to declare itself in reaction to the rush of alien ideas, fashions and temptations.

Add the rapid pace of technological change with its effect on behaviour, and the likelihood that groups like women, native people and the young — and perhaps the old as well in the next decade — will sustain their pressure for a world that is more just. With all these new forces coming into play, one does not need to succumb to prophecy to declare that we are facing an era of change as unpredictable but probably as important as any in the past.

A Selected Bibliography

In this selected bibliography I have set out to provide what I feel will be a useful reading list for those interested in the aspects of Canadian history treated in this book. For this reason I have tended, among historical studies, to choose those that have a considerable social content and to avoid those that are narrowly political or military or pedantically obscure. I have also included a number of contemporary documents — memoirs, journals, etc. — which give a direct flavour of the times when they were written. In addition to these more specific books I would draw attention to those useful and informative compilations which, now they have appeared, seem indispensible to the student of the Canadian past. They are the *Dictionary of Canadian Biography*, of which the first eleven volumes have now been published, the *Literary History of Canada*, whose most recent three-volume edition appeared in 1976, and the *Historical Atlas of Canada*, whose first volume, carrying us to 1800, was issued in 1987. All these important reference books were published by the University of Toronto Press. Equally valuable for its wealth of references and cross-references is the *Canadian Encyclopedia* (three vols.) which Hurtig Publishers in Edmonton brought out in 1985.

G. P. V. A. Akrigg and Helen B. Akrigg, *British Columbia Chronicle, 1778–1840*. Vancouver, 1975.

Susan Allison, *A Pioneer Gentlewoman in British Columbia: The Recollections of Susan Allison*. Ed. Margaret A. Ormsby. Vancouver, 1976.

Pierre Berton, *Flames across the Border*. Toronto, 1981.
—————, *Klondike*. Toronto, 1958.
—————, *The Invasion of Canada*. Toronto, 1980.
—————, *The Last Spike*. Toronto, 1971.

Peter Turner Bone, *When the Steel Went Through: Reminiscences of a Railroad Pioneer*. Toronto, 1947.

R. H. Bonnycastle, *The Canadas in 1841*. 2 vols. London, 1841.

J. J. Brown, *Ideas in Exile: A History of Canadian Inventors*. Toronto, 1967.

Robert Craig Brown, and Ramsay Cook, *Canada 1896–1921*. Toronto, 1974.

William Francis Butler, *The Great Lone Land*. London, 1872.
———————————, *The Wild North Land*. London, 1873.

J. M. S. Careless, and R. Craig Brown, eds., *The Canadians, 1867–1967*. Toronto, 1967.

St John Chadwick, *Newfoundland: Island into Province*. Cambridge, 1967.

Samuel de Champlain, *The Works of Samuel de Champlain*. Ed. H. P. Biggar. 6 vols. Toronto, 1922–26.

Guillaume Charette, *Vanishing Spaces: Memoirs of Louis Goulet*. Trans. Ray Ellenwood. Winnipeg, 1980.

James Cheadle and Lord Milton, *The North West Passage by Land*. London, 1865.

Ramsay Cook, *Canada and the French Canadian Question*. Toronto, 1966.
———————, *The Regenerators: Social Criticism in Late Victorian Canada*. Toronto, 1985.

Ramsay Cook and Wendy Mitchison, *The Proper Sphere: Women's Place in Canadian Society*. Toronto, 1976.

Donald Creighton, *Dominion of the North*, rev. ed. Toronto, 1967.
———————————, *The Empire of the St Lawrence*. Toronto, 1956.
———————————, *The Forked Road, 1939–1957*. Toronto, 1976.

Lord Dalhousie, *The Dalhousie Journals*, Ed. Marjorie Whitelaw. Ottawa, 1978.

Peter Drucker, *Indians of the Northwest Coast*. New York, 1955.

Lady Dufferin, *My Canadian Journal, 1872–3*. London, 1891.

William Dunlop, *Statistical Sketches of Upper Canada for the Benefit of Emigrants: by a Backwoodsman*. London, 1832.

Lord Durham, *Report on the Affairs of British North America.* London, 1839.

W. J. Eccles, *Canada under Louis XIV, 1663–1701.* Toronto, 1964.

——————, *Essays on New France.* Toronto, 1987.

——————, *Frontenac, The Courtier Governor.* Toronto, 1959.

Gordon R. Elliott, *Barkerville, Quesnel & the Cariboo Gold Rush.* Vancouver, 1958.

Simon Fraser, *Letters and Journals, 1806–1808.* Ed. with an intro. by W. Kaye Lamb. Toronto, 1960.

J. S. Galbraith, *The Little Emperor: Governor Simpson of the Hudson's Bay Company.* Toronto, 1976.

Marcel Giraud, *The Métis in the Canadian West.* Trans. by George Woodcock. 2 vols. Edmonton, 1986.

G. P. de T. Glazebrook, *A History of Transportation in Canada.* Toronto, 1938.

——————————, *The Story of Toronto.* Toronto, 1971.

Alan Gowans, *Building Canada: An Architectural History of Canada.* Toronto, 1966.

J. L. Granatstein, *Canada, 1957–1967: The Years of Uncertainty and Innovation.* Toronto, 1986.

George Munro Grant, *Ocean to Ocean: Sandford Fleming's Expedition through Canada in 1872.* Toronto, 1873.

James H. Gray, *The Winter Years: The Depression in the Prairies.* Toronto, 1966.

Frederick Philip Grove, *Over Prairie Trails.* Toronto, 1922.

Edwin C. Guillet, *The Story of Canadian Roads.* Toronto, 1967.

Richard Hakluyt, *The Principal Navigations, Voyages, Traffics, and Discoveries of the English Nation . . .* 12 vols. London, 1903–5.

Daniel Williams Harmon, *A Journal of Voyages and Travels in the Interior of North America . . .* Andover, 1820.

J. Russell Harper, *Painting in Canada: A History.* Toronto, 1966.

Samuel Hearne, *A Journey from Prince of Wales' Fort, in Hudson's Bay, to the Northern Ocean* . . .London, 1795.

John Sebastian Helmcken, *The Reminiscences of John Sebastian Helmcken.* Ed. Dorothy Blakey Smith. Vancouver, 1975.

Mary Hiemstra, *Gully Farm.* Toronto, 1955.

Joseph Howe, *Western and Eastern Rambles. Travel Sketches of Nova Scotia.* Ed. with an introduction by M. G. Parkes. Toronto, 1973.

John Howison, *Sketches of Upper Canada* . . ., London, 1821.

Harold A. Innis, *The Fur Trade in Canada.* Rev. ed. Toronto, 1956.

Anna Jameson, *Winter Studies and Summer Rambles in Canada.* London, 1838.

Diamond Jenness, *The Indians of Canada.* Ottawa, 1932.

Paul Kane, *Wanderings of an Artist among the Indians of North America.* London, 1859.

Edna Kenton, *The Jesuit Relations and Allied Documents.* Toronto, 1954.

W. H. Kesterton, *A History of Journalism in Canada.* Toronto, 1967.

Robert Kroetsch, *Alberta.* Toronto, 1968.

Anna Langston, *A Gentlewoman of Upper Canada: The Journal of Anna Langston.* Ed. H. H. Langston. Toronto, 1950.

Robin Lizars, and Kathleen M. Lizars, *In the Days of the Canada Company.* Toronto, 1895.

Arthur M. Lower, *Canadians in the Making.* Toronto, 1958.

Nellie McClung, *Clearing in the West: My Own Story.* Toronto, 1935.

Edward McCourt, *Saskatchewan.* Toronto, 1968.

Alexander Mackenzie, *Voyages from Montreal . . . through the Continent of North America, to the Frozen and Pacific Oceans* . . . . London, 1801.

William Lyon Mackenzie, *The Selected Writings of William Lyon Mackenzie, 1824–1837.* Toronto, 1960.

Kenneth McNaught, *A Prophet in Politics: A Biography of J. S. Woodsworth.* Toronto, 1959.

W. S. McNutt, *The Atlantic Provinces, 1712–1857.* Toronto, 1965.

Andrew McPhail, *The Master's Wife.* Toronto, 1939.

Orlo Miller, *The Donnelleys Must Die.* Toronto, 1962.

Susanna Moodie, *Roughing It in the Bush.* London, 1852.
———————————, *Letters of a Lifetime.* Ed. Carl Ballstadt et al. Toronto, 1985.

Brian Moore, *Canada.* New York, 1967.

William Scott Moorsom, *Letters from Nova Scotia.* London, 1830.

Adrian Gabriel Morice, *Fifty Years in Western Canada.* Toronto, 1930.

W. L. Morton, *The Critical Years: The Union of British North America, 1857–1873.* Toronto, 1964.
———————————, *The Kingdom of Canada.* Toronto, 1963.

Farley Mowat, *Canada North.* Toronto, 1967.
———————————, *Ordeal by Ice.* Toronto, 1960.
———————————, *The Polar Passion.* Toronto, 1967.
———————————, *West-Viking.* Toronto, 1965.

Hilda Neatby, *Quebec, the Revolutionary Age: 1760–1791.* Toronto, 1966.

Mary O'Brien, *The Journals of Mary O'Brien, 1828–38.* Ed. Audrey Saunders Miller. Toronto, 1868.

Tryggvii Oleson, *Early Voyages and Northern Approaches, 1000–1632.* Toronto, 1963.

Margaret Ormsby, *British Columbia: A History.* Toronto, 1958.

Fernand Ouellet, *Lower Canada 1791–1840: Social Change and Nationalism.* Toronto, 1980.

R. A. J. Phillips, *Canada's North.* Toronto, 1967.

John Porter, *The Vertical Mosaic.* Toronto, 1965.

Alison Prentiss, and Susan Mann Trofimenkoff, eds., *The Neglected Majority: Essays in Canadian Women's History*, vol. 2. Toronto, 1985.

Colin Read and Ronald J. Stagg, eds., *The Rebellion in Upper Canada: A Collection of Documents*. Toronto, 1985.

Martin Robin, *Radical Politics and Canadian Labour*. Kingston, 1968.

Alexander Ross, *The Red River Settlement*. London, 1856.

André Siegfried, *The Race Question in Canada*. London, 1907.

A. J. M. Smith, *Modern Canadian Verse, in English and French*. Toronto, 1967.

——————————, *The Oxford Book of Canadian Verse, in English and French*. Toronto, 1960.

George F. G. Stanley, *Louis Riel*. Toronto, 1963.

——————————, *New France: The Last Phase*. Toronto, 1968.

——————————, *The Birth of Western Canada*. Toronto, 1936.

——————————, *The War of 1812*. Toronto, 1983.

Samuel B. Steele, *Forty Years in Canada*. Toronto, 1915.

Vilhjalmur Stefansson, *My Life with the Eskimo*. New York, 1913.

——————————, *The Friendly Arctic*. New York, 1921.

Clara Thomas, *Ryerson of Upper Canada*. Toronto, 1969.

William Toye, *A Book of Canada*. Toronto, 1962.

——————————, *The St Lawrence*. Toronto, 1959.

Catharine Parr Traill, *The Backwoods of Canada*. London, 1836.

——————————, *The Canadian Settlers' Guide*. Toronto, 1855.

Susan Mann Trofimenkoff and Alison Prentiss, *The Neglected Majority: Essays in Canadian Women's History*, vol. 1. Toronto, 1977.

Anthony Trollope, *North America*. London, 1862.

Marcel Trudel, *The Beginning of New France, 1524–1663*. Toronto, 1973.

Mason Wade, ed., *Canadian Dualism: La Dualité canadienne.* Toronto, 1960.

George, Woodcock, *Canada and the Canadians.* London, 1970.
——————————, *Gabriel Dumont.* Edmonton, 1975.
——————————, *Peoples of the Coast.* Edmonton, 1977.

J. S. Woodsworth, *Strangers within the Gates; or, Coming Canadians.* Toronto, 1909.

Morris Zaslow, *The Opening of the Canadian North, 1870–1914.* Toronto, 1971.

NOTES

1. *The Voyages of Jacques Cartier*, translated by H.P. Biggar, cited in William Toye. *A Book of Canada*. Toronto: Oxford University Press. 1962. p.28.

2. Diamond Jenness. *The Indians of Canada* (Third Edition). Ottawa: National Museum of Man. 1955. p.386.

3. Samuel Hearne. *A Journey to the Northern Ocean*, edited by Richard Glover. Toronto: Macmillan. 1958. p.35.

4. Diamond Jenness. *Op.cit.* p.306.

5. *Life, Letters and Travels of Father Pierre-Jean de Smet*, cited in Jenness, *op.cit.*, p.127-8.

6. Cited in Jenness, *op.cit.*, p.128-9.

7. Cited in *Historical Atlas of Canada*, Vol.1, edited by R. Cole Harris. Toronto: University of Toronto Press. 1987. p.54.

8. Alexander Ross. *The Fur Hunters of the Far West*. London: Smith Elder. 1855. p.173.

9. *The Journals and Letters of Sir Alexander Mackenzie*, edited by W. Kaye Lamb. Cambridge: Hakluyt Society. 1970. p.378.

10. *The Letters and Journals of Simon Fraser 1806-1808*, edited by W. Kaye Lamb. Toronto: Macmillan. 1960. p.96.

11. *Paul Kane's Frontier*, edited by J. Russell Harper. Toronto: University of Toronto Press. 1971. pp.138-9.

12. Isaac Brock. Address to Upper Canada Legislature, July 27, 1812. Cited in John Robert Colombo, *Colombo's Canadian Quotations*. Edmonton: Hurtig Publishers. 1974. p.76.

13. *Lord Durham's Report*, edited by G.M. Craig. Toronto: McClelland & Stewart. 1963. p.150.

14. Frederick C. Cozzens, *Acadia, or a Month with the Blue Noses*, cited in William Scarth Moorsom, *Letters from Nova Scotia*, edited by Marjorie Whitelaw. Ottawa: Oberon Press. 1986. p.25.

15. *Joseph Howe: Voice of Nova Scotia*. A Selection edited by J. Murray Beck. Toronto: McClelland & Stewart. 1964. p.31.

16. Diary of Lieut. Charles W. Wilson, British Columbia Provincial Archives. Cited in *British Columbia: A Centennial Anthology*, edited by Reginald Eyre Watters. Toronto: McClelland & Stewart. 1958. p.18-19.

17. W.J. Eccles. *Frontenac: The Courtier Governor*. Toronto: McClelland & Stewart. 1959. p.54.

18. "Canadian Literature," Vol. 28, 1966. p.47.

19. George Woodcock, *The Canadians*, Toronto: Fitzhenry & Whiteside. 1979. p.99.

20. Woodcock, *op.cit.* p.105.

21. Susanna Moodie. *Roughing it in the Bush or, Forest Life in Canada.* Toronto: Bell & Cockburn. 1913. p.xv.

22. Alexander Ross. *The Red River Settlement.* London: Smith Elder. 1856. p.255-6.

23. Cited in Colombo, *op.cit.* p.471.

24. Cited in Colombo, *op.cit.* p.132.

25. *The Queen v. Louis Riel*, with introduction by Desmond Morton. Toronto: University of Toronto Press. 1974. p.360.

26. Cited in Colombo, *op.cit.* p.575.

INDEX